Videoconferencing for the Real World

Implementing Effective Visual Communication Systems

Videoconferencing for the Real World

Implementing Effective Visual Communication Systems

by John Rhodes

Focal Press

Boston   Oxford   Auckland   Johannesburg   Melbourne   New Delhi

AMERICAN FORESTS
GLOBAL ReLEAF 2000 — Butterworth–Heinemann supports the efforts of American Forests and the Global ReLeaf program in its campaign for the betterment of trees, forests, and our environment.

Library of Congress Cataloging-in-Publication Data
ISBN 0240-80416-3

British Library Cataloguing-in-Publication Data
A catalogue record for this book is available from the British Library.

The publisher offers special discounts on bulk orders of this book.
For information, please contact:

Manager of Special Sales
Butterworth–Heinemann
225 Wildwood Avenue
Woburn, MA 01801-2041
Tel: 781-904-2500
Fax: 781-904-2620

For information on all Focal Press publications available, contact our World Wide Web home page at: http://www.focalpress.com

10 9 8 7 6 5 4 3 2 1

Printed in the United States of America

This book is fondly dedicated to the memory of my parents

Charlotte and Leo, and grandparents Jean, Abraham, Fanny and Nathan.

Table of Contents

List of Illustrations

Foreword

We have evolved into a speedy society. The technology we invent, market and sell makes it possible for us to send, receive, and participate with minimal downtime. We continue to pursue and perfect technology in our ongoing effort to satisfy our craving for immediacy and speed. This is not a bad thing, because we have become more efficient. Business moves faster, and everyone, it seems, is ahead of the curve.

Not too many years ago, we took great comfort in knowing that a business letter could be mailed and would arrive later in the week. Now we want it overnight. We even jokingly refer to regular mail as "snail mail."

Which brings us to the Internet. Ten years ago, a fax transmission was marveled for its ability to deliver messages quickly. Today, we're pushing the fax toward extinction with our voracious appetite for the Internet and its ability to deliver e-mail almost instantly.

We secretly scoff at the fax because it's clumsy and hard to read, and sometimes comes out on shiny paper. Our frustration is aimed at its lack of speed. Faxes are slower than e-mail, and we've even turned on that technology in favor of the faster Internet.

As Chairman of the International Communications Industries Association, Inc.® (ICIA®), the world's leading trade association for audio, video, and presentation professionals, I want to give you a technological tip. Learn about videoconferencing—it's the next new wave of communication that will satisfy your need for technological speed. ICIA members make it possible for doctors to consult globally, study or assist in operation theaters anywhere. We integrate and interface the audio and video equipment inside the operating room to provide the ultimate teaching tool for the medical profession—a telemedicine event transmitted live throughout the world. Videoconferencing is also used throughout the world in business, sales and marketing, education, and government.

For more than sixty-two years, ICIA has served as the global voice of the audio, video, and presentations products industry. ICIA is headquartered in Fairfax, Virginia, about a twenty-minute drive from Washington, D.C. The association represents more than 2,200 member companies representing more than 10,000 individuals. ICIA members include the world's leading manufacturers that develop the innovative presentations products, the dealers that sell the inventory, and the consumers or technology users that purchase the product.

Other ICIA members are systems installation specialists, resellers and specialty companies, such as consultants and researchers. ICIA members are part of the presentation display market that is literally everywhere, from boardrooms to classrooms, sports arenas, rock concerts and trade shows. ICIA members, through the use of videoconferencing, help bring the world closer together.

John Rhodes' *Videoconferencing for the Real World*, is a one of the world's most comprehensive blueprints for the awesome power of videoconferencing. In a time of trending, information sharing, and an insatiable need for technological speed, we invite you to read this A-to-Z primer on videoconferencing applications, systems, installations, and uses.

As you will see after reading *Videoconferencing for the Real World*, the remarkable thing is that we can instantaneously communicate, whether for business or pleasure, with anyone in the world at lower costs than ever before. Videoconferencing is the hope of your business communications, and this book is a how-to for your technology future.

Brad Caldwell
Chairman of ICIA and president of
Integrated Media Services, Anaheim, California

Acknowledgments

I would like to thank the many people who have helped me during the preparation of this book. Needless to say, any misstatements, misinterpretations, omissions or other goof-ups are my responsibility alone.

Thanks to my partner and best friend, Shonan Noronha. This book would never have been completed without her countless hours of research, editing, advice, and support.

For information that has made this book more useful and relevant to the real-world needs of communication professionals—thanks to Tim Gilbert, Worldroom Consulting; Ira Weinstein, Credit Suisse First Boston; Mike Diodato, Walsh-Lowe; Richard Hezel, Hezel Associates; Donal Leith and Richard Schaphorst, Delta Information Systems; and Warren Ingersol, V-Span. Important information was also extracted from interviews and conversations held over the past several years with Carl Ceregno, Communications Research; Wayne Williams, AG Video; Bob Maier, EDR Systems; Mike Albi, CEAVCO; and Ken Muffley, The Whitlock Group. I am also grateful to the Association of Telehealth Service Providers, AC&E, Elmo, Lucent Technologies, Polycom, Smart Technologies, Tandberg, and VTEL for their contribution of images.

A big shout out to the people involved in bringing this book to press—Marie Lee, publisher; and editors Lilly Roberts and Jennifer Plumley. Many thanks, too, to my fearless preproduction team of Joe Helfenbein, creative director; Bert Jantzer, preproduction manager; Christine DeMarfio, layout artist; and Dave Campbell and Patrick Curran at 4-Front Design.

I would also like to thank the many other people who, though not directly involved in the creation of this book, were instrumental in the development of my understanding of videoconferencing—Henry Grove, Kunio Sano, Hiro Kikawa, Elliot Gold, David Congdon, Joyce Thompson, John McDonnell, and others too numerous to mention here, including many members of the ITVA, ITCA, ICIA, and SMPTE.

To Janet, Jim, Allyssa, Kenny, Catherine, John, Matthew, Mary, Sirikit, Kara, Bianca, Jean, Antonio, Avertano, Dave and Cori, Karen, Chet, and "uncle Eddie"—thanks for your patience, support and understanding during the months I spent preparing this book, though it often interfered with birthday celebrations, press conferences, SciFi Cons, and other important activities.

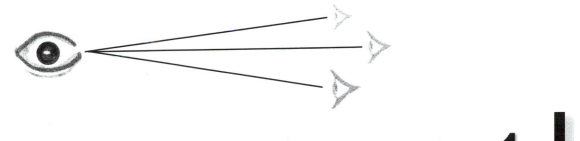

Introduction to Successful Videoconferencing 1

Great Expectations

Interactive video communications can boost productivity, improve morale, and "spread the word" in a powerful and cost-effective way. It can also provide a significant competitive advantage by reducing time-to-market and improving access to geographically dispersed expertise. It can address the need for better coordination of dispersed workgroups, more effective training or a clear channel of communication between corporate layers.

All that is required to harness this force to benefit your organization is to combine the appropriate video technologies with your organization's work process, and provide the support needed to ensure that these tools continue to function as required. This is easy to say, but perhaps a bit more difficult to achieve.

Thanks to recent technological advancements and the dynamics of a fiercely competitive telecommunications market, there are hundreds of powerful, cost-effective video communication solutions and services to choose from. There are also many vendors—ranging from system manufacturers and integrators to network service providers and consultants—all eager to provide you with the "perfect" solution. This wealth of choices can make it difficult to select the best system solutions to address the unique communication needs of your organization.

The Purpose of This Book

This book has been developed to help business and technical managers make informed decisions regarding the deployment of video communications systems. In it, you will find a simple, systematic presentation of the steps required to implement and sustain a useful and cost-effective solution. These steps include analyzing your users' needs, selecting the appropriate technologies, and choosing the best vendors to supply and support your system. Other sections of the book cover issues related to user training, staffing, and system management.

At the beginning of each chapter, you will find a nontechnical Executive Summary of the issues covered in that chapter. The remainder of each section delves into the nuts-and-bolts aspects of that topic, including costs, technical considerations, human factors, and related issues. Where appropriate, I have included real-world examples of both successful and suboptimal applications of these technologies. In some cases, the names of people and organizations have been changed for reasons of confidentiality or to spare some good friends a little embarrassment.

The first two chapters of the book are intended as an introduction to the field, covering the history of videoconferencing, the current state of the art, and the outlook for both the technologies and the business of interactive video communications. Subsequent chapters examine specific aspects of the discipline, such as conducting a needs analysis, multipoint conferencing, and network management, and can be read in sequence or referred to as required. I also have included several appendices including case studies, listings of professional and commercial associations, and technical resources.

What Is Videoconferencing?

There are many names for the tools that make up interactive video communication—Videoconferencing, Video-TeleConferencing (VTC), Multimedia Collaborative Computing, Desktop Conferencing, and Distance Learning. All of these names and others are used somewhere in this book to describe specific applications, but for the sake of clarity and simplicity, I have used *videoconferencing* as a generic term to cover them all. To save ink and trees, I have frequently used the conventional abbreviated form, VTC, one of the original names for the medium.

There are two factors that unify these disparate technologies and applications:
1. They use moving video images (of people, places, and things) to enhance the communication process.
2. The transmission of this video (and the accompanying audio) involves two-way interactive communication.

One-way transmission of video and audio, for video distribution, broadcasting or video-on-demand, is also of great importance. But because a complete analysis of these applications would add many chapters to the length of this modest volume, they will not receive in-depth coverage. However, several of the key issues are discussed in Chapter 4 under the heading Hybrid Desktop, TV/Conferencing Systems.

For interactive video communication, a wide range of technologies and disciplines are usually combined to achieve maximum impact and economy. These include a variety of digital networks and communication protocols, computer graphics, digital audio and video compression, ergonomics, interactive multimedia, application-sharing, acoustical engineering, and many others.

Recently, convergent developments in many of these areas have enhanced two-way interactive video communications and made it even more cost-effective. But this convergence has also increased the number and complexity of available solutions.

The First Steps

The first step in determining the right tools and services for your particular application is a thorough "needs analysis." In Chapter 3, we cover the process of preparing an effective needs analysis, and have included a checklist to simplify the process. Once you have developed a clear picture of your users' needs, you need to know what products and services will actually satisfy those requirements. Subsequent chapters provide you with information to help you to evaluate these products and services, and to plan and implement the best solutions for your organization.

Whatever your role in planning, deploying, and supporting videoconferencing—it will be played out against the background of a medium and an industry in great flux. To ensure that your decisions are as future-proof as possible, it is important to understand the forces that are driving the evolution of this industry. These topics are covered later in the book, but here's a brief overview of a few of the key issues and trends in videoconferencing that are likely to have an impact on your deliberations.

The Inside Track

The evolution of videoconferencing and other forms of video communications reflects the movement of this medium from an exclusively one-to-many (broadcast) model, to a form that expresses the many-to-many (networked/interactive) nature of our wired society. Most of the trends and key issues facing managers and users of videoconferencing today reflect this general trend.

Over the last ten years, the growth of videoconferencing has been nothing short of phenomenal. During this period, the number of conferencing endpoints (dedicated rooms, rollabout systems, desktop units, etc.) has grown from less than 5,000 to several hundred thousand.

This rise in popularity has been due, in large part, to lower costs, better quality, greater ease of use, and improved reliability. The rapid expansion of usage (and the attendant publicity) have served to fuel increased demand and raise user expectations. As more users seek to take advantage of the power of videoconferencing, network, technical, and communications managers are faced with several apparently contradictory demands. These managers are called upon to provide adequate support for an expanding, largely inexperienced user base, who often have had their expectations inflated by industry hype and popular science fiction. At the same time, managers are also being asked to deliver ever more sophisticated communication services, such as desktop, multipoint, and collaborative multimedia videoconferencing, at ever lower costs.

In response to these demands (and the potential profits to be derived from satisfying them), the VTC industry has developed solutions intended to make it even easier and more cost-effective to deploy, manage, and support video networks. These include: integration of video with the local area network (LAN) and wide area network (WAN), set-top systems with simplified setup and user interfaces, remote system management, and a smorgasbord of support services.

Key Issues and Trends

Although there has been tremendous progress in videoconferencing over the last few years, specific technologies within the field have sometimes been promoted before they were "ready for prime time." Here is a quick reality check on some of the current hot topics in video communications:

H.323 and Packet-Switched Networks

Networking professionals have long dreamed of the fully integrated network, capable of combining data, voice, video, fax, and other services into a cost-effective and easy to maintain communications system. To integrate VTC into the information technology (IT) mainstream and to reduce expenditures for switched digital telephone circuits, there is a widespread effort to transform videoconferencing into another service in the packet-switched LAN/WAN environment.

The recently adopted H.323 family of standards addresses this issue, and there is a strong movement to implement these standards on the part of virtually every manufacturer and service provider in the industry. H.323 provides a framework for video, audio, and other content requiring a high quality of service (QoS) to be carried by Ethernet LANs, Frame Relay WANs, and even the Internet. Internet protocol telephony (VoIP) is one H.323 application that has already achieved some limited acceptance.

To perform successfully, H.323 videoconferencing solutions require fast, well-managed LANs and WANs with low latency and proper QoS. The tremendous potential of packet-switched videoconferencing has been well documented. Many pilot projects have been successfully completed, though they have often required heavy technical support. The ongoing saga of H.323 video is covered in some detail in Chapter 5 under the heading "Ethernet and IP Video." But the state of the art can be summed up in a single sentence: There are many promising developments in this area, but we are probably still a couple of years away from widespread, high quality, cost-effective deployment.

Set-top Systems Versus Desktop Conferencing

Gone are the days when a staff of engineers could be kept "on call" to instantly address any problem encountered with a boardroom videoconferencing system. Today, at some sites, we are lucky to have anyone who knows the difference between a BRI and 10Base-T.

While many high-end room systems are still being deployed, the current trend is toward simple, easy to use "set-top" units that provide reasonable quality for $2,000 to $15,000 per location. These units are, for the most part, easy to install, simple to use, and many even provide advanced features such as remote diagnostics, Web integration, and built-in multipoint conferencing capabilities.

The user interfaces of most set-top systems are simple, icon-based, and menu-driven. While they vary in quality and features, even the least sophisticated of these systems are no more difficult to use than a typical office copier. Set-top units have become so attractive to users and system managers that they are even replacing desktop conferencing system in some applications.

Desktop videoconferencing (DVC) involves the use of a personal computer (PC) as an electronic platform to support videoconferencing, collaborative computing, telecommuting and other advanced forms of communication. While these units are seen as a key component of the integrated H.323 network of the future, almost all of the currently installed base of DVC systems use an integrated services digital network (ISDN), that is, a readily available switched digital phone service, rather than LAN connections. Virtually any current PC can be upgraded to DVC at a cost that ranges from $500 to $3,000, depending on the speed of the network connection desired and other features.

The fact that a DVC system is a "part" of a PC is both its greatest strength and a sometimes-critical weakness. PC integration provides users with the ability to instantly merge spreadsheets, reports, graphics and other information into their interactive video communication. Unfortunately, the current state of the art in networked PCs includes occasional crashes, software and hardware conflicts, and assorted bugs and gremlins. These problems are sometimes aggravated through the addition of a DVC "card set" and software to the PC. If you combine these challenges with the less-than-perfect user interface of many DVC systems, and the expense and hassles involved in providing ISDN to the desktop, it is no wonder that the recent growth rate of DVC usage has been good, but not great.

As mentioned earlier, set-top systems are replacing DVC units in several application areas. Since many DVC systems are used in small conference rooms and other shared spaces, the greater reliability and ease of use of the set-top systems makes them an attractive choice for these applications. Even in executive offices, set-tops are seen as a DVC alternative that is easier to use and easier to support.

Don't get me wrong—I love DVC—but it is no magic bullet, just another powerful communication tool that can provide great benefits when used appropriately. More specific information on the state of the art in desktop and set-top conferencing is included in Chapter 4, "Choosing the Right System."

The Role of Telecommunications Service Providers

By far, the biggest expense involved in the deployment of VTC systems is the cost of network services—also known as the phone bill. A small room system with a purchase price of $10,000 and a yearly support budget of $4,000 may easily generate $15,000 to $20,000 in revenues for the company that supplies it with 384 kbps ISDN connectivity. This level of expense is not necessarily a problem for the user organization—a system that attracts hundred of hours of use per year is probably returning ten times its costs in increased productivity and reduced travel expenses. Nevertheless, it is important to understand this balance of costs and revenues for the following reasons:

1. Carriers will aggressively market any technology or application that will increase users' need for bandwidth.
2. Occasionally, marketing efforts run ahead of the ability to deliver reliable, economical solutions.
3. A good relationship with a telecom service provider can provide low-cost access to valuable expertise.
4. That technical expertise will become more valuable and less accessible as videoconferencing becomes more of a commodity.

Pay Me Now—Or Pay Me Later

As the cost of individual room systems and other customer premises equipment (CPE) has continued to fall, the level of pre- and postsales technical assistance provided by manufacturers has continued to decline. Even though Web-based support tools are moderating the impact of this decline, most users still find it necessary to seek the assistance of integrators and consultants in configuring, installing, and maintaining their VTC systems. Unfortunately, the same falling costs and increasing competition that have constricted manufacturers' support budgets have also reduced the amount of free or low-cost help that can be expected from system integrators. As someone who has worked on all four levels (manufacturer, integrator, consultant, and system manager), I can offer three good pieces of advice to those who wish to avoid being caught between this rock and that hard place. They may sound complicated, but they are just good, common sense:

1. Deal only with vendors who provide you with a detailed, realistic plan and budget for the design, installation, and support of your system. The total costs presented in a comprehensive proposal may be higher than the bottom line of a quick, bare bones quote, but ignorance of a necessary expense will not make it disappear.

2. Nothing is plug-and-play for very long. Service contracts save sanity and jobs. Get a quote for the level of technical support that will fully satisfy your users' needs for continuity of service, and include it in your minimum budget for the project.
3. Get everything in writing. "We'll take care of that" is generally not sufficient assurance for the success of mission-critical communication systems. Your request for proposal (RFP) should be very specific about every required function and service, including the terms of "acceptance" and the demarcation of responsibilities.

For a detailed look at the process of creating a bullet-proof RFP, take a look at Chapter 6, "Putting It All Together—The Challenges of Integration."

Operations and Network Management

To make it possible for a relatively small staff to support a large number of remote videoconferencing users and locations, many tools and techniques are being borrowed from the arsenal of LAN/WAN management. These include simple network management protocol (SNMP), and the use of remote control software, such as pcAnywhere. Web-based applications and services for scheduling, presentations, and collaborative computing are also becoming easier to buy and use.

Cost-conscious managers can get help from service providers and integrators with outsourcing of conferencing management and operations. The provision of these services was common practice in the early days of videoconferencing, when critical hardware and expertise were concentrated with the major carriers. Over the years, many companies and institutions developed in-house expertise to deal with their own unique blend of complex system technologies and user needs. As user organizations slim down to competitive shape, and as conferencing technologies and practices become more standardized, outsourcing is once again becoming a viable alternative. Bundled services range from simple scheduling and bridging of multipoint conferences to turnkey system operations and even room coordination (refreshments at a slight additional charge).

The Human Factors

The biggest challenges in videoconferencing are less about the technology itself and more about the way that organizations deal with the impact of these technologies in their way of doing business. For example, the decision-making process within an organization can be totally revamped with the use of video-conferencing, compressing the time required to bring new products to market. This in turn will have an impact on the manufacturing and marketing processes. The jobs of people responsible for these processes will no doubt be affected. Who will prepare the organization for these changes? While forward looking executives are pushing this technology further down the management chain, resistance to change and other related factors can create many challenges to modernization.

There is also a real need to provide effective training for the wide range of employees who could potentially use this technology to increase their productivity. At one end of the spectrum are the enthusiastic "early adopter" types, some of whom may harbor unrealistic expectations. At the other end are technology-resistant types and technophobes, who find the technology difficult to use and may see it as a threat to their accustomed way of doing business or even their jobs.

Example: A major metropolitan district attorney's office installed desktop conferencing systems in police precinct houses to expedite arraignment processes. One of the expected benefits was the reduction of the thousands of "unproductive" overtime hours required for officers and witnesses to travel downtown to give statements. An unaccountably large number of maintenance problems, particularly broken headsets, were reported. This problem was alleged to be due to the actions of a few officers who did not see the drastic reduction in overtime as a benefit. On the positive side, assistant district attorneys were enthusiastic, reporting that they were able to more easily gain the cooperation of witnesses who would have otherwise been reluctant to "take the trip downtown."

Cost-effective user training, help desk support, and meeting services that will allay fears and boost conference productivity are among the highest priorities for those charged with the management of conferencing systems. This topic is covered in some detail in Chapter 7, "Managing the Conferencing Process."

In preparing this book, I have attempted to distill the insights gained from ten years of experience in designing and implementing videoconferencing solutions. It is my hope that readers will benefit from these observations and tips.

While technologies and user needs will continue to change, the principles involved in selecting, implementing, and supporting effective communication systems that are presented here should endure for at least a few more years.

Videoconferencing Applications

2

Executive Summary

This chapter provides an overview of the most popular and productive applications for videoconferencing. It also includes some examples of innovative uses that may help you to discover the best ways to use VTC to improve communications and productivity within your organization. Since there are hundreds of applications for videoconferencing technology, this chapter is not intended to serve as a comprehensive description of the potential applications, but rather as a starting point for the development of your own solution.

While the mature application areas of videoconferencing—distance learning, telemedicine, and executive communications are continuing to experience significant growth—the use of the technology for increased productivity in sales and marketing, workgroup collaboration, and a wide range of vertical applications is steadily approaching mainstream status.

Powered by a variety of technical, economic, and social developments, the use of videoconferencing is growing rapidly in conventional areas and gaining widespread acceptance for new applications. The ease of use, powerful features, and low capital cost of new systems, along with the decreasing cost of transmission, are making a significant impact in all business sectors—delivering increased productivity and decreased costs for travel, meetings, and training.

To take maximum advantage of these new productivity-enhancing tools, it is helpful for decision-makers to become familiar with the various types of applications—how different solutions have solved specific communication needs. Examples of successful videoconferencing applications are useful for at least two reasons:

1. They provide ideas on how VTC can be used to solve similar communication needs for other organizations.
2. They provide documentation and support for those who need to convince their management that VTC has been productive and cost-effective in solving similar communication needs for other organizations.

In Appendix A, you will find case studies describing the challenges, solutions, and successes of each selected project. These case studies also provide a format for writing reports that can be used in proposals to upper management. It is a good idea to develop a "clippings" folder of application articles published in electronic and hard-copy trade journals and magazines. Manufacturers and integrators also publish success stories on their Web sites. Particularly useful are research data and case studies specific to your organization's industry.

As the use of collaborative computing, Internet telephony, and other new media tools continue to expand, users are discovering new and innovative applications for VTC. Some of these emerging applications are also discussed in this chapter.

Application Areas

The uses of videoconferencing can be divided into several major application groups:

1. General business applications
   These include meeting and collaborative work support for management, sales, accounting, manufacturing, customer service, engineering, training, and other functions.

2. Distance Learning (DL)
   DL encompasses a wide range of uses by institutions focused on K-12, college-level, and professional instruction. This area also includes many aspects of corporate and institutional training.

3. Government applications
   This area includes law enforcement, military, and other specialized applications group, as well as the use of VTC by federal, state and local governments for more conventional uses.

4. Vertical business applications

Many businesses have specialized needs that can be served by specific videoconferencing solutions. These include banking, aerospace, pharmaceutical, and other companies with distinct ways of conducting their business.

5. Telemedicine

Telemedicine employs videoconferencing and a variety of VTC and other remote communication technologies (*see* Figure 2-1) to diagnose and treat illnesses and injuries. It is one of the oldest applications for VTC, and its steady growth has accelerated recently, primarily due to increasing public pressure to provide widespread access to cost-effective health care.

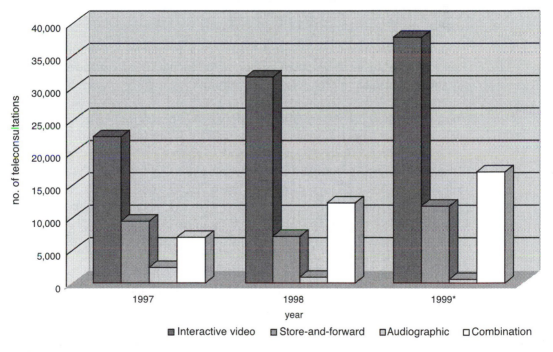

*Based on 1st quarter projections

Figure 2-1 Use of different technologies over time, 1997 to 1998*. (Source: Association of Telehealth Service Providers)

General Business Applications

Executive Support

Videoconferencing first came into prominence as a management support tool, enabling top executives at major multinational corporations like Sears, Citicorp, Merck, Sony, and others to hold important meetings without the delay and inconvenience of travel. The high level of expense and technical support requirements of the early VTC networks were not critical issues because the need for immediacy and the great value placed on the time of participants far outweighed any expense. As a result, room systems costing hundreds of thousands of dollars were supported by skilled engineers and conferencing managers at every site and were often connected via dedicated, leased T1 lines costing $10,000 or more per month.

Even with all that technical and networking firepower, connections were not always reliable, the equipment was temperamental, and enhancements such as graphics and data collaboration were primitive by today's standards.

Now that the cost of reliable group systems has fallen below $10,000, and telecom costs have plummeted to around $1 per minute, many organizations are adopting videoconferencing as a collaborative tool for all levels of management. "Forward looking companies are pushing this technology further down the management chain," says Seymour Friedel, CEO and cofounder of Zydacron. "These companies have discovered that in many instances, the equipment pays for itself after one use. This level of return on investment cannot be ignored."

Teamwork

VTC is a great tool to facilitate teamwork and to increase the productivity of knowledge workers who are separated by time and distance. This is particularly true in situations where mergers, downsizing, and competition for specialized skills have made remote access to expertise an important solution. For example, Boeing, with facilities scattered around the Seattle, Washington, area, was one of the first companies to realize the substantial time savings and increased productivity that could be realized from videoconferencing. For more than ten years, engineers and other project personnel have "met" regularly via VTC, thereby saving many hours that otherwise would have been wasted. At Sony, VTC meetings between U.S.- and Japan-based members of product development teams had become a routine occurrence as early as 1991.

Not only does this type of long-distance collaboration drastically reduce project completion times, it often results in higher-quality decision making. This is due largely to the freedom that VTC brings to the composition of a meeting. Travel expenses and other restrictions could deprive the attendees at a mission-critical meeting of the advice of an important specialist. Before VTC was widely deployed at Sony, attendees at major product planning meetings in Japan had to be limited to senior department managers. After VTC became easily accessible, junior team members (e.g., an interface design engineer) could immediately be brought into discussions where their specialized expertise was needed.

Sales and Marketing

Since the work of corporate sales and marketing divisions involves communication media, it is no surprise that videoconferencing has become a favorite tool of sales and marketing management. The uses range from product planning to face-to-face sales calls—wherever there is an advantage to be gained from instant visual communication. Marketers use VTC for meetings with advertising and public relations agencies, press briefings and interviews, product development meetings with engineering and manufacturing departments, focus group sessions, and meetings with suppliers and strategic partners. Sales managers use VTC to reach out to branch offices and field sales personnel, for training and motivational meetings, follow-up meetings with important customers, and presentations to just about anyone. In business-to-business sales, VTC makes salespeople more accessible to their accounts and reduces the cost of maintaining personal contact with customers.

Example: One financial services company provides turnkey desktop videoconferencing systems to key clients. This not only provides a direct conduit of personalized multimedia communication, it gives the account manager the opportunity to "conference in" experts to help the client make the best possible decisions.

Systems for Sales and Marketing
Good presentation graphics capabilities as well as superior room lighting are important aspects of well-designed sales and marketing VTC systems. The first, because PowerPoint is the lifeblood of sales and marketing management, and the second, because good lighting helps to produce a healthy looking and relaxed impression at the far end of the connection.

Service

For high-level service operations and customer service, VTC provides an opportunity to solve problems quickly and maintain a personal and positive relationship with customers. VTC also provides a cost-effective alternative to on-site service training.

Example: A major airline set up VTC systems that enabled service crews to consult with experts at the company's headquarters. A typical meeting involved the transmission of detailed images of a worn or damaged part with a discussion of the problem and the best course of remedial action.

Systems for Service

It is important that the serviceable part under discussion, whether it is an engine part or a piece of software, be clearly visible at both ends of the conference. For this reason special care needs to be paid to the graphics capture systems, and to software programs that facilitate visual collaboration.

Human Resources

Many organizations require that several departments conduct interviews before a candidate is hired. The travel and delays involved in an extended series of interviews can make it difficult to make timely hiring decisions. This is particularly important when the position being filled is at a branch office or in an industry where there is a shortage of qualified employees. Since many human resources (HR) professionals have found VTC to be a useful hiring tool, agencies like Management Recruiters International (MRI) have set up VTC networks to serve that market. MRI created ConferView, its 350-site videoconferencing network, primarily to allow clients to conduct face-to-face interviews with candidates at a distance. Additional uses that have proved beneficial to HR include personnel planning and management, training, and, on occasion, employee evaluations and performance reviews.

Systems for Human Resources

Several VTC system options could serve HR departments well. However, since the functions of HR are varied, it is important to conduct a thorough need analysis, because requirements can vary from desktop systems for interviews and an employee information kiosk, to full-blown conference and training rooms with a wide range of multimedia support. Additionally, there may be special privacy requirements that must be met, and other needs such as the video documentation of meetings.

Training

To remain competitive, companies are realizing the need to upgrade employee skills in a rapid and cost-effective manner. Employee training within corporations and institutions is rapidly widening its reach from classroom-based instructor-led learning to a variety of delivery technologies, including videotapes, computer-based training (CBT), CD-ROM, DVD, the corporate intranet, satellite, videoconferencing, and the Internet.

National Technological University (NTU), a leading provider of advanced technical education and training, reports that over 1,200 working professionals and managers were admitted to its degree programs in 1998–99. NTU offers a wide range of courses from a working alliance of universities and training organizations, delivered via multiple platforms, including satellite and the Internet.

The delivery of programs directly to the work site, coupled with the ability to record broadcasts for student viewing at home, eliminates student travel costs and significant time away from the job. According to NTU, removing these components of traditional corporate training costs can save its customers as much as 45 percent of their total training expenses.

According to a report on trends in corporate training by W.R. Hambrecht & Co., corporate e-learning is one of the fastest growing markets in the education industry. The report notes that the online training market is expected to nearly double in size every year, reaching approximately $11.5 billion by 2003.

Point-to-point instructor-led group training is the most common form of VTC-based training, as it maximizes the reach of instructors, and minimizes travel expenses and employee down time while maintaining a high degree of interactivity and maximizing student assimilation of course materials. This form of instruction has been widely used by such leading companies as AT&T, Hewlett-Packard (HP), and Sony. Many organizations seek to further expand the reach of instructor expertise through the use of multipoint conferencing. While this can be very effective, great care must be taken to maintain good audio, video, and graphics quality, and to maximize opportunities for instructor-student interaction.

Sometimes one-on-one videoconferencing is the best choice for training. Tim Gilbert, president of VisioComUSA, a company that designs and delivers VTC and Web-based technical training courses for executives at large corporations, notes, "One-on-one videoconferencing with applications sharing can facilitate high-intensity coaching-style learning environments where intermediate and advanced skills are the subject. These skills are almost invariably applied in ways that are very specific to the learner and are therefore perfectly suited to transfer in a one-on-one environment. If the skill is specific to a computer software application, either business or technical, the applications sharing capabilities of desktop videoconferencing is a fantastic way to teach and learn."

Gilbert cautions training managers that videoconferencing is still a tool with unacceptably high error rates, compared to, say, the telephone: "So, always remember to have contingency plans in place and ready to go." VTC based-training requires careful preparation: "Always test your distance training program prior to going live," Gilbert advises. "You will need to validate the content, the delivery, and the trainer. Assessment and certification in all these areas should be a constant and ongoing process. As a mantra, the training industry should use the word: interaction. Everything you do is amplified in a videoconference. So, as boring as linear delivery of content is in a classroom, it is even worse in a videoconference."

Matrix Resources, an Atlanta-based staffing company for IT professionals, is using videoconferencing to conduct distance training for its employees located in its Atlanta, Dallas, Phoenix, and Raleigh, North Carolina, offices. As might be expected from a company that leaves and breathes high-tech, the Matrix network takes advantage of the latest technologies—including VTEL Galaxy systems and Cisco routers, along with Qwest's ATM backbone. According to Andy Hall, director of information systems, the company has been working to improve the quality of conducting video over its private ATM network. "We see the IP world evolving over the next couple of years as the mainstream vehicle for videoconferencing," notes Hall.

Systems for Training

Videoconferencing systems that are to be used for training should strive to maximize image quality and to provide teaching tools that are easy to use. To assure maximum throughput of instructional content, systems should communicate at speeds of 384 kbps or higher and employ high-quality cameras, microphones, and lighting in the instructor-side system. Student-side systems should be equipped with larger-than-average monitors, or even video-data projectors. Teaching support tools, such as electronic whiteboards, copy-stand cameras, and slide projectors, should be fully integrated into the instructor system whenever possible and should have a common control interface.

Systems that have been optimized for training and distance learning are available from VTEL, Tandberg, and a number of value-added resellers (VARs) and system integrators who are specialists in the design and implementation of educational systems.

Distance Learning

Distance learning is one of the more mature application areas of teleconferencing technologies. Initially, satellite broadcasting was the primary delivery technology for education and training, with switched digital lines playing a steadily increasing role over the years. Recently there has been a greater convergence of delivery technologies, with various combinations of digital satellite broadcasting, interactive H.320/323 conferencing, Web-based instruction, and streaming media. Figure 2-2 shows a videoconferencing classroom.

Partnerships between academic organizations and business are becoming more

Figure 2-2 An elementary school distance learning classroom. (Photo: VTEL)

popular as schools look for a greater return on their intellectual resources, and corporations try to retain and develop high-level personnel. Videoconferencing provides an ideal solution for both sides of the equation. Colleges and universities maximize the reach of their faculty without the cost of branch campuses and additional administrative overhead; and companies improve the skills and morale of their employees, with no downtime for travel. While the academic institutions provide the content, their business partners are in a better position to provide the technical infrastructure to distribute the programs.

Several distance education networks provide good examples of the benefits of partnering and the convergence of technology.

Ohio SchoolNet

The state of Ohio is supplying videoconferencing systems for its Next Generation Internet initiative, the Interactive Video Distance Learning Project (IVDLP). Using live, two-way video and other multimedia applications on a computer network, the $9.2-million pilot project aims to develop teaching methods for advanced math and science concepts, as well as community outreach and career development programs.

The IVDLP is one of the first statewide private networks to push the envelope of PC-based videoconferencing by incorporating streaming video, multicasting, and video-on-demand into traditional two-way conferencing activities. System partners Ameritech, Mnet, VTEL, and FVC.com have committed to making IVDLP a model program for Ohio and the integration of multimedia technologies and the Internet. Established in 1998 by the Ohio General Assembly, IVDLP is a $9.2-million competitive grant program to provide funds for interactive video distance learning systems in public high schools. The program also funds the piloting of an Asynchronous Transfer Mode (ATM) network, a faster standard for transmitting digital video, audio, and data. To date, 128 high schools, representing seventeen consortia and two single high schools, have been awarded IVDLP grants ranging from $45,000 to $100,000.

Georgia's Statewide System

Established in 1992, the Georgia Statewide Academic and Medical System (GSAMS), one of the world's largest two-way interactive video and audio networks, has conducted over 100,000 videoconferences over its multimedia network. GSAMS enables students to interact directly from their community with teachers and students in other GSAMS classrooms throughout Georgia.

With the multipoint, gateway-enabled system that reaches across the world, they have access to a multitude of previously unavailable programs and courses and exposure to a wide variety of instruction.

Any GSAMS distance learning classroom can be connected to any other GSAMS classroom point-to-point or up to a sixteen-classroom multipoint configuration. These classrooms are used to teach traditional subjects in non-technical ways and communicate administrative issues, such as staff development, administrative policy meetings, student debates, and faculty interviews. "Citizens throughout Georgia are gaining exposure and access to resources they never would have had without the system. They receive the education or information they need while in their community without having to expend extra time and incur costs associated with traveling," notes Kelly Thomas, video product strategy manager for Georgia's Department of Administrative Services, Information Technology Services.

According to Thomas, "GSAMS has allowed state government to run more efficiently and effectively as well as increased collaboration among agencies." GSAMS is also being used to provide telemedicine programs, telemedicine consultations, and special conferences, meetings, public and legislative hearings and updates, educational field trips, and other communications.

VTEL Managed Solutions, one of the network's main hardware maintenance providers, serves as the system's call manager, connecting and maintaining a majority of the four hundred sites within the GSAMS network.

Government

Government use of VTC dates back to the earliest days of the technology. In the military, where personal command and consultation are so much a part of the basic fabric of management, VTC has played a major role in extending the reach of command and enabled mission-critical meetings to be held without regard for distance or travel restrictions. The Defense Commercial Telecommunications Network (DCTN), constructed by AT&T for the armed forces in the 1980s and 1990s, provided the first secure, reliable, high-quality two-way video network for many major military installations.

In recent years, Defense Information Systems Video Network has made VTC a normal, day-to-day tool for military commanders around the world. It provides interactive multimedia support for discussion of critical issues, adding a personal dimension to the transmission of orders, and even contact with loved ones for members of the armed forces. The U.S. Army Teletraining Network is one of the largest two-way training networks in the world. It uses both terrestrial and satellite communications to deliver more than eighteen hours of training per day to army personnel in more than seventeen different countries around the world.

Today virtually every branch of the federal government, from the White House to the Department of Energy and the National Institutes of Health, uses VTC as a basic communication tool to increase productivity and reduce travel costs. For example, the U.S. Patent Office has set up a special VTC program to enable applicants and their patent examiners to meet at a distance, saving time and money for all concerned. States and localities have also learned to use VTC as a powerful tool to make government more efficient and responsive to the needs of their constituents. Beginning with distance learning and telemedicine, VTC quickly found a home in law enforcement.

Justice for All

Overburdened courts and police department found that they could do their job a bit better with the help of videoconferencing. The Manhattan District Attorney's office in New York City has been using desktop conferencing units for years to make the wheels of justice turn a little more smoothly. Remote units installed at police precinct houses around the city enable assistant district attorneys (ADAs) to instantly take statements from witnesses, complainants, and police officers. This saves the city millions of dollars in overtime previously paid to officers who had to travel downtown and sometimes wait for hours to provide statements. It also makes it easier for ADAs to get statements from witnesses and victims who might otherwise have been reluctant to become involved.

El Paso, Texas, and other municipalities have gone one step further, adding video arraignment to their arsenal of time- and cost-saving tools. One of the biggest costs involved in law enforcement is the transportation of prisoners for arraignment, and arraignment by videoconferencing has proved to be a popular and cost-effective application. El Paso, Texas, made VTC-based arraignment even more cost-effective by reducing the network costs—hooking up their widely dispersed locations using a variety of existing T1 and single-mode-fiber connections. They did this with the help of First Virtual Corporation (FVC), which supplied ATM adapters, switches, software, and (most important) creative technical expertise. With sophisticated multipoint capabilities and an ATM/ISDN gateway to allow law enforcement personnel to consult with colleagues outside the area, the El Paso system is perhaps a prototype for future mixed-network systems. "The learning curve was significant particularly in the area of having adequate tools, training, and troubleshooting skills," reported Jake Nicholson, director of data processing for the county. "Our success, and the ITCA Excellence Award we received for this application, will help foster increased collaboration between local governments and law enforcement agencies," he said, "and it will also serve to help decision-makers recognize the value of investing in leading-edge technologies."

But the use of VTC in law enforcement doesn't stop at the courthouse. The Hillsborough County Corrections Facility in Florida has a Video Visitation System consisting of 124 conference rooms and stations—74 for inmates and 50 for visitors. In addition to increasing the number of hour-long visits the facility could safely handle (from ten to over fifty per day), the system (designed by Atlanta-based Brinckman & Associates) also improves inmate access to legal counsel. The county public defender's office is now equipped with more than eighty desktop videoconferencing units, allowing lawyers to confer with their clients without the need to travel to the facility from their offices.

Industry-Specific Applications

Several industries were in the vanguard when it came to the adoption of videoconferencing. Some of the most prominent "early adopters" include pharmaceuticals, aerospace, banking, and electronics. These were generally involved in businesses that met all of the following criteria:

1. Widely dispersed management workgroups. This could involve many offices scattered around a city (e.g., Boeing) or major offices scattered around the world (e.g., Citicorp).
2. Geographically concentrated expensive expertise, such as leading scientists, financial industry "market makers," and world-class managers. VTC enables them be present in two places (or more) at one time.
3. Short product cycles or the need for rapid strategic decision-making.

In some industries, such as consumer electronics or women's apparel, shaving even a few days off a product development cycle can spell the difference between success and failure. In others, such as pharmaceuticals, the travel time saved by conducting videoconferences can cut months from the time required to bring a new medicine to market.

Banking and Financial Services

Perhaps nowhere else does the time- and travel-saving aspects of teleconferencing translate so directly into increased profits as in the international financial services industry. With Citicorp, Credit Suisse First Boston and other giants leading the way, videoconferencing and collaborative technologies have quickly migrated from the boardroom to virtually every aspect of day-to-day financial services business. Some banks have already completed pilot projects involving VTC-enabled kiosks that bring "personal banking" services to remote locations like the outback of Australia.

The key application of VTC in the fast-paced financial services industry is still the support of workgroup meetings for all levels of management, from the army of IT scientists they employ to the relatively few "seniors" whose time is worth thousands of dollars an hour.

The Citicorp videoconferencing program stretches back to the earliest days of the medium, when CLI's (Compression Lab, Inc.'s) Rembrandt Codec serial number 001 was installed in the company's San Francisco regional headquarters. Under the direction of Citicorp Global Information Network's senior vice president Joyce Thompson, the VTC network has grown to connect hundreds of locations in every corner of the globe. It was the first corporate network to deploy multipoint control units (MCUs) at multiple locations, the first to remotely manage the operation of dozens of systems, and has set the standard for technically astute organization and dedication to excellent customer service. The company's New York City boardroom system, designed jointly by David Congdon, a vice president at Citicorp, and the engineers of Pierce Phelps, still stands as one of the technical marvels of the golden age of videoconferencing. Multiple 3-CCD cameras, walls of monitors, banks of codecs, in-house MCUs, and a powerful Madge network switching facility ensure that all the senior executives of this financial giant can meet instantly, face-to-face, whenever necessary.

The Credit Suisse First Boston (CSFB) video network began as a grassroots program, with business units and offices adding systems as required, but with no centralized control over network configuration or equipment purchasing. In late 1996, CSFB formed the Global Media Services department, with the purpose of improving the reliability and quality of meetings, increasing the cost-effectiveness of all videoconferencing activities, and generally bringing "order out of chaos." Since that time, vice president and department head, Ira Weinstein has established rigorous technical standards and testing procedures, helped develop a strategic plan for the worldwide deployment of VTC technology, and managed the expansion of the network to include more than 150 systems worldwide. A dedicated staff of more than thirty five members support all VTC activities, including the remote management of systems all over the world, and the operation of CSFB's state-of-the-art, 24-port Accord MCU-100.

The Advantages of In-house Capability

According to Weinstein, the recent deployment of the MCU-100, and the parallel deployment of a cable and wireless virtual private network (VPN), has led to a tremendous reduction in the cost of multipoint conferencing. For example, the cost of including a London site in a multipoint conference at 384 kbps has been reduced from $460 to $90 per hour. With almost 30 percent of CSFB's video-conferences requiring the use of a multipoint bridge, the savings have been enormous. A single, 28-point videoconference with the new MCU and network could cost as much as $80,000 less than a similar meeting conducted through a multipoint service provider. The management of a big MCU and major multipoint meetings is not a simple task and requires well-trained, in-house, 24x7 technical staff, as well as a solid escalation strategy for high-level technical support when required. But it can be an ideal solution for some users who have both heavy multipoint conferencing needs and progressive management ready to provide the resources required for successful deployment.

Electronics and Aerospace

Both of these industries have tight product-development cycles, widely dispersed workgroups, complex project-management requirements, and the need to expedite workgroup communications with a variety of partners, suppliers, and major customer organizations. VTC use has been a key element in the growth of IBM, HP, Sony, Apple, and dozens of other high-tech companies, as it has been in aerospace giants such as Lockheed and Grumman.

Systems developed for use in these industries are designed to maximize collaborative work processes by providing a variety of interactive tools, such as screen and application sharing. It is also important to provide sufficient bandwidth to allow virtually instant transmission of high-resolution graphics, including blueprints and CAD/CAM diagrams. Display devices that enable these graphics to be easily viewed by the entire group, such as large multiscan monitors or video-data projectors, are also important to the success of VTC systems intended for technical communications.

Pharmaceuticals

Multinational drug companies, such as Pfizer and Merck, were early adopters of videoconferencing due to their need for rapid high-quality communication between management and scientific workgroups spread around the world. Other factors attributed to the rapid deployment of VTC systems within this industry include intensive training requirements, the need to optimize communications with regulatory bodies (e.g., the Food and Drug Administration) and with academic and medical communities.

Telemedicine

Few professions are better suited for videoconferencing than the practice of medicine. The expertise of medical doctors and scientists is very expensive, and if even the best medical centers do not have local access to high-level specialists in every area, how much more difficult is the plight of disadvantaged or remote communities? Telemedicine is one of the most important solutions to the conflicting imperatives of better medical care and lower costs. Recent progress in resolving difficult regulatory and technical issues (i.e., insurance and licensing, remote sensing and imaging) has fueled even greater growth in this important application.

Uses of Telehealth Networks

Health care providers to patients located at a distance traditionally have focused the use of telemedicine networks on clinical applications, such as teleconsultations (*see* Figure 2-3). In recent years, the networks have increasingly been used

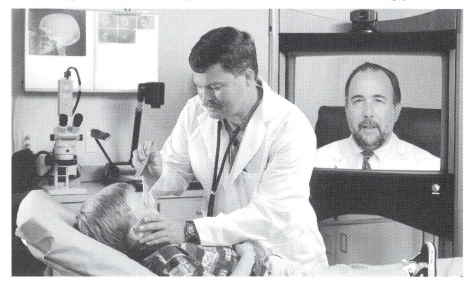

Figure 2-3 A telemedicine VTC facility. (Photo: VTEL)

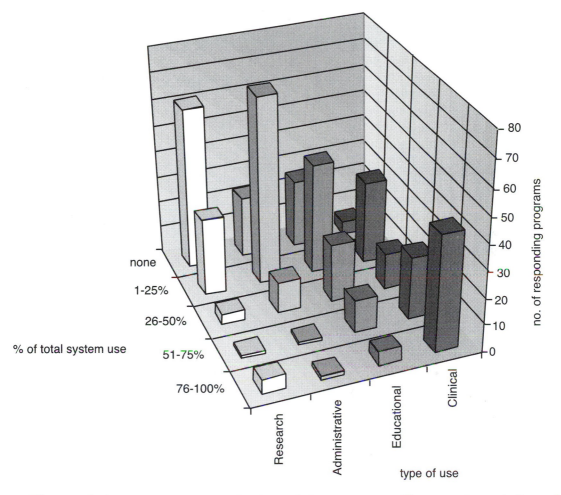

Figure 2-4 Reported uses of telemedicine systems. (Source: Association of Telehealth Providers)

for nonclinical applications such as administrative, educational, research and organizational functions (*see* Figure 2-4); hence the term *telehealth networks* is now frequently used in the industry.

According to the 1999 Report on U.S. Telemedicine Activity published by the Association of Telehealth Service Providers (ATSP), the primary use of telemedicine systems is for clinical applications. The ATSP survey respondents listed the following top clinical services provided by their networks:

- Specialist referrals and second opinions

- Ongoing management of patients' clinical conditions (e.g., chronic disease management)
- Medical/surgical follow-up
- Specialist clinics
- Medication management (often used in conjunction with mental health applications)
- Diagnostic exam interpretation
- Emergency room/triage
- Patient case review (cancer patient review)
- Patient screening
- Home health
- Facilitate family/patient interaction
- Rehabilitation
- Pain management
- Physiological monitoring
- Nursing home/assisted living care
- Fetal ultrasound
- Patient education
- Legal/judicial
- Patient triage
- Mobile emergency response

Among the nonclinical uses of telehealth systems, education was the most frequently reported activity. In general, education included continuing medical education, grand rounds (including staff development, morning reports, and resident education), distance education, and patient/community education. Almost 5,000 continuing medical education courses were offered in 1998, involving some 28,000 participants. Other educational applications included continuing nursing education, demonstrations, tumor boards, family support, and infection control orientation.

Videoconferencing is used by telehealth networks for administrative activities such as meetings among telehealth network participants, board of director meetings, and to facilitate network supervision. The benefits realized have been in the savings of time and travel-related expenses, and increased internal communication.

Research activities involving the use of videoconferencing have been limited. Most of the documented applications in this area are within military programs that are examining a wide range of telemedicine applications suitable for battlefield situations.

Typical Telemedical Applications

A wide range of health care providers are recognizing telemedicine as a core business component and a tool to extend the geographic reach of their institutions and doctors, particularly to better serve rural and economically disadvantaged areas.

Clinical

The Charles R. Drew University of Medicine and Science in Los Angeles administers the Carmelitos Prevention Eye Care Center, an urban telemedicine project that provides primary medical care to 1,800 residents of Los Carmelitos, an inner-city public housing development in southern California. The Carmelitos clinic shows how teleopthalmology is a cost-effective solution to improve health care in underserved urban communities. "The ability to integrate VTEL systems into our ATM network environment was the key factor in determining the success and proliferation of telemedicine here at the King/Drew Medical Center," said Dr. Charles W. Flowers, director of telemedicine at King/Drew Medical Center. "We can now distribute expertise throughout our campus and out to neighborhood clinics seamlessly. VTEL has consistently stayed on the cutting edge of videoconferencing technology, enabling us to develop custom applications and better serve the population."

Clinical and Nonclinical

The Eastern Montana Telemedicine Network makes clinical, mental health, education, and administrative services available to twelve network sites in isolated rural communities in eastern Montana. "The members of the Eastern Montana Telemedicine Network have embraced telemedicine technology as a cost-effective means of providing improved access to medical care and continuing health education, shrinking the distance faced in rural eastern Montana," said Thelma McClosky Armstrong, director of telemedicine at the Eastern Montana Telemedicine Network.

Distance Education

The Inland Northwest Telehealth Services program in Spokane, Washington, is a consortium of five hospitals and fifteen rural sites. Over 50 percent of the use of its telemedicine system is devoted to distance education. The most common use is for grand rounds in trauma, pediatrics, psychiatry, orthopedics and genetics, which are broadcast to all fifteen sites. They connect monthly with a pediatric oncologist at the University of Washington to do tumor board case reviews for breast cancer.

Research

The Telemedicine Directorate, based at Walter Reed Army Medical Center in Washington, D.C., has several research projects either underway or starting in 2000. Ask-A-Doc is a low-cost electronic e-mail consultation system available to all health care providers throughout the North Atlantic Regional Medical Command (NARMC), TRICARE (the military health care system), and the U.S. Army Medical Department (AMEDD). It provides clinical expertise, supported by the house staff of Walter Reed Army Medical Center, to military health care providers. Ask-A-Doc owes its success to rapid response capability, and it has been providing approximately one hundred consultations per month to requesting clinical providers, mostly connecting them to internal medicine specialties. Using the system for triage, they reportedly have decreased referrals to specialists and reduced costs. Another research study involves teledentistry. A recently developed Web site enables army, navy and air force dentists to send consults, including images, to specialists who review the requests and provide consultation on diagnosis and treatment. There is also a section on the Web site devoted to distance learning. Dentists can view archived cases, set up a video-conferencing schedule for continuing education purposes, search dental abstracts, and listen to online lectures.

Systems for Telemedicine

Videoconferencing systems for use in telemedicine run the gambit from simple desktop units to some of the most advanced remote imaging and collaboration systems in the world. In general, VTC systems for telemedicine applications must interface with a wide range of diagnostic instruments (microscopes, X-ray scanners, etc.), and may need to comply with strict regulations in regard to their electrical and mechanical characteristics. Tandberg, VTEL, NEC, and several specialized VARs manufacture VTC systems designed for use in telemedicine.

Conclusion

It is becoming easier and less expensive to deploy and operate effective video-conferencing systems for a wide range of applications. The cost of equipment and network services is decreasing, while the selection of manufacturers and service providers is increasing.

If there is a downside to this increased availability and reduced cost, it is the commoditization of VTC and the resulting "one size fits all" approach of a number of vendors. While it is true that current low-cost set-top and desktop systems are more powerful than some room systems of just a few years ago, they can be worse than useless if not properly customized for user-specific communications needs. The options required could be something as simple as an extra monitor and camera for a teacher in a distance learning classroom, or as complex as an inband teleradiology unit for a desktop telemedicine station. As long as the unique communication needs of users are understood and effectively addressed, the system will be a success.

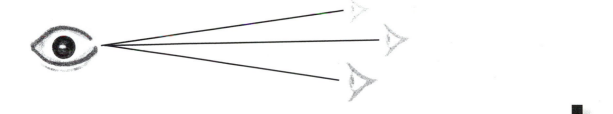

Needs Analysis—Defining Your Ideal System 3

Executive Summary

Could your organization benefit from the use of videoconferencing or some other mode of video communication? The answer is almost surely yes. But what are the specific communication needs that such a solution would address, and, are the benefits worth the effort and expenditure? To find out the answers to these questions and to zero in on the right video solution for your needs, you first need to know who will use it, how often, and for what purpose. In order to maximize the return on investment (ROI), you need to make sure that the sysem will actually meet the communication needs of potential users. To ensure that users' needs will be addressed, you need to know all about their current "style" of meeting—content, size, type, visual aids, and, last but not least, who they meet with and where those people work. This chapter provides a step-by-step method for conducting your own needs analysis. A needs analysis and deployment checklist at the end of the chapter (*see* Figure 3-5) should help you cover all the bases, and keep your project on track toward a successful deployment.

Conducting a Needs Analysis

Nothing is more important to the success of a video communications system than a thorough, systematic, and honest needs analysis.

Thorough—because "the devil is in the details," and a successful system must incorporate, or at least allow for, every foreseeable need likely to be encountered during its planned lifetime. Imagine the embarrassment involved in explaining to a chief financial officer, who has just finished paying the bills for a new video network, that he can't show his budget spreadsheet to the chief executive officer during a conference.

Systematic—because the components of a videoconferencing system derive from many separate technologies—from telecommunications and computing to audio, video, and machine control. What trade-offs and accommodations you will need to make to blend these varied technologies can be discovered by systematically combining the needs of your users with the hard realities of the available time, tools, and budget.

Honest—because there is sometimes a difference between the stated objectives of a system, and the real needs and priorities of its most important users.

Major Steps

The major steps in a needs analysis are:
1. Determine the scope of your project.
2. Identify potential users, their locations, and communications needs.
3. Develop a prioritized list of functional requirements.
4. Project and quantify future needs and requirements.
5. Compile a master list of present and future functional requirements.
6. Investigate your existing digital communication infrastructure.
7. (Optional) Prepare and distribute a request for information (RFI).
8. Develop one or more preliminary solution plans.
9. Develop one or more preliminary budgets.
10. Analyze the cost/benefits of your alternate solutions.
11. Evaluate and modify your preliminary plans and budgets.
12. Prepare a final needs analysis report.

Request for Proposal

After completing your needs analysis, you will be ready to prepare a request for proposal (RFP). This document is important even for projects as simple as a "packaged" two-location, dial-up, small group system. It serves as a baseline reference to which you and your vendors can refer, and which can be used to define the "scope of work" that each vendor agrees to undertake. Without this defined scope of work for each vendor, small but vital elements may be left to chance. In the case of a simple dial-up system, issues that might "fall through the cracks" could include: testing and troubleshooting the ISDN service, training remote users, and even the provision of adapters such as NT-1s and AC power strips.

RFPs can also be used as a tool for developing preliminary budgets, although many vendors will respond to requests for information with proposals containing costs. Detailed information on creating an RFP is provided in Chapter 6.

The Twelve Steps

There are many ways to prepare an effective needs analysis. What follows is one method that has proven useful over the years. You can use it as a template, or modify it to suit your needs. It may be too complex for some simple projects, or not complete enough for the most complex. Even if you already have developed a satisfactory method of analyzing your user and system requirements, you may find a few helpful ideas in this section.

1. Determine the scope of your project.
It may seem obvious, but determining or defining the scope of your project in writing is a step that is often neglected or glossed over. To do this, you need to formulate, list, and confirm the specific goals of your project, the resources available, and the time that has been allotted for its completion. If you are investigating the long-term potential benefits and costs of videoconferencing for your organization, you will take one approach. On the other hand, if you have a mandate to develop a predefined solution for a limited group of users within a specified budget and schedule, your task takes on an entirely different shape. In either case, the first seven or eight steps of your needs analysis will proceed in pretty much the same manner, differing only in the amount of attention and detail devoted to specific areas. A strategic plan, for example, might deal more thoroughly with future user needs, emerging technologies, and relevant trends in networking. A targeted implementation with an established budget, on the other hand, might focus on determining which specific products and services will satisfy the most important user needs—on time and under budget.

2. Identify potential users, their locations, and communications needs.
When compiling a list of probable users for your system, it is first helpful to classify them according to the following criteria:
  • Name, title, department, division, etc.
  • Location or Locations. Be specific—include not only town or city, but building, floor, etc. If the users are "mobile," include a list of locations from where they may participate in meetings.

You need to know as much as possible about their meeting habits. One simple method to accomplish this is to ask users only about meetings they organized or chaired during the last year. A more thorough and exhaustive process involves asking them about every meeting they have attended during this period. This can be a task of daunting proportions, especially in a large organization. In either case, your primary interest should be in meetings that are attended by people from other locations. Whatever your approach, the more that you know about the meeting habits and requirements of your key users, the more likely it is that your videoconferencing solution will become a real success.

Note: In the case of senior management, I have found that an executive's administrative assistant can often provide this information more easily than the execs themselves. Assistants can at least provide you with a list of dates and attendees with which to prompt the memory of a busy boss.

For each major user or group of users, you can determine needs by combining current meeting style and habits with their expectations (if any) for the new system. Keep in mind that the purpose of a good system is to enhance the existing meeting process and to empower users with more effective communication tools. A system that forces users to communicate in unfamiliar or uncomfortable ways will not be successful.

For example, a group comptroller might be accustomed to presenting budget analyses spreadsheets using a laptop computer with a 1,024 x 768 display and a LCD projector. She does this at monthly meetings of accounting managers who travel from five branch offices to headquarters to attend. During the meetings, it is necessary for everyone to hear the comments of all attendees, and to easily identify who has said what. Substantial savings in both time and travel expenses could be realized if these meetings were conducted via videoconference. Unfortunately, many "packaged" videoconferencing solutions are not equipped to receive and display high-resolution (hi-res) images of this kind. Spreadsheets could be reformatted with larger type, a copy-stand camera could be used to magnify the cells under discussion, or copies could be faxed to all attendees beforehand. None of these are optimal solutions, as they require a change in meeting style and process. Fortunately, there are several options that will satisfy these meeting needs without requiring users to modify their work style, though they do add some expense and complexity to the system. Which solution you finally implement will depend on an evaluation of the sum total of all your users' needs and the available resources. Your list of needs for this hypothetical user should include the ability to connect her laptop directly to the system, and to have the content transmitted and displayed at hi-res at all the required remote sites.

What follows is a brief description of the key issues that need to be addressed to create a clear picture of your system's requirements. I have also included a sample list of questions (*see* Figure 3-1, pg 43) that can be used to gather information from your end users, as well as several spreadsheets that show one way that this information can be organized.

A. Number and Identity of Potential Users

This should include all the likely participants at each site and meeting. The average and maximum number of participants at a typical meeting or training session is an important factor in system design. Equipment suitable for small groups is very different from what is appropriate for larger groups. The ideal number, position, and type of cameras, microphones, and monitors vary depending on the size of the group. Even the speed (and cost) of the network connection may need to be increased to transmit a clear picture of larger groups.

The identity of probable meeting attendees is also of great importance. Their title or job function will give you a clearer picture of the actual meeting process. Engineers generally conduct meetings in a very different way than accountants or marketing people. User interfaces that are ideal for technical types are also usually far too complex for senior managers.

It will also help you to prioritize needs in a way that conforms to your organization's culture. For example, the meeting needs of senior vice presidents usually carry more weight than those of product managers.

The amount of travel currently required for people to attend a meeting is of great importance. This information should help you to calculate how travel expenses (and time lost to travel) could be reduced if a videoconferencing network is deployed.

Key Question: Is there someone whose attendance would have contributed to achieving the goals of this meeting who did not attend due to the travel expense involved, or a need to be at another location? This question highlights one of the greatest hidden benefits of videoconferencing—the ability to include remote expertise in a meeting.

B. Type of Presentation Materials

This list should include all the visual aids currently used at meeting, as well as those that are under consideration for future use. These might include: overhead transparencies of spreadsheets, PowerPoint presentations (on disk, laptop, or LAN), photographs, ad layouts, CAD drawings, or 3-D objects (e.g., product samples), or any of a hundred other media. Your list should also include the equipment currently used to display these media, such as LCD projectors, large video monitors, or overhead projectors. This list of visual media and display equipment will become a key factor in the determination of the right combination of cameras, graphics transmission hardware and software, and display devices at the remote sites. In some cases, it will also influence decisions about network type and bandwidth. It may be necessary to test several solutions for critical applications, as the definition of "acceptable" image quality can be a very subjective call.

Example: In one system installed at several locations for a famous designer and manufacturer of clothing, samples of fabric and garments were routinely pinned to the wall for group review. Close-up views of clothing details also needed to be shared with remote attendees. The simple solution was to mount a remote control camera on the side of the room facing the "clothing wall," and to install a hi-res (3-chip) copy-stand camera for detailed views.

C. Meeting or Session Type and Style

Are typical meetings formal or informal, roundtable, podium speaker/presenter, structured brainstorming, or free-form with lots of movement? The answers to these and related questions will influence the design of the videoconferencing room, position and type of cameras, microphones, and a host of other elements.

Are there any special meetings (such as quarterly reviews) that differ from the typical meetings described above in size, character, or special requirements? The size, frequency, and importance of these meetings will determine whether your basic system must be changed to fit them, or whether ad hoc arrangements will do.

Example: The average expected videoconference attendance at branch offices of a financial services company was less than ten. At the end of each quarter, the division head wanted to address all the "troops" simultaneously. Rather than enlarge the conference rooms to gigantic proportions, the simple solution was to distribute the sound and picture to the cafeteria TVs, and to include wiring for an extra camera and microphone at that location.

Are any special technologies currently used in these meetings or sessions, such as speakerphones, computers (for e-mail or document sharing), fax machines, whiteboards, projectors, etc.? The answer to this question will not only alert you to specific hardware requirements for new rooms, it will help you to design a system that integrates new and old technologies in a synergistic way.

Are these meetings internal or do they include presentations to customers or other groups outside your organization? If key clients, vendors, or strategic partners are regularly included in the list of attendees, you might want to add them to your list of users. Find out if they already have videoconferencing capabilities. If they do, these "outsider" systems are particularly important in that you have no control over their system and network configurations, and you may need to adapt your plans to ensure effective communication.

How far in advance are these meetings usually scheduled? Who handles these arrangements? Collating the answers to these questions will help you to select the right scheduling software or system.

D. Locations

Where are the meetings currently held? The list of locations should include a description of both the current location(s) for the meetings and the probable locations from which remote participants would join a "videoconferenced" version of the same meetings.

Do participants typically use specific rooms or facilities for their meetings? List the address, room number, and as much detail about facilities and equipment as you can.

Example: The monthly regional budget review is held in the 4th floor conference room in the office at 10 Main Street in New City. The room measures 15' x 20' with no windows, seats twelve people at a rectangular conference table, and is equipped with an LCD projector and screen, a computer connected to the LAN, and a table-top speakerphone. There is good air conditioning with in-room temperature control, and four, 4-foot fluorescent fixtures (spaced 3 feet apart) with individual switches. The office at that location has one ISDN line (BRI), which is currently used for shared Internet and remote computer access.

The more complete your "picture" of the room and facility, the easier will be the task of selecting and installing a system for that location. If possible, you should have a copy of the floor plan of the facility, including the room in question and any others that could be used for videoconferencing. Details such as lighting, location of electrical outlets, windows, and doors are all significant. Before finalizing the plans for a particular location it is always a good idea to make a site survey. This will alert you to any differences that exist between drawings or reports and the current reality.

If desktop conferencing is being considered as a possible alternative, list the locations of potential desktop conferees, and (if possible) their computer type, LAN and phone connections, size of office or cubicle, etc. Mobile managers frequently use laptops with docking stations as their primary computer, and these are not suitable for many desktop conferencing applications. In such a case, there is a choice to be made between a dedicated PC for conferencing, a set-top system, or one of the new units with a universal serial bus (USB) interface such as the Polycom ViaVideo.

E. Picture and Sound Quality

Are there any special needs related to video or audio quality? It is very important to determine if there are special requirements for a high level of video or audio quality—as distinct from the need for hi-res graphics for spreadsheets, ad layouts, CAD files, and similar documents.

The basic functional need involved in seeing and hearing the distant members of a meeting is related to the size of the group and the physical characteristics of the room, and can be determined objectively, as described in Chapter 4, "Choosing the Right System."

There are special objective needs based on the content or conduct of meetings. These could include anything from the need to see the delicate movements of a surgeon's scalpel to a requirement for the accurate rendition of recorded musical selections.

There are also special subjective needs related to the communications process. When a high-ranking member of your organization expresses these in a business context, they obviously carry tremendous weight.

Example: One senior vice president of a major corporation planning to use videoconferencing for high-pressure business negotiations said, "I want to see them sweat." He got his wish, despite the substantial increase in cost for the additional bandwidth and high-quality hardware required.

If, on the other hand, the need for high-quality video is driven by a vague notion that conferences should "look like *Nightline*," it may be necessary to take a more active role in managing user expectations. This can sometimes be accomplished through a simple demonstration of the various quality levels available, accompanied by a presentation of the relative costs involved.

<u>*Note*</u>: In addition to better cameras and other hardware, higher picture and sound quality usually requires higher-speed communication, which can result in substantially higher cost of operation, up to three or four times.

F. Other Important Considerations

• Legal and security issues: Are there any considerations that may be unique to your organization and that shape the conduct of current meetings? These might include legal or security concerns, or record keeping procedures—and could trigger the need for the recording of conferences, the implementation of encryption procedures, or other specialized processes. For example, in certain financial institutions, it is customary (and sometimes mandatory) to tape discussions with customers about the prospective purchase or sale of securities.

• Access: Access for workers with special needs related to limited sight or hearing can be easily integrated into videoconferencing systems if the requirement is included in the needs analysis. For example, it is a relatively simple matter to "design-in" a separate graphics monitor for a regular attendee who would have difficulty reading from a main monitor or projection screen. This task, if left to the last minute, can become an expensive cabling and equipment hassle.

• Corporate culture: Is there anything special about the arrangements for your meetings or the way in which you conduct them? This covers a multitude of issues, some simple and logical, and some right out of *The X-Files*. The answer could be something as simple as the need to provide two chairs at the head of the conference table, or to have fresh coffee always available. Or it could be something as arcane as the need to play the company song at the beginning of each meeting (a real example), or to have all remote controls in the company color (another real one). You or your key meeting participants will know if there is anything special about the meetings in question.

• Who's the real boss?: Organizational politics are an unfortunate fact of life in many work situations. Even if you write your notes in disappearing ink, you need to factor in the political and other possibly irrational factors that might impact system design. As a Japanese friend, an assistant general manager for the world's largest electronics company, used to say, "There is the truth of truth, and then there is the truth of survival."

I have prepared a detailed list of questions to help you compile information about user needs (*see* Figure 3-1). Please consider it only as a starting point and modify the list to suit your situation.

3. Develop a list of functional requirements.

Once you have queried your prospective users, you need to compile a prioritized list of their needs. There are many ways to do this, and the best method for you to follow depends on your preferred method of digesting information, and the scope of your project. My favorite method for larger systems is to consolidate the list of "needs" questions on a spreadsheet, and compile the responses under the corresponding query (*see* Figure 3-2, Functional requirements by user).

At the same time that I usually compile a list of weighted responses to each needs question, I create a weighted profile of the needs for each location (*see* Figure 3-3, Needs profile for a single location). The weighting process often involves more than translating users' requirements into a hierarchy of needs. Rank has its prerogatives in most organizations, and for good or bad, the wants of senior management sometimes outweighs the needs of lower-level work-groups. In some cases, conflicting needs that cannot be harmonized may need to be compiled and kicked upstairs for resolution.

4. Project and quantify future needs and requirements.

This may take a little digging, but the answers are usually there for the asking. So ask your key users:

- How might your meeting needs change over the next 3 (or 2 or 5) years?
- How do you expect the nature of your meetings or group work processes to change over the next 2 years?
- Do you expect the number of your meetings or the number of people involved in them to increase or decrease over the same period?
- If so, by how much? Will the location of these people be different from those currently involved in your meetings or collaborative process?
- If so, how? Do you plan or expect to use new tools, processes, or ways of presenting and sharing information. (Examples?)
- If videoconferencing becomes available to you, how do you expect this to effect the size, type, or number of your meetings? Please explain.

5. Compile a master list of present and future functional requirements.

The best method to use in the compilation of a master list should be simple enough for you to put together and, of course, makes sense to you and those who will read it. I just expand my spreadsheet, as illustrated in Figure 3-4, List of requirements by location.

6. Investigate your existing digital communication infrastructure.

If you haven't already done so, this might be a good time to talk to your network and telecommunications managers and share some or all of the

Figure 3-1 User Needs Survey

Depending on the complexity and extent of your system and organization, it may be helpful to create a separate user needs survey report for each location, for key users or departments, or even for important meetings that are scheduled on a regular basis. You should gather information on the following items:

1. User name, title, department, division.

2. Specific location of meetings (address, including room number and description).

3. Typical size of meetings.

4. Maximum meeting size.

5. Frequency of meetings.

6. How far in advance is each meeting scheduled and by whom?

7. Primary participants (job function or title).

8. Attendees from outside the organization (specify)?

9. People that typically travel to the meeting?

      A. Location, title and function
      B. Travel method and approximate expenses

10. Non-attendees whose participation would have been useful.

      A. Location, title, and function
      B. Did not attend due to:
         i. Travel expense
         ii. Travel time
         iii. Other (specify)

11. Purpose of the meeting (e.g., budget review, staff meeting, sales meeting).

12. Type of meeting?

      A. Presentation (standing, with or w/o podium)
      B. Presentation (seated)
      C. Group interaction
      D. Training
      E. Hands-on (specify)
      F. Other

13. Meeting style?

      A. Formal
      B. Shirtsleeves
      C. Active collaboration (amount of movement?)
      D. Other

continued >>

Figure 3-1 User Needs Survey (continued)

14. Graphics or other presentation materials used (or desired).

    A. Electronic presentations: type and content
       (e.g., PowerPoint with product photos)
    B. Computer graphics: source, type, and content (e.g., 1,024 x 768 CAD drawings)
    C. Printed text: size and content (e.g., 8.5" x 11" spreadsheets, 10-point type)
    D. Printed graphics: size and content (e.g., 11" x 14" color ad layouts)
    E. 35mm slides or overhead transparencies
    F. Video: source and content (e.g., VHS cassette of site surveys)
    G. 3-D objects: type and content (e.g., products, scale models, machine parts)
    H. Other

15. Graphics annotation required or desired?

16. How are graphics currently displayed?

    A. Projector: type and model (e.g., LCD, Epson EDP-3600)
    B. TV/Monitor: type, size, and model (video, Sony KV-36FS10)
    C. Whiteboard: type and model (e.g. Virtual Ink mimio)
    D. Flipchart
    E. Cork-board, pin-ups
    F. Other

17. Are there any other special meeting needs?

    A. Audio or video playback or recording
    B. Food service
    C. Security/confidentiality
    D. Handicapped access
    E. Other

18. Is a speakerphone used during the meetings?

    A. Names, function, and locations of other parties
    B. Type of speakerphone currently used at this location
    C. Is a conference bridging (conference call) service used?

19. Are there any other meeting technologies in use or anticipated (e.g., fax machine, collaborative computing via NetMeeting)?

20. How do you expect your meetings to change over the next two to three years?

    A. Frequency
    B. Number of participants
    C. Type (leader controlled, interactive, collaborative)
    D. Technologies required

Figure 3-2 Functional requirements by user.

	Functional requirements by user				Banco Binkara				Compiled: 05/05/00		
User Name/Title	Location	Meeting Type	Meeting Style/Type	Frequency	Attendees	Current Travel	Presentation Needs	Other Locations	Other Factors and Needs	Current Meeting Tech.
BN, CEO	Rockville	Board	Formal (Podium) Financial, Strat. & Bus. Presentation	Quarterly	12 Board Members	1 transcon 6 int'l. 3 air shuttle	Overheads, LCD proj., PowerPoint w/video, Lectern	NYC, London, LA, Cinci, Kuala, Mumbai MP (Multipoint)	Highest-quality. Continuous Presence for multipoint (7+ locations)	In-person (with extensive travel), LCD proj.
BN, CEO	Rockville	Direct Rpts. Staff	Informal Financial, Strat. & Bus. Presentation	Monthly	Pres. & 6 Senior VPs	1 transcon 3 int'l. 1 air shuttle	PowerPoint, Overheads, LCD proj.	NYC, London, LA, Cinci, Kuala, Mumbai (MP)	Continuous Presence for multipoint (up to 7 locations)	LCD proj., Audioconference
SN, CFO	NYC	Budget Review	Formal Financial Presentation	Quarterly	CEO, 6 Senior VPs, 2-3 Fin. Staff	CEO via air shuttle	PowerPoint w/ Excel, Overheads, LCD proj.			LCD proj.
SN, CFO	NYC	Staff	Informal Financial Presentation	Weekly	VP Finance, 2 Dirs., 4-6 Staff	No	PowerPoint w/ Excel, Overheads, LCD proj.			LCD proj.
DR, VP- S&Mkt.	NYC	Qtr. Review	Formal	Quarterly	CEO, CFO, CTO, 2 Dirs. 6 Mgrs.	12 air shuttle 1 transcon 2 int'l.	PowerPoint w/Excel, LCD proj. w/remote & laser pointer	Rockville London, LA, Cinci, Kuala, Mumbai (MP)	Audio-add plus Web presentation for remote staff	LCD proj.
DR, VP- S&Mkt.	NYC	Weekly Call/ Briefing	Informal Presentation Sales and Strategy	Weekly	2 Dirs., 8 Mgrs. Want to broadcast to desks of 32 remote staff	No. Due to expense and time	PowerPoint w/Excel, LCD proj. w/remote & laser pointer	Rockville London, LA, Cinci, Kuala, Mumbai (MP)	Audio-add plus Web Presentation for remote staff	LCD proj.
KN, VP- IS	Rockville	Staff	Informal Tech. and Strat. Presentation	Informal Technical and Stretegy	2 IS Dirs, 6+ IS Mgrs.	Yes. 2 air shuttle, others rarely due to expense and time	Overheads, LCD proj., PowerPoint w/MS Project & Visio, Electronic Whiteboard	NYC, London, Cinci, LA (Mumbai, Kuala) MP	Audiographic add, for remote experts	LCD proj., Audioconferencing service, screen-sharing via WAN
KN, VP- IS	Rockville	Status	Shirtsleeve, Collaborative, Technical Presentation	Weekly	2 IS Dirs, 6+ IS Mgrs, 6+ Senior Tech staff	Yes, but rarely, due to expense	Overheads, LCD proj., PowerPoint w/MS Project & Visio, Electronic Whiteboard	NYC, London, Cinci, LA (Mumbai, Kuala) MP	Audiographic add, for remote experts	LCD proj., Audioconferencing service, screen-sharing via WAN

Figure 3-3 Needs profile for a single location.

	Needs profile for a single location				Banco Binkara	Compiled: 05/05/00
	Headquarters location: Rockville, M:				Location requirements prioritized	
Proposed location	Number of Local Participants	Local Attendees	Meeting Styles/Types	Meeting Needs	Presentation Needs	Other Factors
Existing Conference Room "B", 15'x25', large window east exposure. Will require at least some added lighting and soundproofing. Check AC. See drawings rkvlconfb.jpeg	Priority: Room must be able to seat 12 for Board meetings. Typical: Meetings range from 2 to 12+ participants. Most meetings with 4-6 major local participants.	Executives, senior technical and financial management	Priority: Must support current Board meeting style. Typical: Formal and informal Financial, Strat. & Bus. presentations. Informal technical workgroup meetings and presentations. May be used for distance training in the future.	Priority: Must support high-quality video and financial presentations (PowerPoint), with simple controls for executive level meetings. General: High-quality, full motion videoconferencing, multipoint with Continuous Presence (up to	Priority: Video/data projectors must provide easily readable displays of local and remote spreadsheets for executive meetings. General: Data projector (ceiling mount, SXVGA, 1,000+ lumens), networked-PC with wireless mouse, Copy-stand camera (data and vi	Priority: All furniture and fixtures must be of Boardroom caliber. General: Need VCR/DVD/CD theater system for client meetings, breaks, (and WNBA games).

Figure 3-4 List of requirements by location.

List of requirements by location

Headquarters location: Rockville, Maryland, USA

Banco Binkara

Compiled 05/05/00

Proposed location	Room Functions	VTC Capacity	System	Telecomm (Preliminary)	Displays	Other VTC	Presentation Needs	Environment	Notes
Rockville	VTC, local presentations and meetings	6 to 12+	Dual-screen rollabout or built-in, 1.54 Mbps, 4CIF graphics, audio add, main and Presenter pit cameras, Touch-screen and handheld remotes, high-speed user-data	1.54 Mbps, managed dial-up. More if MCU location (e.g., 3+ PRI)	One 32" video monitor, one 32" video/data monitor, one SXVGA (1,000+ lumens) projector, one 10" video monitor (copy-stand), one 17" XVGA Monitor (PC)	MCU with Continuous Presence (up to 7 remote locations) hub to manage bandwidth	Networked-PC with wireless mouse, Copy-stand camera (data and video out), Presenter camera, Electronic Whiteboard projection screen, VGA-in and AC jacks at table, VCR/DVD/CD, Cable TV	Boardroom quality fixtures, add 30A power, air cond, soundproof walls, VTC lighting, 15' x 6' motorized curtain	Get early estimates from architects. Prepare data on MCU "buy vs service"
NYC	VTC, local presentations and meetings and (staff and clients)	6 to 12	Dual-screen rollabout or set-top, 384+ kbps, 4CIF graphics, high-speed user-data, audio add	384 kbps dial-up	One 32" video monitor, one 32" video/data monitor, one SXVGA projector (1,000+ lumens), one 10" video monitor (copy-stand), one 17" XVGA Monitor (PC)	Hub to manage/share bandwidth, H.323 gateway etc.	Networked-PC with wireless mouse, Copy-stand camera (data and video out), Presenter camera, Electronic Whiteboard projection screen	Needs new conf table, Add soundproofing (2 walls) and 2 VTC ceiling fluorescent fixtures	Check noise level from elevator; may need to use/rebuild other room

requirements you have discovered and compiled. Not only will they be able to tell you about current and planned digital communication links within your organization; they often posses considerable expertise in this area and their active participation can be of great importance in the successful completion of your project. Among the things you want to know are:

- What capabilities currently exist within your organization for digital communication between the locations (e.g., T1, ISDN, frame relay)?
- Is there existing capacity that could be used for videoconferencing between these locations, or could existing capacity be expanded to accommodate these needs?
- Is any expansion of these capabilities planned for that would be useful in satisfying the communication needs you have identified?
- What would be the most economical way to satisfy the networking requirements of the identified needs for videoconferencing?
- What is the best way to translate your projected need for digital communications for videoconferencing between these locations into planned, budgeted, and managed network capabilities? (Translation: I'll scratch your back.)

In some cases, the bandwidth you need for video can become part of the planned or existing network infrastructure. In other situations you will be given useful advice and contacts, and told to arrange for separate lines or service (Translation: Keep that pesky video off my network). In any case, this is an opportunity to make powerful allies by proactively involving them in your decision-making process.

Note: After completing the first six steps of this needs analysis, you may have developed a basic picture of the type of technologies and services that will satisfy your users' needs. This might be a good time to read the specific chapters of this book that cover these issues, surf some of the Web sites listed in Appendices B and C, or even to prepare and circulate a request for information.

7. (Optional) Prepare and distribute a request for information (RFI).

You might find it useful to communicate your requirements to potential vendors for their comments and suggestions. Manufacturers, integrators, network service providers (these used to be called phone companies), and consulting and design firms are among those whose free advice you might want to solicit. Be prepared for sales inquiries in response; this is a frequent method of "qualifying" you as a potential customer and determining whether your project justifies the time and expense of generating a comprehensive reply to your RFI. At the very least, you will receive selected (and usually helpful) brochures and white papers. At best, you will establish a good relationship with people or companies that will prove to be important partners in the deployment of your system. In Appendix C you will find a categorized list of vendors that may serve as a useful starting point for this process.

Note: Preparing and distributing an RFI based on your preliminary analyses can be very helpful in zeroing in on an ideal solution. Because they face similar challenges every day and are in touch with a wide variety of emerging technologies, vendors can often suggest better or more economical ways to satisfy your users' needs.

8. Develop one or more preliminary solution plans.

After investigating a number of possible solutions that fit your requirements, you need to put together one or more preliminary solutions plans. Simply put, this is a list of:

- The electronic equipment required for each location.
- The network services and infrastructure required for communication between all your locations.
- The additional furniture, carpentry, lighting, electricity, and air conditioning required for each location. Even a well-designed conference room usually requires some modification for VTC use. Frequently, the room dedicated for VTC was not originally designed as a conference room. In this case, additional electrical outlets, network and phone wiring, fluorescent fixtures, and air conditioning are usually required. Air conditioning in the area in which most plans shortchange users as a videoconferencing system, and related equipment can add several thousand BTUs to the heat load in a room.

Example: A large storage room with poor ventilation at one location was converted for VTC use and became an unofficial sauna every time the conference system went online. Additional air conditioning was hastily routed to the room, and the noise from impromptu, uninsulated ductwork caused only minor problems with the system's audio quality.

In Chapter 4, "Choosing the Right System," there are some useful tips and criteria for room selection and design, under the heading "Room Systems."

- The additional personnel or outsourced services needed to assure that users will be properly trained, and that conferences will be properly scheduled, coordinated, and supported. This is the area where necessary resources are most likely to be underestimated. If you think that these tasks can be accomplished using existing human resources, be sure to carefully compile the required skills and man hours required. For example: A typical group meeting usually requires at least a half hour of premeeting setup and support by a "room coordinator." This person will probably have had at least four hours of training on the use of the system. Each location usually requires at least two people with "coordinator" training to allow for vacations, sick days, and other leaves of absence. For more information on this topic, see Chapter 7, "Managing the Conference Process."

9. Develop one or more preliminary budgets.

Obtain quotes for all the components and services contained in your preliminary solution plans. Compile a preliminary list of all these costs, including all hardware, software, transmission costs, and estimated expenses for delivery, installation, extended warranties, and support services. Don't forget to add the cost of furniture, carpentry, electrical work, and any internal costs associated with the installation and maintainance of each solution. Your budget(s) should list the total estimated cost of each solution, and:

- The cost per location.
- The cost per meeting per hour of operation.
- Any other cost factors commonly used in your organization (e.g., cost per department or budget code, per year, amortized costs, etc.).

Note: One cost that is sometimes overlooked in the creation of preliminary videoconferencing budgets is the cost of ongoing support services, including room coordination and technical support for meetings. Whether these jobs are performed by existing personnel, new hires, or are outsourced to service providers or consultants, they occupy the time of somebody's paid staff.

10. Prepare a cost/benefits analysis of your alternate solutions.

This analysis should include a comparison of the most important cost-related differentiating factors for each prospective solution, such as picture quality and number of locations. This process can give you a clearer picture of the trade-offs involved in the selection of various features and functions. For example, the cost for three set-top units in one building might equal the cost of a single higher-end room system at that same location. Which solution you choose might depend on whether it's more important for you to have the capacity for simultaneous meetings or only a single higher-quality videoconference at one time.

11. Evaluate and modify your preliminary plans and budgets.

Get feedback from your colleagues, management, and potential users. Once you have clarified user needs and organizational priorities, costs can frequently be trimmed without sacrificing significant benefits. This step also helps to spread the "ownership" of the solution and to build a consensus that will make the chosen solution easier to implement.

Note: This is also a good time to manage the expectations of key potential users. If possible, arrange to demonstrate the differences in picture quality between solutions at varying price points. Other sensitive factors include audio quality, transmission costs, and individual reactions to the selected user interface.

12. Prepare a final needs analysis report.

This summation will probably have at least two iterations. First, you may want to create a complete project report, listing every detailed cost, consideration, and conclusion related to your final solution(s). This document can be of great value in developing your RFP, and for future reference. Second, you will need to create condensed reports, formatted appropriately for the managers who will be involved in the final decisions regarding your project.

If you follow these twelve steps, or something similar that is customized to your real-world situation, you should have a clear and objective picture of the needs that your system must address.

What follows is a checklist of the major steps involved in planning and deploying a successful videoconferencing system, including some items to keep in mind as you move from concept to completion. Please use the list only as a starting point, and modify it to fit your situation. While most of the steps listed are necessary for both large and small projects, some may not be required for your particular deployment. Likewise, your unique circumstances may require certain processes or procedures not mentioned here.

Figure 3-5 Needs analysis and deployment checklist.

Company: Banco Binkara

Tasks	Date Completed	
	System-wide	Location 1/2/3/n

1. Determine the initial scope of your project and plan.
   A. Determine the strategic and specific goals for the project
      i. Establish clear and attainable strategic goals
      ii. Establish realistic specific goals for the project
      iii. Define operational changes that need to be accomplished as a result of the project
   B. Resources allocated or available:
      i. Funds
      ii. Facilities
      iii. People
      iv. Time
   C. Are the goals and resources consistent with a reasonable expectation of success?

2. Identify potential users, their locations, and communications needs.
   A. Identify and list each key user or user group by Name, Title, Department/Division
   B. Identify and list each specific location
   C. Question each user/group to determine their communication requirements (see Figures 3-1 and 3-2)
      i. Size, type, and style of meetings
      ii. Graphics, audio and video
      iii. Bandwidth requirements
      iv. Special requirements (legal, human, etc.)
      v. Future requirements
   D. Conduct site surveys of every potential location
      i. Determine suitability of available room(s) at each location (see Chapter 4, "Choosing the Right System")
      ii. Compile detailed description of existing room, fixtures, utilities, etc.
      iii. Compile list of required alterations, new wiring, air conditioning, furniture, etc.
   E. Compile a prioritized list of requirements for each potential location/site (see Figures 3-3 and 3-4)
   F. Project future needs and requirements and modify your site requirement lists accordingly

     Ask your key users and groups the following questions:
      i. How might your meeting needs change over the next three to five years?
      ii. How do you expect the nature of your meetings to change over the next three to five years?
      iii. How will the size or number of your meetings increase or decrease over the same period?
      iv. Will people from different locations need to be added to your meetings?
      v. What new ways of sharing information do you expect to use in the future?
      vi. How will VTC affect the future size, type, or number of your meetings?

5. Prepare and distribute an RFI (request for information).
   A. Seek the opinions of experts on the best ways to satisfy your users' needs
      i. Send questions based on your needs analysis to vendors and consultants
      ii. Send questions based on your need analysis to telecommunication and networking service providers

6. Determine the most economical and supportable transmission services
   A. Discuss users' transmission/communication needs with IS/Telecommunications management
   B. Create a preliminary budget for digital service installation, usage, and support

7. Develop one or more preliminary solution plans.
   A. Allow generous leeway in projecting completion schedules
   B. Preliminary plan should include complete functional descriptions of all facilities and services

8. Develop one or more preliminary budget(s).
   A. Include costs of all equipment and services
      i. Hardware purchase, lease or rental
      ii. Software purchases and contracts for future upgrades
      iii. Design, consulting and integration services
      iv. Service contracts and technical support

Figure 3-5 Needs analysis and deployment checklist (continued).

    B. Include the estimated cost of site modifications (carpentry, electrical, air conditioning)

    C. Include the total cost per location

    D. Include the estimated costs per meeting/hour of operation

    E. Include costs for training and internal marketing programs

    F. Include "fudge factors" to allow for inevitable changes and delays (Murphy's Law)

    G. Include other cost factors commonly used in your organization

9. Analyze the cost/benefits of your alternate solutions.

    A. Look carefully for large costs that produce small gains (e.g., custom fixtures, excess bandwidth)

10. Evaluate and modify your preliminary plans and budgets.

    A. Obtain key user consensus on high cost options (bandwidth, custom work)

    B. Consider classifying marginal, future, or "special interest" functions as options

11. Prepare a final needs analysis report and action plan with recommendations

    A. Include a preliminary roll-out schedule (with substantial leeway).

    B. Include cost and function "fudge factors" to allow for changes and delays (Murphy's Law)

    C. Prepare a complete (technical) report and a "strategic" version for senior management

12. Secure management approval and allocation of resources.

    A. May the Force be with you.

13. Prepare and issue an RFP (see Chapter 6, "Putting It All Together"), including:

    A. A complete set of technical requirements

    B. A complete list of all required equipment and services

    C. Specific criteria for minimum acceptable system performance

    D. A clear statement of work, and demarcation of vendor responsibilities

    E. User and technical training and support required for proper operation

    F. A project schedule with key mileposts to be met by vendors

    G. Room for comments and suggestions from vendor experts

    H. Requirements that all products and services comply with applicable regulations

    I. Legal safeguards related to safety, copyrights, and other potential liabilities

14. Select vendors.

    A. Don't decide on bid price alone

      i. Vendors reputation and ability to deliver as promised are paramount

      ii. A complete and professional proposal will include all related costs

      iii. Get in writing everything related to deliverables and acceptance criteria

15. Complete project, on-time and under budget.

    A. Ascertain that all vendors have met acceptance criteria

    B. Implement training and internal marketing programs (see Chapter 7, "Managing the Conferening Process")

16. Take much deserved vacation.

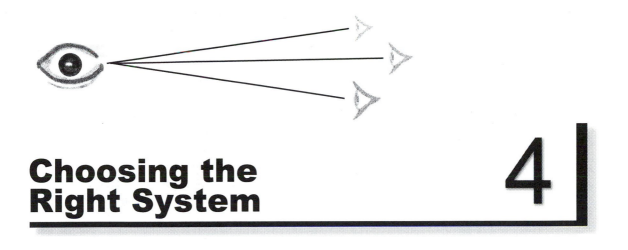

Choosing the Right System

4

Executive Summary

Selecting the right systems to meet your users' needs is a key step in building a successful videoconferencing network. In this chapter, we will cover the four basic types of systems, the advantages and disadvantages of each for various applications, and how to select and configure the right system(s) for your needs. The four types are: desktop (PC) systems, set-top systems for use with TV monitors, integrated rollabout systems, and custom-built room systems. The most important consideration in selecting the optimum system is to choose one that suits the room, the number of users, and their special meeting needs in a cost-effective manner. The second priority is to guard against rapid obsolescence by picking a system that can be easily expanded to meet your user and network requirements for at least the next two to three years.

Basic System Selection

The most critical aspect of your videoconferencing system is the interface between the users and the system itself. What they see, hear, and touch will ultimately determine the quality of their conferencing experience. This is true whether you select a simple desktop unit or a custom room system. The best electronics and networking services in the world can do little to save a system that is hard to operate, difficult to see, and impossible to hear. By applying a few simple guidelines to your users' needs, it is easy to come up with a system that will do the job and still not break the bank.

Selection Guidelines

Here are some factors to consider in the selection of a system, and a few rules of thumb that should help you to make good choices.

1. Display Devices

Your system should have an adequate number of TV/monitors to display the required information, and they should be large enough for comfortable viewing. Select displays that make it possible to read charts from the rear-most seats.

Example: If your meetings involve basic PowerPoint presentations to audiences of eight to twelve people; a dual monitor system with 32-inch monitors should enable everyone to easily see both the speaker and the slides at the same time.

2. Transmission Speed

Your system should operate at a communication speed that produces acceptable picture quality at a reasonable cost. Low-speed, 128 kbps videoconferencing is economical, requiring the use of just a single inexpensive ISDN-BRI connection. But the picture quality is barely adequate for one-on-one conferences between people who already have a working relationship. At 128 kbps the picture is fuzzy, movement is not smooth, and the lack of resolution makes it difficult to pickup subtle cues and facial expressions, particularly with larger groups. Desktop videoconferencing (DVC), particularly when collaborative computing (e.g., the sharing of spreadsheets) is of primary importance, is one application where a 128 kbps connection is usually acceptable. Most group videoconferencing takes place at transmission rates of 384 kbps or higher. This speed usually provides sharper pictures, smoother motion (30 frames per second), and adequate bandwidth-to-spare for good quality audio and fast transmission of graphics. The cost of 384 kbps transmission is typically less than seven simultaneous phone calls, and this speed offers a good compromise between cost (of transmission and equipment), and comfortable viewing and listening quality. Slightly higher speeds (e.g., 512 kbps) provide some additional picture quality at a one-third increase in transmission cost. Though transmission speeds of 768 kbps to 1.54 Mbps provide even better picture quality, the additional costs make them a questionable choice for most routine conferencing applications. These costs may include several thousand dollars for a faster codec, and more importantly, a two- to four-fold increase in transmission charges.

3. Audio Enhancement

Because the spoken word is the most important part of virtually every videoconference, your audio subsystem should be able to produce "stress-free" and "shout-free" conferencing in your real-world application. Room size and acoustics, number of people, planned use (e.g., presentation or brainstorming), and typical noise level—all need to be taken into consideration.

It is almost impossible to overstate the importance of good-quality audio to the success of a videoconferencing system. Any modern rollabout or set-top video-conferencing system can usually provide acceptable sound quality for one or two people in a small, quiet, well-soundproofed, windowless conference room. Other situations may require additional equipment or room treatment. A knowledgeable consultant or sales engineer should be able to provide you with several alternative solutions with varying costs and benefits.

Example: A relatively large, "live" room (with many hard, reflective surfaces), with high background noise might require a very-high-grade echo canceller (such as the Voicecrafter from Biamp), multiple microphones placed very close to meeting participants, and an automatic mixer at a cost of $2,500 to $6,000. Depending on the precise situation, soundproofing that same room with acoustic wall treatments and curtains could provide a simpler and more cost-effective solution.

4. Video Capture

Your system should be equipped with a sufficient number of cameras of the right type to clearly and easily "pick-up" both the people and the documents that are important to your meetings. The standard CCD (charge-coupled device) cameras typically supplied with VTC systems can provide clear, crisp pictures at reasonable levels of illumination. At a minimum, bright and even fluorescent lighting should be provided.

Example: A single remote control, pan-tilt camera should be sufficient for a meeting where four to eight people sit facing the camera and presentations are fed directly to the system from a laptop or other computer. Add a presenter in front of the group and you will probably need a second camera. If your meetings involve the presentation of paper documents (or 3-D objects), consider a copy-stand camera from Elmo, Sony, Canon, or Sanyo. Adding these cameras is easy with a little advance planning, and they are simple to connect and a snap to use. Just make sure that the system you select will accept the number and type of inputs you will need. Plan in advance for installation of the required video and power cables to avoid the prospect of sloppy wiring or expensive add-on construction.

5. Simple Controls

Don't assume that everyone who will use your systems has the same degree of technical sophistication as you and your colleagues. Select a control system that will present no problems to the least technical people in your user group. Most packaged systems either have very basic handheld remotes that control easy-to-read on-screen menus, or are equipped with simplified AMX/Panja or Crestron touch-screen control panels. See Figure 4-1, a basic wireless handheld remote control, and Figure 4-2, a basic layout for a touch-screen controller.

It is a good idea to have actual end-users attend demo sessions to test various remote controls for ease of use. If possible, have one of your most technophobic users test a system to see how foolproof the controls really are.

Example: We demonstrated both the handheld remote and the simple, standard touch-screen controllers of one system to an important executive. He had trouble with the handheld remote and was irritated by the layers of menus on the touch-screen. We decided to customize the panel for his conference room, and had the integrator program his touch-screen to show only a simplified "phone book" screen when the system powered up.

6. Basic Multipoint Conferencing

The ability to conference with many locations at one time has been an important part of VTC since its early days. Some set-top and rollabout systems, such as the Polycom ViewStation MP and the Sony Contact, offer basic multipoint conferencing as an option. While full-featured, standards-based multipoint conferencing can be a complex and expensive undertaking, these systems offer low-bit-rate multipoint conferencing between three or four similar units. Multipoint conferencing is discussed at length in the next chapter, but these "integrated" multipoint systems are worth a look if you frequently require informal conferences between several locations.

Example: A "small" investment bank wanted videoconferencing to be used primarily as a meeting tool between small groups of senior management in their three main offices. Sony rollabout systems with built-in, proprietary multipoint capability enabled them to conduct low-speed, dial-up multipoint conferences of adequate quality at a reasonable cost.

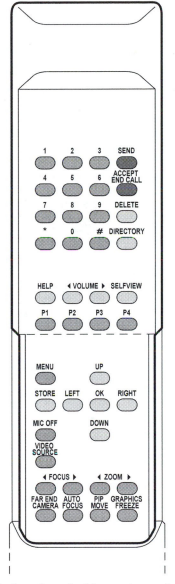

Figure 4-1 A basic wireless handheld remote control. (Photo: Tandberg)

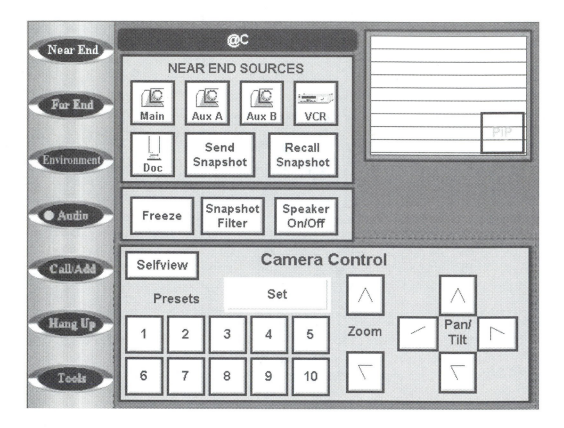

Figure 4-2 Basic layout for a touch-screen controller. (Photo: Crestron)

Overview of Basic Systems

The videoconferencing systems currently available can be divided into four general categories: Desktop, Set-top, Rollabout, and Room Systems. Videophones and portable systems hold great promise, but do not yet answer many real business communication needs in a cost-effective way.

Here's an overview of the four basic types of practical systems, followed by an in-depth look at the ergonomic and technical considerations involved in their deployment. The divisions between these categories are widely accepted today, but evolving technology and dynamic market forces continue to blur the lines between them. For example, there are super-powerful desktop systems; set-tops that embody the features and functions of rollabouts; rollabouts with heavy-duty room capabilities; and cameras that can fit many set-top features into the palm of your hand. It would appear that the process of Hegelian synthesis (thesis, antithesis, synthesis) is as active in communications systems markets as in the world of geopolitics—with one new synthesis of existing technologies giving birth to its opposite, and to a constant churning process of innovation and electronic Darwinism. The examples given are current as of this writing—but time marches on, and the standards-based systems that you can buy when you read this will probably be cheaper, smaller, and better than the ones described. Based on their track records, any current system from PictureTel, Polycom, Sony, Tandberg, VTEL, VCON, or Zydacron should provide solid performance and value for several years after installation.

1. Desktop Systems

Desktop videoconferencing systems usually consist of a PC with a small camera mounted above the monitor (*see* Figure 4-3). They are most suitable for individual users of three types:
  • Those who want to add simple "picture phone" capabilities to their PCs.
  • Users who wish to employ document conferencing, application sharing, and interactive computing in addition to simple face-to-face communication.
  • Users who need both desktop delivery of video programming and face-to-face videoconferencing.

Advantages: DVC is simple to use, relatively inexpensive, and many systems enable the integration of computer applications and broadcast video into videoconferences.

Figure 4-3 User at a desktop videoconferencing unit. (Photo: Lucent Technologies)

Figure 4-4 A typical set-top system. (Photo: Polycom)

Disadvantages: Desktop systems are suitable for use by only one or two people at a time, per unit. With the exception of some high-end units, the picture and sound quality of these systems is also somewhat limited.

Since desktop systems make for many single-user units (instead of fewer group systems), they frequently increase training and support requirements. For the same reason, deployment of desktop units increases the need for multipoint bridging services and equipment.

Cost: Typically, $500 to $3,000 per desktop, plus the cost of a PC and monitor.

2. Set-top Systems

These popular units integrate camera, microphone, speakers, codec, network interface, and other components into a single box that sits, as the name implies, on top of a TV set or monitor (*see* Figure 4-4). They are a good choice for small groups (two to six people) and routine meetings.

Though originally aimed at the low-cost workgroup market, these units (like the compact car) keep getting bigger and more powerful, and the latest offerings in this category are equal to many rollabout systems in cost and capabilities. Some current set-top systems include such advanced features as built-in Web servers to enhance presentation capabilities and remote systems management.

Advantages: Set-top systems are economical, simple to set up, easy to use, and powerful enough for most normal uses.

Disadvantages: Many set-tops have very limited capabilities for future upgrades and expansion.

Cost: Approximately $3,000 to $9,000.

3. Rollabout Systems

Rollabout systems usually consist of a variety of audio, video, telecommunications and control systems electronics mounted in a wheeled cabinet, topped by one or two monitors, and crowned with a pan/tilt camera (*see* Figure 4-5). For more than fifteen years these systems have been the workhorses of the videoconferencing community. The integrated, modular construction of rollabout systems make them a flexible, easy-to-maintain solution for applications ranging from workgroups to boardrooms, and distance learning to telemedicine.

Advantages: Rollabouts are relatively simple to install and use. They are easy to expand and modify to fit changing requirements. Audio, graphics, and camera subsystems can be customized to produce the best results for specific applications and environments (e.g., remote training or large-group presentations).

Disadvantages: They have a higher purchase price than many comparable set-top systems and are more difficult to set up and move.

Cost: Approximately $10,000 to $30,000.

Figure 4-5 Rollabout systems can be powerful and elegant. (Photo:Tandberg)

4. Room Systems

For the ultimate in performance and ease of use, nothing equals a custom room system that has been designed to match your specific conferencing requirements. A well-implemented room system can make users forget the distance and time that separates them from their conferees, and even make VTC sessions more productive than a face-to-face meeting in a conventional facility.

Disadvantages: The cost of implementation and support of custom designed room systems has been the major limiting factor in their use by all but the largest organizations. Though simple room enhancements, such as soundproofing and hidden wiring can be implemented at relatively low cost, the budget for a high-end custom boardroom, classroom, or studio can easily climb into the mid-six figures.

Cost: From around $30,000 to over $1,000,000.

Analysis of Basic Systems

Let's take a closer look at the characteristics of each type of system and examine some of the issues involved in selecting the ideal system for your users' needs.

1. Desktop Systems

From the outside, most desktop systems look the same—a PC with a camera on top. There are, however, some very basic differences between the following classes of desktop systems.

Software Codec Systems

The most basic desktop systems use the PC's microprocessor and graphics card to handle the capture and compression of audio and video. They do this by running a special program called a software codec. This method is less expensive than using separate chips or boards for the important task of coding and compressing sound and pictures, but it has several important limitations. When the computer's CPU is asked to do the work of a codec (coder/decoder), it has less power to devote to displaying PowerPoint presentations or crunching spreadsheets. The better the picture and sound quality required, the slower normal computing gets. And even the fastest PCs are limited in the compressed image quality they can produce without the help of a hardware codec.

Recent advances from Lucent Technologies and others take advantage of new, faster CPUs (e.g., 600 MHz Pentium III) to produce usable IP-based videoconferencing, while leaving enough processing power to handle routine tasks like word processing and spreadsheet calculations. But even these systems require a hardware codec board to encode higher-quality video. For this reason, systems like Lucent's iCosm are best suited for semibroadcast applications, such as training, where a single hardware-equipped machine provides high-quality video to many remote users—who in turn transmit only the low-frame-rate video required for such tasks as Q&A.

Keeping all this in mind, there are still some situations where software codecs can shine. For example, if your videoconferencing needs are limited to basic face-to-face collaborations over a high-speed LAN or WAN combined with collaborative computing, you might want to go the software codec route. Factors to consider in selecting a software codec-based system include:

- Will the system work smoothly within your network architecture? Issues such as network traffic load and quality of service (QoS) must be satisfactorily addressed.
- What is the percentage of CPU capacity used by the conferencing engine, and is the remaining capacity sufficient for simultaneous use by other applications?
- Are the video and audio quality high enough for comfortable use by your typical users?
- Is the system reliable enough? Does the application cause crashes under normal use? Does the manufacturer provide remote diagnostic and management tools to deal efficiently with user and system problems?

This last question is important for the entire range of desktop videoconferencing systems, but particularly for IP-based VTC systems. This emerging technology still requires at least some expert support to work in most network environments.

Desktop Card-sets and Kits

Manufacturers such as Zydacron, PictureTel, and VCON provide "kits" for the purpose of upgrading everyday PCs into ISDN and IP-based desktop videoconferencing systems. These units generally work well once configured and provide a simple, relatively inexpensive and reliable solution to the need for personal videoconferencing. Kits are available in a wide range of quality, features, and pricepoints—from $1,500 to over $10,000.

At the bottom of the scale, we have basic fixed-camera systems with 128 kbps

ISDN (H.320) and IP-LAN (H.323) communication capabilities that sell for under $1,500. One example of this class is the PictureTel Live 550. It provides T.120 (data collaboration) support through integration with Microsoft NetMeeting and has full duplex audio with echo cancellation for use with small speakers. An upgrade kit is available for under $1,500 that increases the ISDN communication speed to 384 kbps and allows for "business quality," 30 frames per second (fps) conferencing over three inexpensive BRI-ISDN lines through the use of a built-in IMUX (Inverse Multiplexer). An IMUX is a device that combines three or more low-speed (128 kbps) BRI-ISDN lines into a single, high-speed connection of 384 kbps or more. A unit equipped to interface with a WAN or ISDN MUX (multiplexer) via a V.35 connection should cost several hundred less than one that includes an IMUX.

It should take a VTC-savvy technician no more than two to four hours to add these components to an existing PC and configure the software, hardware, and network interface. Add one or two hours of user training (which can be done online), for a total basic cost of under $2,000. This does not include the cost of the PC, monitor, and, of course, the line charges from your friendly tele-communication service provider.

Desktop Deluxe

Zydacron and VCON are among those companies that offer high-end desktop kits that incorporate many of the functions and capabilities previously associated with room systems. These products, covered at greater length in the Rooms Systems section, include pan/tilt cameras, microphones, cables, and a range of powerful hardware, software, and connectivity options.

Codec in a Camera

Polycom recently introduced an USB desktop camera with built-in video and audio processing for H.323 conferencing over packet-switched networks at a cost of about $600. By the time you read this, other manufacturers will, no doubt, have jumped on the codec-in-a-camera bandwagon and you will be able to choose between several similar units. Key factors to consider are audio quality and ease of use with collaborative computing applications (e.g., MS NetMeeting). Prior to this introduction it was not practical to achieve business quality (FCIF 30 fps) videoconferencing with a digital camera alone. An expensive PC hardware codec board typically had to be installed in the user's PC, opening the door to a range of potential software, hardware, and service-related problems.

Desktop Extras

"Extras" that may increase the performance and raise the cost of a desktop system include pan/tilt cameras, echo-cancelling speakers, larger monitors, and graphics enhancements. Wherever possible, it is good practice to order these enhancements from the same kit manufacturer that supplied the basic system. Whether these add-ons are ordered at the time of the initial purchase or as upgrades, obtaining them from a single source assures compatibility, and, more importantly, gives you a single place to call if something goes wrong. The practice of buck-passing is not unique to the videoconferencing business, but VTC's complex relationships between video, audio, computing, and datacom functions have helped raise "not me" to a true art form. This important topic is covered in greater detail in Chapter 6, "Putting It All Together."

Pan/tilt cameras: For executive and small workgroup desktop systems, it is useful to add a pan/tilt/zoom camera with a wireless remote control. These units allow users to sit comfortably in various locations within the workspace. Most units include preset positions to enable an easy change of image composition (i.e., from a closeup of one person to a group shot). High-quality pan/tilt cameras, such as the Sony EVI-D30 and the Canon VC-C3, cost about $1,000.

Audio enhancements: Some low-end desktop systems are equipped with echo cancelling and suppression circuitry suitable only for headset use. Add-on speakers with built-in echo cancellers enable a more natural and relaxed mode of communication. The SoundPoint PC from Polycom, and similar units, add full duplex speaker sound to headset-only systems for under $500.

Copy-stand cameras, scanners, graphics tablets, and other input devices, as well as desktop microphones and VCRs, are also useful for some specialized desktop applications and are covered in detail in the section on system peripherals at the end of this chapter.

Packaged Desktop Systems

Many videoconferencing system integrators offer turnkey desktop systems incorporating high-quality board kits from Zydacron, VCON, and other OEMs. There are three reasons to purchase a packaged desktop system from either a manufacturer or integrator:

1. These systems provide the highest level of integration—everything from remote diagnostics services to complete sets of productivity and collaborative software.
2. They provide a single point of contact and responsibility. This can be

particularly important if you are responsible for the installation and support of these systems, but your management has neglected to clone your support technicians or substantially increase your support budget.

3. On the high end, integrated desktop systems like the VCON 8000 are really PC-based room systems that offer large-screen VGA displays, collaborative computing functions, and support high-speed ISDN and IP-based conferencing.

Hybrid Desktop, TV/ Conferencing Systems

Solutions have also been created for organizations whose needs are focused primarily on video distribution but that also have a requirement for limited face-to-face desktop conferencing. These can be divided into two groups: IP-based solutions suitable for high-speed, up-to-the-minute LANs and WANs; and "overlay" systems, for older networks and systems that require many channels of video information.

The Lucent iCosm is a good example of a system that relies on IP infrastructure to move multimedia content between desktops. These systems are suitable for organizations with fast, well-managed networks with high-speed PCs that will not be bogged down by the heavy additional traffic. This innovative application provides multiparty videoconferencing, video distribution, and data collaboration—without the need for an expensive videoconferencing MCU (multipoint control unit), or hardware codecs at each user location. Video and audio quality can be automatically scaled to fit individual user's connection speeds and system capabilities. In its simplest form, iCosm is a low-cost (approximately $100) software application that runs on any fast Pentium and enables basic multimedia collaboration via IP LAN or WAN. But if even one PC in the network is upgraded to the Pro version (approximately $8,000 to $10,000), you get scaleable video-on-demand and business-quality multipoint videoconferencing. Conferencing capabilities extend from low bandwidth H.323 "talking heads" all the way up to near-broadcast-quality Motion JPEG (MJPEG). There are numerous applications for iCosm, including remote collaboration, training, and access to video databases of news and product information. Like most really good technology, it is both cost-effective and flexible enough to be adaptable to your special ideas and needs. For more information on iCosm, go to http://lucent.com/enterprise/ipapps/conferencing.

Some desktop systems from VCON and Zydacron also support various forms of IP-based multicasting and TV distribution, such as Cisco IP-TV.

Analog Overlay Systems

This is a more moderate, even conservative approach taken by U.K.-based Cabletime for its MediaStar system. It employs an "overlay" methodology, using extra or unused pairs of Category 5 LAN wiring to carry analog video and audio—and only requires the LAN to carry small bits of control information. The result is a video network that provides dozens of channels of very-high-quality video and audio, and full-motion "video intercom," with virtually no load on the network. For wide area conferencing, codecs and digital lines are deployed as shared resources, resulting in significant cost savings relative to ISDN-to-the-desktop-systems. These systems are very popular with organizations that require multiple channels of video distribution as well as face-to-face conferencing. They are widely deployed in investment banks, schools, and publishing companies—all applications where access to broadcast programming is of great importance.

At the New York City School for the Deaf, where students, teachers, and administrators use American Sign Language as their primary means of communication, this overlay technology will be used to provide "video intercom" and "video PA" functions as well as TV distribution and conventional distance learning capabilities (*see* Figure 4-6, TV distribution and videoconferencing over unshielded twisted pair (UTP)). Michael Davies, a consultant on communication technologies to the New York City Board of Education, expects the system to provide unprecedented access to new educational opportunities for hearing-impaired students, their classmates and their teachers. The system was designed by a team, including Gurdeep Seehra of Pinacl, engineers at Cabletime, Davies and myself.

In each classroom, a camera is located underneath a wall-mounted TV/monitor. Teachers can select programming, or initiate a video call using a handheld wireless remote or a virtual remote on their PC screens. Content from the Internet or the school's LAN can be displayed on the main monitor via a down-converter. Television or distance learning video programs can also be displayed on classroom computer screens. A desktop camera and an on-screen message generator in the principal's office make it easy to announce special events and even changes in the lunch menu. Currently, the system is equipped with H.320 codecs for wide area access, and programming sources include VCRs and cable TV. Future upgrades may include H.323 connectivity and video-on-demand from disc-based video servers. Cabletime's products are distributed in the United States by Pinacl Communications. Similar systems are available from Corel Video, and Avistar.

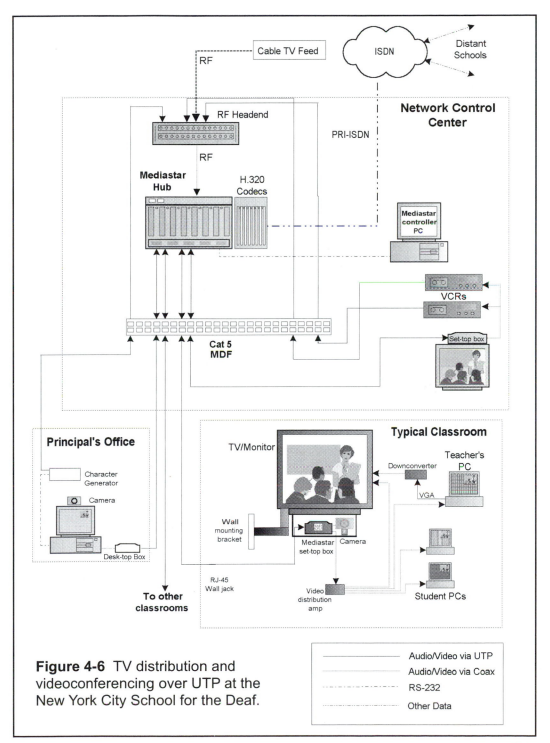

Figure 4-6 TV distribution and videoconferencing over UTP at the New York City School for the Deaf.

2. Set-top Systems

Just a few years ago this category did not exist, but it is now the most common choice for small-group videoconferencing. The original concept was simple and elegant—everything required for basic videoconferencing from the camera to the network interface would sit on top of a typical office TV/monitor, cost less than $5,000, and be as easy to hook up and use as a VCR. The first units (from PictureTel) were limited to a single camera, simple audio, and 128 kbps BRI-ISDN connectivity. The units received a warm welcome in the marketplace. Prices plummeted to under $3,000 as electronic giants like Philips geared up production, and features multiplied as innovative companies, such as Polycom, packed room system capabilities into tiny boxes. See Figure 4-7, drawing of a generic set-top system.

Today, the set-top form function conceals a wide range of capabilites; and price-points range from around $2,000 to over $10,000. Key factors to look at when considering a set-top system include:

Expandability
If you select a set-top system based solely on your current needs, you may be painting yourself into a corner. This is not as important if you will be able to "hand down" systems to branch offices or other smaller locations as your needs grow. Most users, however, will do better to select systems that incorporate an economical upgrade path that can satisfy projected usage requirements for at least two years. The Sony Contact is a modular unit that is capable of relatively easy hardware upgrades, and software for the Polycom ViewStation can be upgraded automatically over either IP or ISDN connections.

Network and Speed
Make sure that your set-top system operates at transmission rates high enough for your current needs and provides an upgrade path to speeds that will satisfy your needs over the next two to three years. Select a unit that provides both ISDN (H.320) and IP (H.323) capabilities to allow for use over packet switched networks in the near future.

Low speed, 128 kbps videoconferencing over ISDN lines is economical, but the picture quality is suitable only for the simplest of conferencing applications between people who already have a working relationship. For conferences with more than two people at each location, or those that involve important business relationships or processes, 384 kbps (via either ISDN or IP) still represents the best compromise between cost and quality. For large group, technical, or distance learning applications, transmission speeds of 512 to 768 kbps may be advisable.

Cameras

Most set-top systems include a single, built-in pan-tilt camera that will adequately cover two to six people seated at a table located 4 to 12 feet in front of the

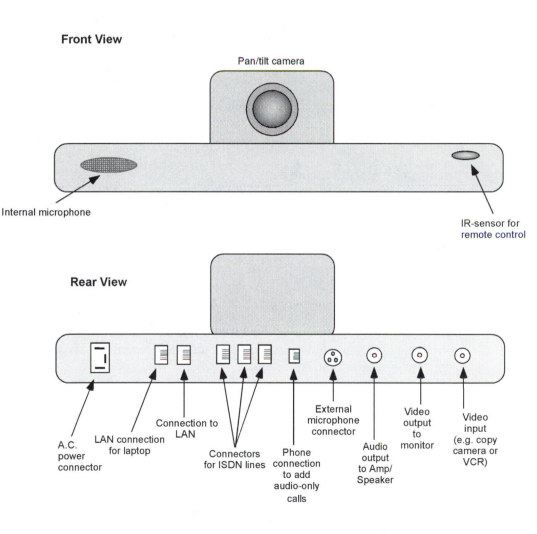

Figure 4-7 Drawing of a generic set-top system.

TV/monitor. Most set-tops will also accept video or S-Video input from a "copy-stand" camera that can be used used to view printed material and small objects. Make sure that the system you select also provides extras video inputs (e.g., for a second pan/tilt camera) if you plan to use your system for stand-up presentations or training, larger group conferences, or other specialized applications.

Audio Quality

Most set-top systems are equipped with audio systems that work well for groups of two to four people sitting at a small conference table in a reasonably quiet room. Progress has been rapid in this area, with Polycom, PictureTel, and others leapfrogging each other each year with improved audio quality and room coverage. Though set-top audio does not yet equal the quality and flexibility achieved with discrete rollabout or room audio subsystems, the gap is closing rapidly. Among the most popular set-top audio options are extension microphone modules for use in larger conference rooms, stand-up presentations, and distance training applications. Conference Technology Group in Hartford, Connecticut, produces a popular audio add-on system for most major brands of set-top units.

Multipoint Conferencing

Some high-end set-top systems, like the Sony Contact-ME and the Polycom ViewStation MP, offer basic multipoint capabilities—allowing up to four sites to simultaneously participate in a low-speed (128 to 256 kbps) video call. Systems with this capability typically cost around $10,000 per location.

3. Rollabout Systems

Rollabouts usually consist of a variety of electronics mounted in a wheeled cabinet, topped by one or two monitors, and crowned with a pan/tilt camera (*see* Figure 4-8). They are easy-to-maintain, flexible, and satisfy the needs of a wide range of users and applications.

Rollabout systems come in various sizes and speeds, from basic single 21-inch monitor units designed to operate at 128 kbps, to dual 40-inch plasma display systems that work at speeds of up to 1.54 Mbps (T1) and higher.

These systems are also available from a wide range of reliable vendors, including Tandberg, VTEL, Sony, PictureTel, Aethra, VCON, and others. In addition, manufacturers such as RSI and Panasonic provide the guts for an "instant" high-performance system in a single box—just add your choice of monitors, cameras, microphones, and other peripherals.

PC or Non-PC Systems

Rollabouts, for the most part, are either based on Wintel PC platforms or on proprietary software/hardware platforms developed specifically for video-conferencing use. Virtually all currently available systems of both types are interoperable with most other H.320/H.323 standards-compliant systems. Each brand and model, irrespective of platform, also offers compatibility with its own smorgasbord of special "standards" (e.g., IP-TV) and enhancements such as 4CIF (four times common intermediate format, which is 704 x 576 luminance pixels).

What, then, are the differences between PC and non-PC based systems? PC-based systems, like those from VTEL and VCON, are often easier to adapt to collaborative computing applications and offer a more open physical architecture for adding network interfaces, graphic adapters, and other components. Systems that are not based on a PC platform may provide a more reliable computing environment than those that must lean on the current version of Microsoft's OS. Proprietary hardware

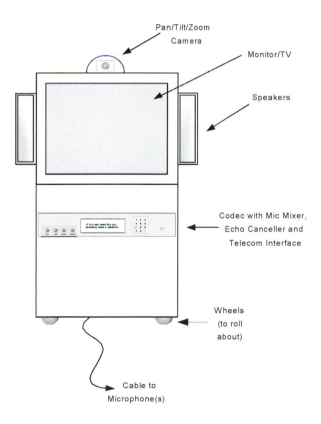

Figure 4-8 Drawing of a generic rollabout system.

can also provide better performance than Intel's multipurpose architecture.

The bottom line? Pick any rollabout from a major manufacturer that meets all of your requirements irrespective of platform. In my humble opinion, cost, performance, and ease of use are more important than these, mostly theoretical, issues.

Guideliness for Rollabout Selection

Here are guidelines for choosing the best rollabout for your group video-conferencing system:

* Pick a system with a user interface that will be comfortable and non-threatening even to your least technical users.
* Look for key features that may be important to your specific needs. For example, VTEL's remote diagnostics and management of an individual VTC system via Simple Network Management Protocol (SNMP) could be a life saver for a far-flung VTC network with scant local tech support. Likewise, the ability of Tandberg's Vision 7000 to dial-up a three-way 384 kbps multipoint conference could be critical for an organization with users in several major locations.
* Take a close look at warranties and on-site service contract costs. Important meetings that must be cancelled due to VTC system failure are bad for business, and for the careers of system managers. Rapid and effective response at the first hint of trouble can usually save the day. Same day on-site service is a must for mission-critical systems, while "Express Replacement or Exchange" contracts can be cost-effective for systems with more mundane workgroup functions. Expect to pay 10 to 14 percent of purchase price per year for same day on-site service, and 8 percent or less for remote support with rapid parts replacement.
* Simple, cost-effective upgrade paths are very important for VTC systems. In a field with rapidly evolving standards, exciting new functions like 4FCIF (for high-res graphics) may become de rigueur in a matter of months. Other options, such as full T1 conferencing or even MPEG-2 video may become desirable long before you are ready to retire your "new" systems. Ask pointed questions about upgrade costs and trade-in policies, and look for written assurances on key points.

Optional Accessories

Rollabout manufacturers and integrators typically offer a full range of optional peripherals such as copy-stand cameras, whiteboards, and extra microphones. Some even offer special options targeted at training and technical applications. Before making a final system selection, be sure that your chosen system will accept the peripherals that your users will want to use—without extensive modification or custom software drivers.

4. Room Systems

There is a widespread misconception in the communication industry that custom-designed room videoconferencing systems are superexpensive and suitable only for the boardrooms of Fortune 500 corporations. It is true that some high-end custom systems and "war rooms" built for major banks and other international powerhouses cost well into the high six figures. But the advantages of a system optimized for an organization's specific needs can often be had for little more than the cost of a fully loaded rollabout. In fact, the final cost of a simple but well-designed custom room can often be less than a Rube Goldberg facility that has grown from inadequate to unwieldy under the tender ministrations of a series of project managers and committees.

For example, a major Wall Street technology company had not figured out who should manage its VTC network. The project was passed from department to department and manager to manager like a valuable hot potato. After a few years of this process, the company had an international assortment of rooms with dissimilar codecs and controllers, no assigned support staff, and a VTC network that consisted of dozens of dial-up line lines with no relationship to the corporate WAN or IS management process. The "flagship" boardroom system was an unwieldy mass of components that were only marginally compatible. The result was videoconferencing that was, more often than not, unreliable and irritating to use.

Expert Help
An experienced videoconferencing room designer can often suggest subtle and inexpensive room modifications that will produce major gains in audio, video, and overall meeting quality. This expert assistance can be solicited as part of your RFI or RFP, but often a pre-RFI consultation can clarify your room design options at an early stage of system development. In any case, carefully developed electrical, air conditioning, and functional floor plans can have a major positive impact on your communication process and user satisfaction.

Kits and Modules
Kits and modules from VTEL, Zydacron, VCON, and others can take a lot of the mystery out of the electronics part of small room design. Zydacron's powerful Small Group Videoconferencing products are also available in kit form. These

do-it-yourself room systems include everything but the room and your choice of a fast PC chassis to act as a platform. The company's comCenter applications for managing collaborative computing and the wide range of connectivity options make these kits a good bet for situations where integration into the everyday computing life of an organization is the goal. These options include an H.323 Gateway, MCUs, video routers, and a variety of network communications cards to facilitate connection through LANs, PBXs, and ISDN lines. VTEL's higher-end PC-based Galaxy codecs can also serve as the basis for a room system that is easy to integrate with an existing computer network.

Make Room, Make Room

The most common error in room design is trying to cram too much equipment and too many people into too small a space. Sometimes this is a result of poor planning or a lack of understanding of the difference between a conference room and a videoconferencing room. Typically a well-designed videoconferencing room will require 25 to 50 percent more space than an "old-fashioned" conference or board room. Not only does the additional equipment take up significant floor space, but the people in the room must be arranged so as to see and be seen by their distant conferees.

You would never think of seating people in a meeting with their backs to each other, yet many poorly thought out videoconferencing rooms require people to sit with their backs or sides to the screen. It helps if you think of a video-conferencing room as being just half of a larger room, separated by a virtual window or one-way mirror from its distant twin (*see* Figure 4-9). Here's a list of the approximate space required for different aspects of a typical videoconferencing room:

Conference Table and People: At least 9 square feet of space extending out from the edge of the conference table, and 6 square feet of table surface for each participant. An additional 2 feet of isle space should be left behind every participant.

VTC System: At least 9 square feet for a single monitor system and 18 square feet for a dual monitor system. If a rollout is used, the system's back should be placed 6 to 12 inches from the wall, and its front 4 to 8 feet from the front of the conference table. At least 3 feet of clearance on either side of the system cabinet (18 sq. ft.) is advisable, to allow technicians easy access to the unit's rear. A built-in unit requires considerably more space.

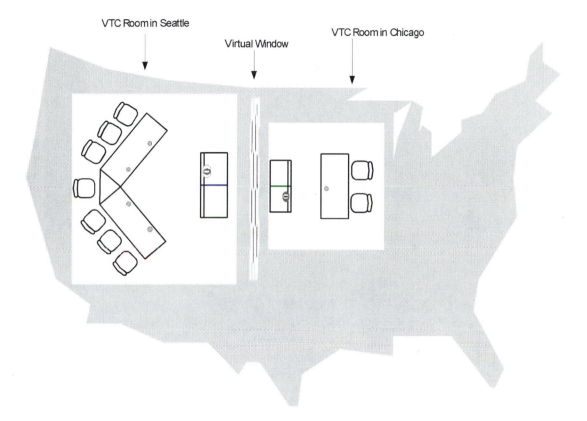

Figure 4-9 Two distant VTC rooms separated only by a virtual window.

Graphics/Copy-Stand Camera: It is a good idea to keep this unit off the main conference table, and to provide a separate small table for its support. This adds 8 square feet of space for the table and standing room for the user.

Whiteboard or projection screen: space must be allowed for a presenter to stand next to these units; allow for 8 to 12 square feet.

Other Space Eaters: Fax machines (4 sq. ft.), coffee pot (2 sq. ft.), PC and chair (8 sq. ft.), audience with chairs (8 sq. ft.) each.

Depending on table shape and the location of doors, a typical videoconference room for eight users with a dual monitor rollabout system could require at least 250 square feet of space and measure 14 x 18 feet or more.

It is of critical importance to create a realistic diagram of your future room using Visio, AutoCAD, or even paper and pencil. In that diagram, you should include all present system elements and probable future add-ons (such as fax machines and whiteboards), and allow for the normal movement of people within the room during a typical meeting (*see* Figure 4-10). Remember, people take up space when they are sitting down and when they are moving around the room. I don't have enough fingers and toes to count the number of videoconferencing rooms I've seen that turn a simple move to the whiteboard into a game of *Twister*, as an apologizing presenter attempts to squeeze past a portly participant.

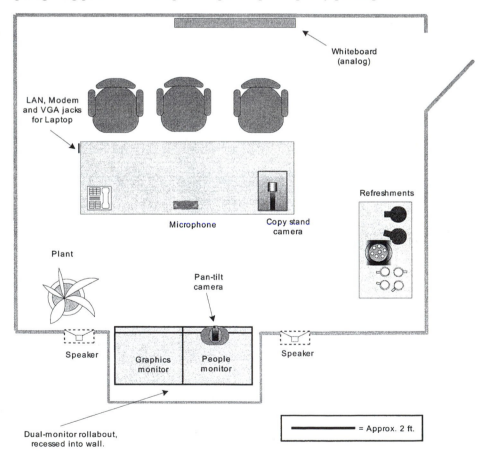

Figure 4-10 Drawing of a basic room system.

Cool It—Air Conditioning

Another major faux pas of VTC room design is the lack of adequate air conditioning. Thousands of BTUs of extra heat are typically generated by the monitors, codecs, audio equipment, and extra lighting that populate even a relatively simple VTC room. Add an LCD projector, a copy-stand with lights, assorted PCs, and a half dozen people, and these rooms can easily turn into a good imitation of a sauna.

If at all possible, add additional soundproofed air conditioning feed ducts (and returns), and make sure that the conferees have control over room temperature. There's no point in freezing early arrivals in anticipation of the buildup of heat from a long meeting.

What Did He Say?

Some years ago, BellCore conducted a study that evaluated the different types of information exchanged during a multimedia videoconference. By a significant margin, audio (voice) was ranked as being of greater importance than video. Despite the obvious truth of this finding, the factors that contribute to the achievement of high-quality audio are given relatively little attention. I have visited manufacturer's demo rooms that produce really awful audio due to lack of proper acoustic conditioning and an inappropriate sound system design. And, I can't begin to count the times that I've heard someone ask, "What did he say?" or "Excuse me, could you please repeat that," during a videoconference.

It is very difficult to achieve excellent audio in group videoconferences. When audio is compressed by a codec and sent over a digital network there are several factors that introduce delays and distortion. Without adequate compensation for delays, you will hear your own voice loop back to you (through the distant speakers and mics), in a variety of echoing effects more suitable to new wave rock-and-roll than to a serious meeting. High compression levels, poor microphone placement and other factors can also reduce the fidelity of conference audio, making a vice president of sales sound like Marlon Brando with a mouth full of marbles. Modern VTC systems use a variety of techniques to control these phenomena, but the task of achieving perfect audio for VTC is no trivial pursuit. As long as the room is small and relatively "dead" (echo-free), the acoustic echo-cancellers that are built into most packaged systems perform reasonably well. For more challenging situations, the acoustic engineer can employ a variety of problem-solving tools. High-quality, dedicated echo cancellers from Gentner, ASPI, and other manufacturers are one solution. Gated microphones, automatic mic mixers, and parametric equalizers are among the other weapons in the war against garbled audio. But each problem-solving component added to your audio system design can lead to further challenges. For example, multiple microphones can make the voice of each speaker easier to hear, but they require additional mixing and processing equipment to produce a balanced, echo-free sound. Sort of like the man who got a cat to catch mice and then needed a cow to provide milk for the cat, a boy to protect the cow, and so forth—you get the point.

The strong air conditioning required to keep a VTC room at a comfortable temperature can also pose a real challenge to the achievement of good quality audio. Noise from air conditioning ducts that have not been properly routed or soundproofed can wreak havoc with a VTC audio system. If you can hear a clear difference in the background noise of a room when the air conditioning goes on and off—the performance of sensitive microphones, echo cancellers and automatic mixers built into your system will, almost surely, be adversely effected. If you cannot reroute air conditioning ducts, at least have them wrapped with sound deadening material, and add extra soundproofing material to the ceiling and walls in that part of the room. In his excellent book, *Videoconferencing and Videotelephony: Technology and Standards*, Richard Schaphorst, a leading expert in VTC system technologies, writes that the background noise level in a well-designed videoconferencing room should be under 45 dB, room reverberation should be between 0.3 and 0.5 seconds, and its absorption coefficient should be between 0.25 and 0.45.

Adequate soundproofing of the room itself is probably the most important and most cost-effective step that you can take to turn a "normal" conference room into a top-notch VTC facility. Here are a few tips for room design to ensure better audio during videoconferences:

• Acoustical consultants: If you have a potential problem (big windows, hard walls or ceiling, high ambient noise) get the advice of a qualified acoustical consultant. You can find one through the ICIA or the AES. If you cannot afford an acoustic consultant, one will not be appointed for you—but you can usually get good free advice from a reputable installer of echo cancellers or acoustic treatment materials. You can also get good advice and referrals from audio equipment manufacturers like Gentner, Shure, and Sound Control Technologies.

• Use the right tools: Don't use audio systems designed for desktop or small group use in a large group or conference room environment. They don't have the required processing power or memory to compensate for the longer and more complex echo patterns in those environments.

• Budget for padding: Allocate a sufficient portion of your budget for soundproofing and acoustic treatment. Wall tiles and curtains are always a good investment, and will do much more for meeting satisfaction than the fanciest chairs and table. There are dozens of types, styles, and brands of acoustic treatment material for walls, ceilings, and even doors. Costs vary from less than one dollar a square foot for basic ceiling tiles to hundreds of dollar-a-piece for high-quality cloth-covered wall panels. Materials for soundproofing a conference room are available from Acoustics First, Silent Source, and other suppliers.

Lighting Up the Room

Automatic video systems and codecs are quite limited in their tolerance for poor-quality, high-contrast lighting. If you must have dramatic pin-spot lighting for your "war room," that's A-okay. But please also install some well-diffused fluorescent lighting between your participants and your VTC cameras—and turn off the spotlights during videoconferences unless your want your execs to look like blurry extras in a remake of *Night of the Living Dead*. Recommended lighting levels are at least 30 average footcandles of flat, diffused 4500K fluorescent light (incident light measured at the face level of participant's seats). Another codec-friendly lighting trick is to use a light-toned, neutral-color table. This will bounce some overhead light back up on to your participants' faces, alleviating the dark eye-socket look sometimes referred to as "racoon eyes."

Lighting Fixtures: Ask your lighting supplier or room integrator about angled louvers for overhead fluorescent fixtures that will channel light toward your conferees and away from the TV/monitors. These can significantly improve the rendition and transmission of facial expressions, and cut down reflected lamp glare from TV/monitor screens. Installing Navitar Hi-Lites or similar units is an easy way to improve the quality of your VTC image. Hi-Lites are fixtures that hang at an adjustable angle from the ceiling of your conference room and cast flat, dimmable, fluorescent light to help produce the best possible picture for transmission. Two or three of these sub-$1,000 units should be sufficient for most average-size conference rooms, replacing four or more in-ceiling fixtures.

A good lighting consultant with VTC experience can create a sophisticated and efficient lighting design for your room—with diffused backlighting for increased visual depth and other effects. But if you do not have the option of securing professional assistance in this area, your solution is clear—equip the room with as many 4500K diffused fluorescent fixtures as it will comfortably hold.

A Window Full of Trouble: The last thing a designer wants to see in a potential

VTC room is a big bright window. Not only will it harden the room's acoustics, it can wreak havoc with the room's lighting. Moving shadows and highlights are guaranteed to give your camera and codec a nervous breakdown, as are the alternating light and dark patterns from venetian blinds. Daylight also varies in color temperature with the time of day, causing the side of a person facing the window to appear to be redder or bluer than their other side.

The solution to unwanted windows is simple, though sometimes costly—buy and install opaque drapes. Electrically operated drapes make it easy to both enjoy the view and to conduct a good-looking conference but usually cost several thousand dollars or more (including installation). One of my favorite tricks is to link the drapery controls to the VTC power switch or room control system, automatically closing the drapes at the beginning of a videoconference and opening them at its conclusion. Manual drapes may be inconvenient but do the job just as well for a lot less money. Just make sure that the drapes are opaque, overlap at the center, and block out all light at the window's endpoints.

Control Systems

If your room design is a simple one, the controller that is supplied as standard equipment with your codec will probably do the best job. There are at least two situations that justify the expense and effort of equipping your room with a custom control system:

- If you have reason to believe that key users will be confused or uncomfortable with the standard controller, a simplified touch-screen control panel may be a good idea.
- If you need to control a wide range of optional devices (such as cable TV boxes, DVD players, room lighting, and drapes), you may want to install a custom-programmed, touch-screen controller.

Touch-screen room controllers are available from a number of sources, most notable Crestron and AMX/Panja. They are available in both wired and wireless models and cost between $500 and $5,000, depending on screen size, type (e.g., color or black-and-white, wired or wireless) and the number and type of the devices to be controlled. First check with your codec manufacturer to see if they offer a touch-screen control option that can be reprogrammed to meet your needs. If this is not a practical solution and your room integrator is not an authorized AMX/Panja or Crestron supplier, your next step is to contact one of these manufacturers for a referral to an authorized supplier who can also program the panel for you.

To minimize your programming costs, first write down a list of all the functions you want the touch-screen to control, no matter how trivial they might seem. Work with the programmer to keep the design as simple and intuitive as possible, keeping in mind that some users may have little training and less skill. Be prepared for a few glitches in the initial programming and, most importantly, test the system very thoroughly before final acceptance.

Monitors and Projectors

Monitor size is an important factor in assuring that room users have a comfortable and productive meeting. One rule of thumb is to multiply the number of participants by four to determine the minimum size for a primary monitor. Thus a room designed for eight users should have a primary monitor with at least a 32-inch diagonal picture. If computer graphics and PowerPoint presentations are to be an important part of your conferences, a large VGA monitor or LCD/DLP projector should be used. Unless presentations and graphics are prepared specifically for transmission and display as regular VTC video (e.g., minimum 18- to 24-point type), or sent as data files, they will probably be unreadable at the distant location. Some systems, like the VCON 8000, already utilize a VGA monitor to display graphics. Others, like the newest units from Tandberg, use 4CIF transmission to increase the available image resolution. At the very least, make sure that your system provides VGA/SVGA output of graphics, either from its main electronics unit or through a PC connected to a user data port.

Many recently constructed conference rooms are using video/data projectors to provide a big bright picture that makes it easy for everyone to see all the available picture detail. These units, from Philips, Toshiba, Proxima, and a dozen other vendors have been getting brighter and less expensive over the past few years. For example, the Epson PowerLite 710C provides more than 1,000 ANSI lumens (enough for a normally-lit conference room) of crisp XGA output for about $5,000.

Plasma displays, though still relatively expensive, take up very little space, are very bright, and weigh considerably less than monitors of similar size. The Mitsubishi Leonardo, for example, is a 40-inch diagonal VGA display-only screen that costs about $6,000. Plasma displays are finding particular favor for use in small conference rooms where a large monitor would occupy too much valuable floor space.

The Ergonomics of Room Design

An entire book could be written on the ergonomics of VTC room design. Briefly, there are four major areas of ergonomic concern for VTC systems:

1. Eye Contact: The ideal location for a VTC camera is directly behind the main monitor or display, horizontally centered and about vertically displaced about two-thirds of the way up the screen. This would assure maximum eye contact between distant conferees. Since it is generally impractical to shoot through a screen, cameras are typically positioned above the main (or "people") monitor. If the monitors are to be mounted high on a wall, or if large projection screens are to be used, it might be advisable to mount the camera below the main screen.

2. Posture and Table Design: In many poorly-designed VTC rooms, participants are forced to twist their necks to look at the main screen, or to turn their chairs toward the front of the room at an angle that makes it difficult to write or read documents on the table. For these and many other reasons, traditional VTC table designs were developed to allow all participants to face both the main camera/monitor and the table work surface simultaneously (*see* Figure 4-11).

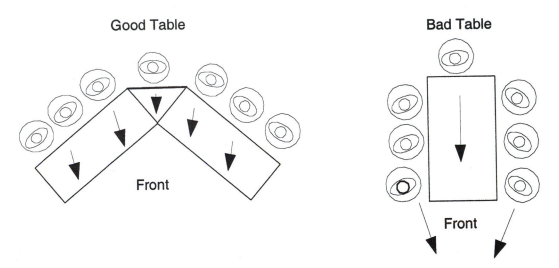

Good Table

Front

Bad Table

Front

Figure 4-11 Good table design, bad table design.

3. Movement Around the Room: The limited space available in conventional conference rooms, combined with the space required for VTC equipment, often leads to a claustrophobic layout for videoconferencing facilities. It is often advisable to reduce the size of the conference table in a room that is being converted for VTC use. This will preserve freedom of movement within the

room and substantially increase the interactivity and productivity of meetings held there. If you follow the design procedures outlined in "Make Room, Make Room," you should be able to avoid "captive meeting syndrome."

Tennis Neck Presentations: Many videoconferencing rooms are laid out with the VTC system at one end of the room and the whiteboard or projection screen at the other. This can create a tennis-match effect during shared presentations, with participants' attention forced to ping-pong back and forth between the live local presenter and the image of their distant conferees.

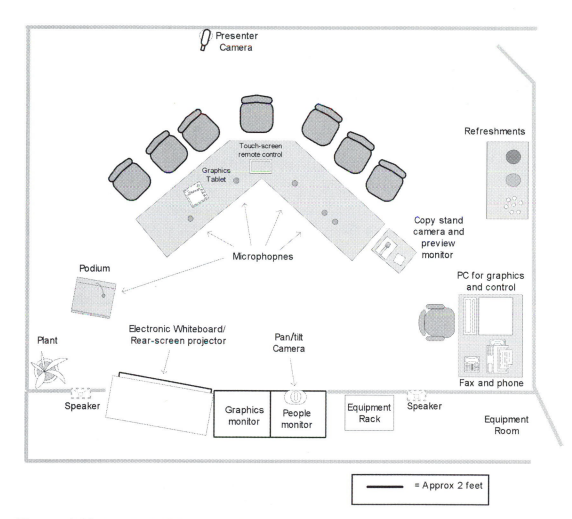

Figure 4-12 A typical VTC presentation room.

There are two simple solutions to this problem. The least expensive cure for ping-pong presentations is to locate an extra TV/monitor or two next to the presenter, displaying the distant end of the conference. This can usually be accomplished by running coaxial video cables from the looping outputs of the main VTC monitor(s). Space (and cabling) for a graphics/copy-stand camera must also be provided at that location.

A more effective (and more expensive) solution requires that we locate the live presenter and his or her tools at the same side of the room as the main VTC system. This maintains a single point of focus for the meeting but requires additional equipment, including a "presenter" camera. In addition, the orientation of the conference table may need to be changed to allow wall space for all the required equipment (*see* Figure 4-12).

Peripherals and Other System Enhancements

Often the right peripheral device can make the difference between a successful VTC system and one that gathers dust. If people can't use the room to meet in a way that is comfortable and familiar, using the skills they have developed over the years, they will look elsewhere for help. Whether users want to project overhead transparencies, run a PowerPoint presentation, draw on the walls, or just stand up in front of the room to deliver their pitch—they will be more comfortable and productive if you integrate the appropriate tools into your system. There are dozens of specialized peripheral enhancements for VTC systems, ranging from simple graphics/copy-stand cameras to touch-sensitive whiteboards equipped for collaborative computing. Here is a look at two of the most useful:

Copy-Stand Cameras

Probably the most common VTC accessory, copy-stand cameras allow users to capture, transmit, and share images of printed documents or 3-D objects (*see* Figure 4-13). They are often used to incorporate printouts of spreadsheets, graphs, and photographs into the meeting process. For general use, the small footprint Elmo DT-100AF (under $1,200) is a good choice. For users requiring high-resolution and flexibility, the powerful Canon DZ-3600U (priced around $5,000) will capture the image of an entire page of 8-point type and feed it into your system via a universal serial bus (USB) or S-Video connection. Sony, Epson, JVC, Panasonic, VideoLabs, and Samsung, also make good-quality copy-stand cameras and "visual presenters."

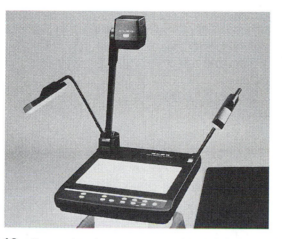

Figure 4-13 Copy-stand cameras enable VTC users to share printed material and images of 3-D objects. (Photo: Elmo)

Depending on your needs and budget, here are some important features and specifications to look for:

• Resolution and type of output: For use with typical set-top or low-end rollabout systems, a single CCD camera with around 400 TVL (TV lines) of horizontal resolution is sufficient. If your system accepts S-Video (Y-C) input, select a camera with this type of output—it will provide a sharper picture.

• Image size: Select a copy-stand camera that will accept documents up to the maximum size you plan to use. Some smaller stands will only handle 8.5" x 11" paper—fine for letter-size printouts, but awkward for spreadsheets and drawings.

• Zoom lens: Important specs are: minimum and maximum image size, power zoom and focus, remote control, and adjustability for room or wall use. For the later function, the lens must rotate to the horizontal position.

• Remote control: A very useful function—often controls zoom, focus, and even transmission of stills.

• Illumination: Copy-stand cameras usually need their own lights to produce a crisp, sharp picture. This is supplied by built-in fluorescent or incandescent lamps on adjustable "wings." A built-in backlight is important if the use of overhead transparencies or 35mm slides is expected.

• Image capture and storage: Some cameras will store multiple frames of graphics (e.g., different groups of spreadsheet cells) and transmit them as required, in a sort of slide show.

• Preview monitor: Some copy-stand cameras are available with small optional "preview" monitors to enable the presenter to see what the camera sees. This allows the presenter to see what the audience sees if he or she is not facing the main monitors, and to arrange or align documents before transmitting.

Electronic Whiteboards

There are many variations of this technology, but basically they all convert anything written or drawn on the board into a digital datastream that can be stored on a disc or transmitted to a distant location. Combined with the right software, electronic whiteboards enable powerful collaborative processes across time and space (*see* Figure 4-14).

Some units, like the MicroTouch Ibid 600, function as a touch-sensitive screen for data projectors, facilitating a truly immersive form of collaborative computing. Units range in price from less than $500 for a desktop tablet model to several thousand dollars for a 4' x 6' projector-enabled unit. The mimio from Virtual Ink (priced under $500) can even convert an old-fashioned whiteboard into an

Figure 4-14 An electronic whiteboard combined with a rear-screen projector and collaborative software. (Photo: Smart Technologies)

electronic one in a few seconds. Key factors in the selection of an electronic whiteboard include:

- The size, weight, resolution, and cost of the unit.
- The cost, if any, for T.120 compliant data collaboration software, and the compatibility of that software with common applications.
- The ability to function as an interactive projection screen—particularly useful for heavy PowerPoint users and for group collaboration.

To maximize the productivity gains from an electronic whiteboard, it is important to provide hands-on training and practice sessions for users.

Choosing the system and peripherals that best suit your needs is a major step toward the deployment of an effective VTC solution. It is also important to develop a sustainable approach to network management and the impact of emerging technologies on videoconferencing. In the next chapter, we take a look at the changing nature of digital networks, video and audio compression, multipoint conferencing, and other important issues.

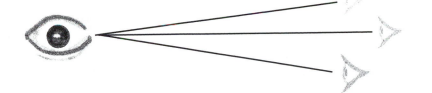

Networks and Advanced Technologies 5

Executive Summary

In contrast to the relatively simple and logical process of choosing a basic video-conferencing system, evaluating network strategies and emerging technologies can be a challenging and sometimes daunting task. These rapidly evolving technologies include multipoint conferencing, collaborative computing, distribution of video-on-demand, mobile applications, Web-based videoconferencing, and, of course, the basic choices involving local and wide area network type and configuration.

This difficulty is due in part to the complex synergetic effect of hundreds of factors, including the technologies themselves, the business factors that will effect their future development, and the impact that all of these will have on the way we communicate and work. It is also sad but true that just because a technology offers significant user benefits, there is no assurance that it will be fully developed in the future, and just because a new tool is readily available, it does not mean that it will be widely used.

For example, asynchronous transfer mode (ATM) to the desktop offered many advantages over Ethernet, yet it is dying a lingering death. Ethernet has been bolstered by ingenious make-do constructions of software and hardware to provide the quality of service (QoS) required for high-quality video, etc., but at a loss of several years and several billion dollars. No two IS experts seem to agree on why this happened, but Byzantine industry politics and the reluctance of technical managers to adopt unfamiliar tools are among the many reasons that have been suggested.

Collaborative computing is perhaps a better example. It has been around for decades, but except in engineering and other specialized uses has failed to make a substantial impact on the way people work. Microsoft NetMeeting is available at no cost on the majority of desktops in the developed world, yet few people even know anyone who uses this powerful tool on a regular basis. Lotus Notes provides the potential for a rich collaborative experience, yet most people use it only as a glorified e-mail application. Why this lack of acceptance of a technology that could do more to increase white-collar productivity than any invention since the paid vacation? Lack of adequate training? Poor marketing? Your guess is as good as mine.

The point is simple—accurately predicting which collaborative multimedia technologies will be widely deployed and well accepted over the next three to five years is almost impossible. Does this mean that we should forgo planning? Of course not. It only means that there is no single right answer to the application puzzle, but that all the right answers begin with substantial, demonstrable user needs, and include contingency plans that allow for the twists and turns of techno-fate.

Developing a Future-proof Strategy for Multimedia Communication

There are at least five tests I like to apply to any proposed solution that involves the use of emerging or advanced technologies:

1. Does the new-technology component of the solution answer a specific, substantial, demonstrable user need?
2. Is there an older, better tested, or more widely accepted technology that will address this need as well as the shiny new tech?
3. Is there more than one source for this new technology, or will I be dependent on the continued ability of a single vendor to supply and support it?
4. Where in its development or deployment life cycle is this technology, and is my organization the appropriate user for it at this time vis-a-vis tech support, mission critical applications, and other considerations?
5. Is there a way that I can implement a phased rollout of this technology, which will not interfere with or endanger existing mission critical applications? Alternately, is there a way to outsource the deployment of this technology that will answer short-term users' needs in a cost-effective and flexible manner? For example, outsourcing to an application service provider (ASP).

Other videoconferencing professionals have their own litmus tests, many of them more stringent than mine. The essential principle is "do no harm" to the flow of important information within the enterprise.

In this chapter, we'll look at some of these emerging communication technologies as they apply to videoconferencing and examine strategies intended to deploy them in the most productive and risk-free manner.

Network Type and Configuration

In order for videoconferencing content to get from one place to another, it almost always needs to travel over a digital network. The exceptions to this rule are rare—even prime-time news "conferences" now ride switched DS3 circuits from coast to coast. The digital networks used for VTC cover a broad range in terms of bandwidth, method of transmission, cost, and other important characteristics.

Warning: I am not an expert in data networking; I only play one on TV. If you have serious technical questions or issues, consult one of the organizations, experts or Web sites listed in "Appendix B: General Resources."

It is unlikely that strategic decisions about your data network infrastructure have been driven primarily by videoconferencing-related concerns. Either VTC will ride on a network created for data and voice, or additional capabilities will be added to the current network to accommodate VTC. In the former case, the impact of video's voracious appetite for bandwidth and QoS may have a significant impact on network performance. In the later situation, the additional capabilities need to be added to the mix with care to avoid unnecessary expenditures or administrative headaches.

In years past, it was not uncommon for videoconferencing managers to arrange for separate digital services for their networks. Many traditional LAN/WAN and telecommunications departments wanted nothing to do with the responsibility and the headaches of this notoriously demanding, complicated, and high-profile application. Today, VTC is generally seen as a lead application in the rush to convergence and broadband networks. Progressive managers of integrated voice and data networks are also more receptive to requests for video services than their more conservative and specialized predecessors might have been. The additional bandwidth and other requirements for IP-Video are not considered a threat by these "new guns." Rather, they are seen as another justification for the next generation networks that they want to deploy in order to provide a wide range of improved services.

Networking and Compression

The relationship of video and audio compression format to network choice is a complex subject, but here is a quick summary of the key issues:

- Higher video quality generally requires higher bandwidth. Whatever network type you use, the greater the available bandwidth, the better the picture (and sound) quality. Packet-switched networks (e.g., Ethernet) often require more raw bandwidth to achieve the same throughput (quality) as circuit-switched (e.g., ISDN), but this difference should be marginal in properly configured networks.
- Specific compression algorithms and standards are most suitable for specific network and transport types. For instance, H.320/H.261 is a perfect match for BRI-ISDN, while H.323/H.263 is custom-made for a 100Base-T Ethernet LAN.
- Specific compression algorithms and standards are designed for specific quality requirements and ranges of bandwidth. For example, MPEG-2 is a high-quality compression method that is used primarily in "digital satellite" TV broadcasting and for the distribution of movies on DVD The target bandwidth range for MPEG-2 is 2 to 20 Mbps, depending on the type of signal and level of picture quality required.
- Different standardized compression algorithms can be used over the same network. For example, H.263, M-JPEG, MPEG-1, MPEG-2, and a host of proprietary methods of compression can be used for video to be transmitted over an Ethernet LAN or an ATM network. The right choice depends on a number of use-specific factors including application, available bandwidth, and cost of hardware.

Each of the compression methods mentioned above will be discussed in more detail later in this chapter under the subheading "Compression," but now, back to the types of networks used for videoconferencing.

ISDN

Traditional videoconferencing runs over integrated switched digital networks (ISDN) and similar networks. This type of VTC is generally governed by the H.320 set of standards approved by the International Telecommunications Union (ITU). These standards tell manufacturers and service providers what they must do to assure that different types of equipment can interoperate, or "talk" to each other. To improve picture quality and other functions, many manufacturers also take advantage of optional capabilities described within the standards. Some vendors also add their own proprietary enhancements that operate only when two or more similar systems are connected.

A detailed examination of the H.320, H.323, and T.120 standards is beyond the scope of this book. An excellent, in-depth analysis of all current and proposed standards and related issues is provided in *Videoconferencing and Videotelephony: Technology and Standards*, Second Edition, by Richard Schaphorst.

ISDN is ideal for videoconferencing. It is relatively inexpensive, reliable, and ubiquitous. Most importantly, it provides the quality of service (QoS) and low latency (delay) required for technically demanding videoconferencing communications. ISDN is available in a variety of forms. The two most common are basic rate interface (BRI) and primary rate interface (PRI).

BRI-ISDN provides dial-up service on two 64 kbps (B) channels, and a separate signaling or data (D) channel of 16 kbps. Each B channel may be used separately for phone, data, or video communication, or the channels can be combined to form a single, higher-speed 128 kbps connection. Many basic desktops video systems employ a single BRI circuit to provide basic videoconferencing and data collaboration. BRI service is inexpensive, sometimes costing less than the two analog business phone lines it replaces. Multiple BRI connections can be combined to create a higher-speed communications link of 256 kbps, 384 kbps, or 512 kbps. This is accomplished with the assistance of an Inverse Multiplexer, or IMUX.

PRI-ISDN provides 24 B channels (in the United States and Japan), one of which is typically reserved for signaling purposes. This leaves 23 B channels (or 1.472 Mbps) for communications purposes, and they can be parceled out for various uses by a Multiplexer (Mux). For example, six channels (384 kbps) can be dedicated for videoconferencing, two channels (128 kbps) for remote access to the Internet through an ISP, and the remaining 15 channels can be connected to a PBX (internal phone system).

<u>Note</u>: PRI uses the T1 (24 B) signaling structure in the United States and Japan, and the E1 (30 B) structure in Europe and elsewhere in the world.

Networks for High-Volume Conferencing

For more flexibility in complex installation, an ISDN hub from Madge or another manufacturer can be installed to manage multiple PRI (and other) circuits and provide bandwidth on demand to a variety of applications (*see* Figure 5-1). This type of setup becomes a necessity when, for example, you expect to have a high volume of calls between a headquarters location and multiple branch offices. In some of these cases, it is more economical to lease one or more dedicated lines to those locations. In others, establishing a virtual private network (VPN) linking all locations will be your best bet. In this context, a VPN refers to network consisting of permanent, high speed (e.g., PRI) links from each location to the nearest point of presence (POP) of your telecommunications provider, and on-demand connections between all those points through secure (virtual) tunnels in the carrier's wide area network. This allows you to "dial-up" a conference with any of your locations, and typically also permits dial-up access to any VTC systems on the public switched telephone network (PSTN).

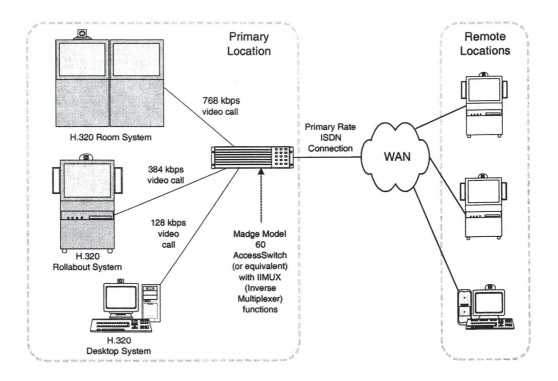

Figure 5-1 Multi-use ISDN network configuration.

Most carriers offer a variety of dial-up and leased ISDN-type services, and it's a good idea to talk to several companies to take advantage of their expertise and get the best deal. Buying the same capabilities under a different name can often save you money every month. For example: eleven BRI circuits usually cost a lot more than the equivalent PRI service. There may be a capital cost for the customer premises equipment (CPE) required to divide the B channel to your various VTC systems, but it's easy to calculate the time required for the savings resulting from lower monthly charges to offset the cost of the equipment. Working with your organization's primary telecommunication services provider to obtain video networking services and equipment can sometimes offer significant advantages, including volume discounts, good advice, and better access to technical support. A partial list of carriers offering these services can be found in "Appendix B: General Resources."

Among the many networking technologies that are important in one way or another to the application of videoconferencing, video over Ethernet is perhaps the key element in the rapidly evolving world of videoconferencing.

Ethernet and IP Video

Ethernet was originally a standard protocol (IEEE 802.3) for 10 Mb/s baseband local area network (LAN) using a variety of transmission media and protocols. In recent years, the capabilities of Ethernet have been enhanced. The maximum bandwidth has been increased to 1 Gb/s (Gigabit Ethernet, IEEE 802.3z), and Ethernet's reach has been extended beyond the local area to the metropolitan area and beyond, covering distances of up to 100 km via single mode fiber optic transmission. Most data exchanged over Ethernet employ TCP/IP protocol, that is, Transmission Control Protocol/Internet Protocol. This is, as the name implies, the same method used to communicate over the Internet. TCP/IP is a full-duplex protocol used over packet-switched networks. Packet switching is a very efficient technique for the routing and transfer of addressed packets of data. It uses the transmission channel only while a packet is being transmitted, giving it up for use by other traffic the instant a packet has been sent. At the receiving end of the circuit, the packets are reassembled in a way that maintains the order of packets, but does not guarantee that they will have the same space (or time) between them. This is fine for static files like e-mail, but can sometimes pose problems for timing-sensitive information such as video or audio.

Why Try Video over IP?

Many methods have been developed to improve the way in which digital video and audio are handled by Ethernet and other packet-switched networks employing TCP/IP. IP networks are cheaper, faster, and more nearly ubiquitous (e.g., office LANs and the Internet) than circuit-switched networks like ISDN. The three most important aspects of an IP network that must be optimized in order for it to effectively handle videoconferencing traffic are:

- Bandwidth
- Latency
- QoS (quality of service)

Bandwidth

No matter what video source, compression method, or transport is used, there is a direct correlation between allocated bandwidth and picture quality. The higher the transmission speed employed, the better will be the perceived quality of the video—within limits. All other things being equal, a 1.54 Mbps transmission using H.261, M-JEG, or MPEG-1 will look better than a 128 kbps transmission using any of these compression methods. Of course, each method has its best range of use. For example, H.261 is optimized for bandwidths from 56 kbps to 1.54 Mbps.

A digitized, uncompressed digital video signal requires at least 75 Mbps of bandwidth for transmission, but most viewers find no significant difference in quality between a direct feed from a broadcast camera and from a 10 Mbps MPEG-2 transmission (when viewed on a standard composite TV monitor). After years of trial and error, most heavy users of videoconferencing industry have settled on 384 kbps as a good compromise bandwidth—the one with the best balance between quality and cost. Most H.320 codecs produce 30 frames per second (fps) of full intermediate common format (FCIF) video at this rate, with enough bandwidth for audio and data. The quality differences between 384 kbps and 768 kbps transmission, while visible, are not dramatic. On the other hand, the transmission costs, using dial-up or VPN-based ISDN, are about twice as high. A one-hour conference that costs about $40 at 384 kbps could cost $80 at 768 kbps. Multiply this by the scores or hundred of conferences a typical VTC facility hosts each year, and pretty soon it adds up to some real money.

The transmission cost differential is more dramatic for ISDN than for Ethernet—

a format where even the smallest "pipe" carries 10 Mbps. As long as the signal is kept on the LAN, the only incremental cost is that of upgrading the infrastructure to handle the increased load. With many organizations already moving to switched 100Base-T to the desktop, and gigabit Ethernet "backbones," the cost of local bandwidth is not a major issue. When the VTC signal gets out on the WAN, where most organizations' payment for connectivity are based on bandwidth, the picture is a little bit different.

Many users are looking to cheaper broadband access to provide "broadcast quality" video using MPEG-2 for video compression. There are three things that make this attractive idea less than practical for many applications:

1. Unless you buy a very large amount of bandwidth to begin with, you will have to buy more to accommodate multiple multi-megabit video streams.
2. High-speed Internet access does not usually translate into high-speed video throughput.
3. Even if you are using leased bandwidth or a VPN for your IP-based WAN, you may have to pay more for the high quality of service (QoS) and low-latency transmission that broadband video requires.

Quality of Service

Quality of service, has very little to do with the merit of the snacks served by an airline. It refers instead to the guaranteed level of throughput, end-to-end, that can be expected from a particular network connection. This generally takes into consideration the stability of the data rate, the bit error rate, jitter, latency (delay), and other factors. The QoS of ISDN and ATM can be guaranteed, while on packet-switched networks QoS usually cannot be guaranteed. Even without guaranteed QoS, video can still be transmitted with good results over IP networks—but competition for priority from other data traffic (and a dozen other variables) can cause dropped frames, poor picture quality, garbled audio, and other problems. Numerous methods have been developed to assure QoS for high priority traffic (e.g., video) on IP networks. These include real-time transport protocol (RTP), the control protocol (RTCP) that works with RTP, the resource reservation protocol (RSVP), and the real-time streaming protocol (RTSP). While it is currently difficult to be sure that your video and audio will make it across the Internet unscathed, there are a number of network services providers and manufacturers that will provide guaranteed QoS for LANs and WANs. These include products from Cisco, VIP Switch, Tollbridge, and many others.

The telecom industry is taking this issue very seriously. A recent study from

Insight Research reported that carrier spending on gateway equipment to help carriers offer guaranteed QoS for voice and other services over IP will grow from $190 million in 2000 to over $2.8 billion in 2004.

What can you do to guarantee that your videoconferencing application will navigate the IP labyrinth and arrive safe and sound at a distant codec? Talk to your network manager or planner, tell them about your planned requirements, and ask about their provisions or plans for guaranteed QoS on your LAN and WAN. The more lead time they have to deal with your QoS requirements, the less expensive it will be to satisfy those needs. It's not necessarily a simple yes-or-no proposition; there may be specific conditions or limitation that might require negotiation and compromise. You may need to limit the length or frequency of IP videoconferences during peak network usage periods, at least until the next planned build-out or upgrade of your LAN. You may also be asked to accept some additional cost for each VTC-equipped desktop or room system that is connected to the LAN/WAN, to offset the cost of new equipment or new telecom services.

Not on My Network

Many organizations have a significant investment in local area networks (LANs) and wide area networks (WANs) based on Ethernet or other TCP/IP-based network types. Managing those networks in a time of increasing user demands and IT personnel scarcity is a very difficult job—even without "crazy video" to worry about.

There have been many attempts over the past ten years to use these networks to transmit various kinds of multimedia content, including videoconferencing. These attempts have, for the most part, been less than successful due to a number of significant factors.

The Top Ten Reasons Why Network Managers Say Videoconferencing Over IP Networks Doesn't Work:

10. It eats up bandwidth needed for more mission critical applications, like financial transactions, e-mail, and interoffice *Quake* tournaments.
9. It would require upgrading the LAN with expensive high-speed switches and other devices to assure sufficient bandwidth, low latency, and guaranteed QoS—and paying more money to carriers for guaranteed QoS over the WAN.
8. Desktop videoconferencing would greatly increase the user support required from an already overburdened, underpaid, and underappreciated IT staff.

7. Who needs desktop video anyway? Not my boss.
6. We tried it before, and it didn't work.
5. It's not budgeted.
4. We need to form a task force to study all the long-term ramifications.
3. It will compromise our firewall security processes.
2. The H.323 standard isn't (standard) yet.
1. Not on my network! This last reaction often comes from an individual wearing a necklace of garlic and brandishing various religious and magical artifacts.

What Is H.323?

H.323 is an umbrella designation for a group of standards and recommendations from the International Telecommunications Union (ITU-T) regarding audio, video, and multimedia conferencing over packet-switched networks. This includes point-to-point and multipoint videoconferencing over Ethernet LANs, WANs, and the Internet; and Internet Telephony (VoIP) and other related applications. The primary components defined in H.323 include:

- Terminals: For our purposes these include VTC user systems, whether room systems, set-tops, or desktop. Most current models of H.320 video conferencing systems either support H.323 or can be upgraded at reasonable cost.
- Gateways: These devices permit the use of an H.320 VTC terminal (e.g., an old room system) on an H.323 network. They also facilitate connection of H.323 terminals and other devices to a circuit-switched WAN (e.g., ISDN).
- Gatekeepers: These devices control the traffic of a group of H.323 terminals and other equipment on a network. Gatekeepers may allow the network administrator to manage the various devices on the network, set privileges, bandwidth allocations, and to set parameters for traffic control that will ensure proper functioning of the H.323 devices and the rest of the net work. Gatekeeper functions also include address translation to simplify a variety of user operations.
- MCUs: The general functions of multipoint control units (MCUs) are covered later in this chapter, but there are some MCU concerns that are unique to the H.323 environment. In the H.323 world, the MCU is divided into two parts; the multipoint processor (MP), which performs all the audio and video mixing and switching; and the multipoint controller (MC), which handles the scheduling, signal routing, and mode negotiations (speed, algorithm, etc.). The increased flexibility of this

model allows multiple MCs to cooperate easily to establish broadcast conferences and add participants on the fly, and to integrate data conferencing into a multipoint videoconference—all difficult tasks for a conventional H.320/H.231 MCU.

Web-based Conferencing

There has been an underground movement afoot for several years promoting the uses of Internet-based videoconferencing. Though this has been occurring mostly in academic institutions, especially those with broadband Internet access, there has been a lot of consumer interest as well. Relatively poor video and audio quality (even for those with high-speed connections) has kept this application out of the mainstream of business communications. Still, tens of thousands of users of CUseeMe and NetMeeting have created an active online community that has helped to develop many of the tools that are pushing the conferencing envelope further into the future. In that future, new networking technologies (including DSL, RSVP, etc.) may make videoconferencing as ubiquitous as the World Wide Web. For a taste of that future, you can visit http://www.cuseeme.com.

What to Do?

What strategies are most likely to provide cost-effective videoconferencing and collaborative computing, without exposing users to the vagaries of QoS on IP WANs? The answer depends on the results of your own needs analysis, but there are some guidelines that should be helpful in the majority of applications. Begin with the assumption that you may need to rely on switched digital services for wide area connectivity for at least a few years. There may be great benefit in pilot projects using H.323 WAN connectivity. But, considering the real state of most of these services it is wise to proceed cautiously. Even when you take the plunge, keep enough wide area ISDN connectivity onboard to handle critical video traffic in an emergency.

For desktop connectivity, H.323 over a robust LAN offers tremendous advantages. It eliminates the substantial cost and hassles of providing multiple ISDN-BRI circuits to each desk. It also provides for high-quality VTC and collaborative computing between local colleagues. To carry IP-videoconferencing traffic, a LAN must be truly robust. Hub-based 10Base-T LANs may handle a few calls, but will be slowed down by the flood of video traffic that can be expected after a successful rollout. Substantial H.323 VTC traffic can even present problems on a well-designed switched 100 Mbps LAN.

If LAN-based VTC looks like it might be a viable solution for your needs, get a professional analysis of your projected network requirements. This is best done in cooperation with your IS management to assure that all future networking needs will be served by a single unified, sustainable, and cost-effective solution. To connect LAN-based desktop VTC systems to ISDN WAN access, you will need to use an H.323/H.320 Gateway, available from Madge, RADVision, FVC.com, and others. Older H.320 room systems can also be connected through an H.323/H.320 Gateway, or directly to your ISDN access. If a number of desktop and room systems are to be set up in the same facility, you will need a way to manage their WAN access and bandwidth. Madge and other vendors supply systems designed for this specific purpose. For a hybrid ISDN and packet-switched network configuration, see Figure 5-2.

Better safe than sorry. Mission-critical and high-use systems should always be provided with backup connectivity wired directly to the terminal location. Three extra ISDN-BRI lines costing around $100 per month will provide dial-up videoconferencing when all else fails, and, consistent with Murphy's law, it probably will. For the particularly paranoid VTC manager, I recommend backup lines from a different carrier than the primary vendor of telecommunication services. By employing IP-LAN and ISDN internal access with wide area connectivity using a combination of

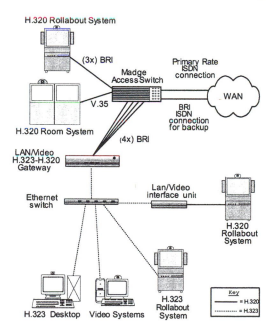

Figure 5-2 A hybrid ISDN and packet-switched network configuration.

IP-WAN, switched public, and virtual private digital network services, you can obtain the best service and maximum bandwidth for the least monthly outlay.

Other Networking Technologies

There are several other types of connectivity that you may encounter in your search for the perfect network. Here's a brief rundown of those networking options and their basic place in the VTC universe.

Asynchronous Transfer Mode (ATM)

ATM is a high-speed switching and multiplexing method using fixed-length cells (packets) of 53 bytes to support multiple types of traffic and reliably route multimedia traffic over the network. ATM currently supports data-transfer rates of 25 to 622 Mbps. It provides guaranteed QoS at various levels, and variable bit rate (VBR) ATM is a natural platform for the delivery of videoconferencing. Unfortunately, ATM to the desktop is not widely supported or encouraged in many networking environments. It is, however, widely used by carriers to support high-speed WAN traffic, and companies like Fore and FVC provide a wide range of ingenious solutions for hybrid (TCP/IP, ISDN, ATM) multimedia networks. FVC's offerings are particularly attractive for those organizations with complex needs that include higher-quality video distribution.

T1

T1 is a dedicated digital connection supporting data rates of approximately 1.54 Mbps. A T1 circuit (sometimes called a DS1) consists of twenty-four individual channels supporting data transfer rates of 56 kbps or 64 kbps. Each channel can carry voice, data, or video traffic. A T1 connection can also be configured to support PRI-ISDN service with 24 B channels, one of which is usually reserved for signaling. E1 is the European equivalent of the T1. It is very similar in form and function, but consists of thirty channels supporting data-transfer rates of up to 64 kbps, for a total bandwidth of approximately 2 Mbps.

DS3

DS3 is a dedicated digital connection supporting data-transfer rates of up to approximately 43 Mbps. It is composed of 672 channels, each supporting a data-transfer rate of 64 kbps. DS3 service is sometimes referred to as T3, and typical uses include connection of ISPs to the Internet backbone and the transport of data and video traffic by financial institutions and other large institutions. Switched DS3 networks are sometimes used by TV networks and production companies for the transmission of broadcast level programming.

Frame Relay

Frame Relay networks use a packet-switching protocol for connecting devices on a wide area network (WAN) and support data transfer rates of up to DS3 (43 Mbps). Most carriers in the United States. provide frame relay service for cost-effective data transfer at rates of 56 kbps to 1.544 Mbps. Many companies have demonstrated H.323 videoconferencing over frame relay networks, and it is one option that should be considered for this application.

DSL

Digital subscriber line (DSL) includes several distinct telecommunication services. All use advanced techniques to pack data onto the tremendous installed base of copper wires between the telephone company's switching stations and businesses and residences. Although DSL provides a very economical "last-mile solution" (actually, the last four miles), wide-area connectivity has been limited in many areas to Internet access and plain old telephone services (POTS). New services promise more flexible connectivity (e.g., QoS, VTC), but as of this writing there has been little high-level deployment. Transmission speeds available for DSL range from services as high as 9 Mbps downstream or 640 kbps upstream for Asymmetric DSL (ADSL), to 3 Mbps both ways for Symmetric DSL (SDSL), to 32 Mbps downstream or 1 Mbps upstream for xDSL.

SONET

It's not a poem by Shakespeare! Synchronous Optical Network (SONET) is a standard for connecting fiber-optic transmission systems in the United States. It defines a hierarchy of interface rates that allow data streams at different rates to be combined without interference. It describes optical carrier (OC) levels from 51.8 Gbps to 2.48 Gbps, the equivalent of over 1,600 T1 circuits.

OC3

One of the more common optical carrier (OC) speeds or services specified for fiber-optic networks compliant with the SONET standard. Other speeds include: OC1 =

51.85 Mbps, OC12 = 622.08 Mbps, OC24 = 1.244 Gbps, and O-48 = 2.488 Gbps.

Compression

As was mentioned earlier in this chapter, virtually every video picture we see has gone through some sort of compression, and the same is true of many audio signals we hear. Even network TV typically is compressed to fit into a 43 Mbps (DS3) pipe at some stage of its trip to our screens. This kind of slight compression results in close to lossless image resolution, and the resulting picture is virtually indistinguishable from the original.

The same cannot be said for most videoconferencing images. In order to fit within the bandwidth limits of the 384 kbps ISDN service typically used for VTC, the signal has been compressed to contain less than 0.3 percent of the data contained in a full-bandwidth digital video signal. A lot of that lost data is unnecessary or redundant (*see* Figure 5-3). Some of it is spatially redundant. We don't need the repetitive data that tells us that every square inch on the rear wall of a conference room in Tokyo is blue; only that it is a blue wall, and that it covers this entire area is sufficient information.

Some video information is temporally (time) redundant: that patch of wall was blue a second ago and guess what, it is still blue. Temporally redundant information is eliminated primarily with interframe compression, that is, by comparing two or more frames of motion video. By eliminating spatially and temporally redundant data and estimating what the rest of the picture should look like, we are able to achieve high compression ratios (up to 1300/1). Though the picture we get at that level of compression (128 kbps) will not win an Emmy for technical excellence, it is good enough to help willing conferees to suspend their disbelief and communicate with each other as though they were face to face. Though this compression process may sound simple, it is actually accomplished with the aid of some extremely sophisticated software called compression algorithms and some very powerful integrated circuits called digital signal processors (DSPs). The combination of these two elements, and a few extra components, make up what we call a hardware codec (coder-decoder). Due to the establishment of videoconferencing standards, the resulting growth in demand, and great advances in the manufacturing of integrated circuits—the cost of a complete video codec kit capable of communication over a single BRI-ISDN line (128 kbps) has been reduced over the last ten years from about $50,000 to under $1,000.

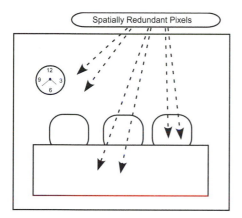

Spatially redundant pixels are points, located in the same area of a picture, that have virtually identical luminance and chrominance values.

Temporally redundant pixels are points whose light and color values remain essentially the same from one frame of a moving picture to the next.

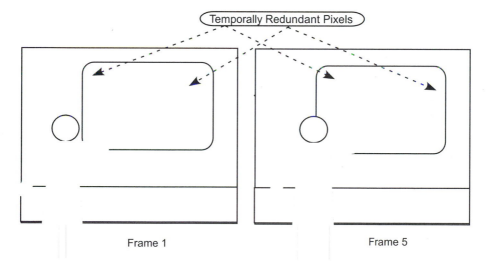

Frame 1   Frame 5

Figure 5-3 Spatial and temporal redundancy in video compression.

DCT and Other Animals

All of the standard video compression algorithms currently in use are based on discrete cosign transform (DCT). These include H.261, H.263, JPEG, MJPEG, MPEG-1, and MPEG-2. There are other newer algorithms based on fractals and vector quantization that do an excellent job, but the process of standardization, which runs several years behind the bleeding age of science, has given us some very powerful and economical tools that we can use to communicate with virtually anybody on the planet.

This is not the place for a thorough technical analysis of DCT and the other compression methods, for that you should read Richard Schaphorst's book referred to earlier in this chapter. What I will try to do here is to describe the most common uses of the various ITU-standard algorithms and their basic differences. Audio compression, though not as critical for bandwidth usage, is equally important for the quality of communication, so a brief description of some relevant audio compression methods is also included.

H.261

H.261 is an ITU-T standard DCT-based interframe compression algorithm used for H.320-based videoconferencing that is most effective in the range of 112 kbps to approximately 2 Mbps. It defines two picture sizes and resolutions, the most widely used of which is full common intermediate format (FCIF), with an effective resolution of 352 x 288 luminance pixels.

H.263

An ITU-T standard, DCT-based interframe compression algorithm, H.263 is similar in many respects to H.261, but H.263 is optimized primarily for H.323-based videoconferencing.

MPEG-1

A standardized, DCT-based interframe compression algorithm, MPEG-1 was developed initially for video recording on CD-ROM, but used today for some streaming video applications. MPEG stands for Motion Picture Expert Group.

MPEG-2

A standard DCT-based interframe compression algorithm, MPEG-2 was developed initially for transmission of "broadcast-quality" video via digital satellite and land lines at speeds of 2 Mbps to 25 Mbps and higher. It is also used in the distribution of video and multimedia on DVD.

M-JPEG

A "motion" version of JPEG, MPEG is a standard, DCT-based intraframe (no frame-to-frame comparison) compression algorithm. JPEG was developed initially for storage and transmission of photographic images. MJPEG is used in video postproduction and similar applications that require every frame of video to contain a maximum amount of video information.

G.711

An ITU standard PCM-based compression algorithm used for the transmission of audio signals at speeds of 48 kbps to 64 kbps with an audio bandwidth of up to 3 kHz.

G.722

G.722 ITU standard ADPCM-based compression algorithm used for the transmission of audio signals at speeds of 48 kbps to 64 kbps with an audio bandwidth of up to 7 kHz.

G.728

G.728 is a lower-quality LD-CELP-based compression algorithm used for the transmission of audio signals at speeds of 16 kbps with a audio bandwidth of up to 3 kHz.

Multipoint Conferencing

Perhaps the biggest challenge faced by managers of videoconferencing systems is that of helping make multipoint conferences live up to the expectations of end users. Users have been led to expect effortless, reliable, and trouble-free multipoint conferencing through news broadcasts, such as *Nightline*, and network advertisements showing instant, broadcast-quality split screens. As a result, users are often disappointed with the quality of their own multipoint conferencing experiences.

To be fair to carriers and hardware suppliers, the industry has made great strides from the proprietary and unreliable solutions of just a few years ago. Today, Accord, Ezenia! (formerly, VideoServer), Lucent, MultiLink, and others provide reliable, standards-based hardware; and specialized network service providers such as V-Span and InView provide user-friendly setup and support for even the most complex multipoint meetings.

Basic Functions of MCUs

A multipoint controller (MCU) allows people at more than two locations to participate in a videoconference. Some VTC systems include a simple built-in MCU for use with two or three other locations, but these MCUs are not expandable and may only permit multipoint conferencing between systems from the same manufacturer. Some built-in MCUs, and all stand-alone units, will work with any H.320 standards-compliant system and comply with the ITUs H.231 and H.243 standards for multipoint conferencing (*see* Appendix C: Commercial Resources).

In the most basic type of multipoint videoconference, the participants at several sites can hear everyone all the time, but can see only the primary speaker. Voice-activated switching routes the picture of the speaker's location to participants' screens. A short, programmable delay in the switching process helps to eliminate the pingpong effect that can be caused by brief comments (and coughs).

Chair control is a useful function included with many MCUs that simply lets the person in charge of the meeting "call on" or recognize a speaker by switching the video to display their picture on everyone's screens.

Graphics are an important part of most videoconferences, whether they are simple bullet-point slides or complex charts and diagrams. Most MCUs allow any site to send a still frame graphic image to all other sites, simultaneously.

Continuous Presence adds the capability of viewing more than one site at a time. There are many ways in which this is accomplished, but generally it appears as a split screen, *Hollywood Squares* style.

Dataconferencing

While there is a set of established standards for dataconferencing and collaboration called T.120, it is expensive and difficult to implement in an H.231/243 (e.g., ISDN-based) multipoint conferencing environment. The cost of adding this capability to a conventional MCU can increase the cost by 50 percent or more. Though this function is supported by some MCUs operated by bridging services, there has reportedly been little call for it. One reason for this lack of demand is the relative simplicity (and low cost) of setting up a Web conference using one of the many services available from WebEx, Astound, Akamai, and others. Web conferences allow users to view PowerPoint slides and other presentation graphics through any browser-equipped computer connected to the Internet. Most services include annotation and other collaborative functions as well.

H.323 MCUs

Several years ago, anticipating the shift of videoconferncing from the realm of circuit ISDN to packet-switched IP-WANs, most MCU manufacturers switched their development focus from H.320-based MCUs to H.323-based units. As a result, most of the recent interesting development in MCU technology has been in this area. As mentioned earlier, H.323 MCUs now have several advantages over their circuit-switched cousins:

- H.323 MCUs can easily add and drop conferees on the fly, enabling more spontaneous, productive uses of the technology.
- They can "invite" and add voice-only conferees in the same manner.
- The cost per port of H.323 MCUs is only a fraction of that of comparable H.320 units; and the differential is getting greater as production and competition ramp up.
- T.120 data conferencing is a relatively inexpensive option for H.323 MCUs, but has remained a prohibitively expensive add-on for H.320 units.
- Even low cost units allow call-in conferencing, operator-free conference setup, simple network management protocol (SNMP) remote configuration, and other advanced user and administrative features.

Multipoint Challenges

Multipoint control equipment and services continue to improve at a rapid pace, becoming more reliable and accessible, and offering additional capabilities to users. The improvements in these critical areas and the resulting increase in demand, combined with the rapid spread of desktop videoconferencing systems, may have created a whole new set of headaches for video network managers.

A typical scenario might go like this. Last month's staff meeting for vice president X consisted of a six-way multipoint at 384 kbps involving twenty-four participants in six well-equipped rooms on the corporate VPN. Because of the good lighting and audio, the easily managed high-bandwidth, copy-stand cameras for charts, the availability of a trained room coordinator to assist with testing and setup, and a variety of other factors resulting from years of planning and development, the meeting went off without a hitch.

Example: This month, vice president X is too busy to break away for the meeting and wishes to conduct it from the new desktop videoconferencing system in her office. On hearing this, directors A, B, and C, who also have shiny new DVC systems, also want to join-in the meeting from their own offices.

With the remaining twenty staff members still spread across six conference rooms (and as many time zones) the total number of locations has now grown from six to ten. If the local MCU does not support this number of ports, we must go to an outside service for bridging, with the attendant added expense and potential for error. If the new desktops have not been certified with that particular provider, additional time must be spent completing that process. But even if you have ports galore, and can handle it all in-house, this may be a mixed blessing. If, as is likely, your executives are not nerds, they will probably need help testing and setting up for conferences—so you have ten "rooms" to set up instead of six, and four of these rooms don't have lighting or acoustics designed for VTC. As a matter of fact, vice president X's system faces a window overlooking the corporate duck pond. With no copy-stand cameras in the executives' offices you are also faced, probably before you or your executive users are ready, with the need to incorporate scanners and PC graphics into a multipoint conference.

As if this isn't enough—three of the desktops have only a single public BRI and typical 128 kbps ISDN connectivity, bringing much of the conference back down to an even lower level of quality and reliability. The same 128 kbps that might look and sound fine for two talking heads doesn't quite cut it anymore for a lively discussion with as many as four people on-screen at once, with many more trying to be heard at the same time.

It's easy to extrapolate on from here—to dissatisfied users, manpower, hardware and budget problems, and a need for increased mental health benefits for videoconferencing managers—but what might be more useful, though less amusing, is a quick look at some of the solutions for these challenges.

Help Is on the Way

Some managers are trying to address these challenges by making it easier for users to become an integral part of their video networks. Networked reservation systems, such as such as VC Wizard from AC&E, can make it easier to schedule diverse users especially if they are coupled with the effective training of administrative personnel. One large financial institution custom developed an MS Access-based reservation system that fit their system and corporate culture, and also created a self-paced presentation to teach desktop users and their administrative assistants how to use the system in the most productive way. Perhaps this kind of outreach offers a better chance of improving the quality of desktop participation in multipoints than some of the more sophisticated technological fixes. Keeping it simple is still often the best solution. An executive familiar with the use of a copy-stand camera with printouts may find it a lot easier to send PowerPoint slides than to learn the latest T.120 compliant collaborative software (which may not yet be usable in a multipoint videoconference). But there is only so much that improved management and training can do in the face of multiplying demand and cost-saving strategies, without some basic improvements in the core communications technologies.

Call setup is the number one obstacle to the success of multipoint conference systems. Approximately 60 percent of multipoint calls experience some setup problems, according to DesignNet, a Boston-based multimedia network operations consulting firm, and the situation can only get worse with the growing deployment of undersupported H.320 desktops and coming proliferation of H.323-based systems.

Hardware and service providers are offering separate but complementary solutions to this challenge. Accord Telecommunication's MCU seeks to ease the pain with its Transcoding Gateway. It has the ability to intelligently mediate between endpoints' video and bandwidth capabilities, and to translate across network technologies. "With our gateway, human expertise is no longer required to set common parameters for all endpoints in a conference, or to resolve incompatibilities arising out of standards implementations," said Amir Shaked, president of Accord U.S.A. Both Accord and VideoServer (now Ezenia!) have introduced technologies that bridge users using different rates, without degrading the video and audio quality of those with higher bandwidth connections. RadVision and Accord are also looking toward Simple Network Management Protocol (SNMP) to provide desktop video users with the same network management safety net now available to networked PC users.

Ezenia! has announced H.323/H.320 bridging with its MCU, and Madge and others have shown simplified multipoint bridging and routing of conference traffic that incorporate RadVision's H.323 bridging technologies. Manufacturers like MultiLink are trying to make the multipoint experience a friendlier one by combining sophisticated systems management tools with customizable dial-in greetings, on-the-fly bridging, and other features already familiar to users of audioconferencing bridges.

The last few years have seen dozens of breakthroughs in multipoint technology, from T.120 and H.323 implementation to futuristic call setup and automation features. But with complexities inherent in the blending of these new technologies, and promotions often outstripping deliverables—it's often a safer bet to arrange for some expanded support services—and let someone else's boss be the beta tester.

Bridging Services

The safest route for multipoint conferencing is still the bridging service, particularly for small and medium-size organizations that cannot afford their own 24/7 (twenty-four hours a day, seven days a week) technical support staff. Bridging services like V-Span and ACT provide a security blanket that you can wrap around even the highest profile virtual meetings.

The better service providers can connect users on different networks (even DSL, cable, and frame relay) at different speeds, in different countries, and do it all with virtually no assistance from your staff or users at remote sites. Other services offered by top-tier bridging-service providers include: managed conferences services for planning and hosting large events; location and booking of public VTC rooms anywhere in the world; and scheduling, reservations, and network management for organizations with their own MCUs and that need assistance in these areas.

The best news about these services is that they can often save users money, particularly those that only occasionally need to conduct large multipoint videoconferences.

Conclusion

The best advice I can offer to anyone responsible for planning the deployment of any of the more complex or advanced videoconferencing technologies is: seek a second opinion and delay your decision until action becomes imperative. In this way, you will avoid falling victim to the sincere hype of technology evangelists, and you will also stand the best chance of addressing real user needs with a sustainable solution.

Putting It All Together— The Challenges of Integration 6

Executive Summary

After you have narrowed down your choices to a few possible systems, network configurations, and vendors, your next challenge involves soliciting proposals, evaluating specific solutions, selecting vendors, and deploying your chosen solution. Every project will require different tactics for moving from this point to completion. The following guidelines should help you separate the wheat from the chaff and assist you in making sure that the solution you deploy performs as advertised and as expected.

Pilot Project

Run a pilot project that will confirm that your solution will work with your users, in your environment, on your network, and with the level of support that you can afford. It is important that your pilot project be conducted over a sufficient period of time (one to three or more months) to allow any network or reliability issues to surface. Depending on the size of your network and current competitive vendor market conditions, you may need to pay for your pilot project. If so, be sure that the bulk of those payments can be applied to your purchase.

Request for Proposal (RFP)

Write a RFP that describes clearly and precisely what you want, when and where you want it, what you expect it to do, and what kind of support you expect. If you are not confident that you can write a bullet-proof RFP, get some help from an independent consulting company. Their fee will probably be balanced out by the resulting savings, not to mention the resulting peace of mind.

117

Responsibilities

In your RFP and all subsequent documents, make sure that the demarcation of responsibilities is crystal clear. These include, among others, the allocation of responsibility between various levels of user hardware and software, communication interfaces, control and switch-room equipment, local area networks, and the WAN or other telecommunication services. This is a critical integration issue for the simple reason that telecommunication and VTC vendors have made an art out of passing the buck. So, even if you have an experienced engineer on staff, you will need all the help you can get to solve problems in a hurry.

Getting Help

Don't hesitate to use consultants to fill the gaps in your available expertise, time, and other resources. From independent "hired guns" to major multifaceted consulting organizations (e.g., Walsh-Lowe), cost-effective help is available to make sure that your system will meet all your needs.

Schedule

Make sure that you allow plenty of "fudge-factor" in your timetable for system deployment. Not only do hardware vendors occasionally provide optimistic delivery estimates, telecommunication service providers are notorious for long delays in the installation and provisioning of video-capable connectivity. Few things are more embarrassing than to have a network crash during a "ribbon cutting" videoconference because insufficient time was allotted to conduct a thorough shakedown.

Staffing

Be realistic about your organization's ability to install, maintain, and support your new system. For all but the simplest systems, this means planning and budgeting for adequate professional assistance. Even the best-staffed, most sophisticated organizations outsource a substantial portion of their technical support requirements.

Project Management

This can be a daunting task for VTC projects. Assign your best available person to manage the integration of your system. The job is a lot more complex than it may seem at first glance, and requires a firm hand, clear thinking, flexibility, and the ability to understand the complex relationships between widely disparate technologies and their vendors.

Keeping Up-to-Date

Make sure that both you and your systems are up-to-date with regard to software and system functionality. Arrange to install software upgrades on a regular basis to take advantage of improved functionality and bug fixes (enhancements of undocumented features). You and your staff can keep abreast of industry developments by reading trade publications, attending seminars and training sessions, and meeting regularly with your system vendors and service providers.

Two of the key steps in moving your VTC solution from idea to reality are the request for proposal and the pilot project. Since a complex solution may go through several iterations before a final purchase order is generated, these two steps can occur in a number of different sequences. For example, an unsuccessful or "lesson learned" pilot project can generate a whole new RFP, which can, in turn, result in several new pilot projects.

Since pilot projects are often helpful in creating a bulletproof RFP, let's first take a closer look at what's involved in a pilot and then move on to an examination of the process of preparing an RFP.

What Is a Pilot Project?

Pilot projects are one of the few ways to make sure that specific hardware, software, or services really match your organization's communication needs and environment.

A pilot project involves testing a solution by installing and using it, for a significant amount of time, under conditions that are as close as possible to the actual work situation of end users. This situation should include a true representation of the network, the physical environment, the type of meetings or communications and, if possible, typical future users of the system. A pilot project usually involves some sort of organized evaluation so the results can be tabulated and compared to other prospective solutions. A well-run pilot will also involve some give and take between the customer and the vendors involved. This allows the system to be tweaked to fit the specific application and helps the prospective customer evaluate a vendor's responsiveness.

More Than Just a Demo

A pilot project is not just a demonstration. A demonstration is usually free, of short duration, and can take place under pretested, controlled, and sometimes vendor-favorable conditions. A pilot project may involve some direct costs, allows enough time for a thorough shake down of the solution, and takes place under the customer's own real-world conditions. Demos are valuable—they let you see what the system or service can do under the best possible circumstances. And. if your requirements are simple, a thorough demo may be all that is required. Mike Diodato, the head of Walsh-Lowe's audio-visual practice, advises that, "If a company is new to VTC technology and simply wants to find a solution for a single user or a single conference room, it is simplest to try off-the-shelf products at the vendor's demo room."

Much can be learned from the installation of system components at several sites and their use over a period of one or two months. To accurately predict the results of deploying a particular solution requires a more scientific approach. In Diodato's view, "If the pilot program is going to define a company's future VTC standards or a large-scale rollout of VTC equipment (both conference and desktop solutions), a small-scale pilot project will rarely provide effective results because it will not reflect real-world conditions. Image and voice quality are subjective, and it is easy to gather user opinions. However, it is more difficult to discern the impact on the network, the computers/servers, and the ISP or bandwidth provider." Since the systems will have many different configurations based on local needs and conditions, the cost and performance of the pilot systems may not be representative of the solutions that would finally be deployed." Diodato cautions that the complexity of planning a thorough pilot project may strain the resources of even the best-staffed department: "At this level, expert advice is required to help define the pilot program, and produce the proper services and equipment to simulate the operational aspects of the network traffic in addition to the VTC equipment."

Some years ago, I had the opportunity to consult for a large financial institution that had established a multidisciplinary team to evaluate the suitability of various desktop videoconferencing solutions. The group included internal experts in videoconferencing, telecommunications, network management, operations, and consultants with expertise in several areas. A preliminary matrix of published specifications was created to help in narrowing down the field to a reasonable number of final candidates. All systems that did not meet minimum criteria (e.g., 384 kbps connectivity) were eliminated at that time.

After further discussions of the technical and organizational priorities, vendor selection criteria were set and a form was created to enable evaluation and comparison of the various finalists. The criteria included: ease of operation, picture and sound quality, ease of installation, technical support, reliable connectivity, and a number of other factors.

Users from the various "expert" groups, as well as more typical end-users, had a chance to use the units for several weeks. The systems were then rotated between users to level the effect of personal preferences and to allow specialists to register their findings on the suitability of each unit. The results were compiled, a comparison matrix chart was prepared, and the final evaluation of each system was presented.

I present this case only as an example of the serious preparation that should be a part of any comprehensive pilot program. Every well-run pilot project has its own specific set of circumstances and a unique set of questions that it is intended to answer. One pilot will have as a primary objective the evaluation of the actual impact of a system on LAN traffic. Another project may seek to determine which desktop system will best withstand the rigors of daily use and abuse on a trading floor. Yet another might plan to discover how well a multimedia room system works in a high-pressure multilingual collaborative environment. The common factor is careful planning to ensure that all of the most important issues are addressed in a manner that is as objective and conclusive as is possible.

Planning Your Pilot

Significant thought and planning should go into the preparation of a pilot program, particularly those involving real end-users. V-Span's Warren Ingersol offers the following important advice: "Make sure that the networks and systems are thoroughly tested before rolling out a pilot program. There is nothing worse than starting a pilot with a failed rollout. There are many senior executives who have never returned to a videoconference room after one bad experience. Technology scares people, and when you are more concerned with the potential problems than the presentation or message, you're done."

The impact of a pilot project on users' expectations can involve significant challenges. Ira Weinstein, who manages Credit Suisse First Boston's (CSFB) mammoth worldwide videoconferencing network offers this advice: "I strongly recommend the use of caution regarding pilot projects. The danger is that you may expose the users to a helpful, yet impossible to deploy tool. For example, that wonderful desktop videoconferencing system that works, most of the time, yet requires a dedicated staff of fifteen to manage. This is an example of a pilot that might be accepted by the users, yet not be realistic to deploy."

Vendors also may harbor unrealistic or at least optimistic expectations in regard to pilot projects. "I suggest making it quite clear to your vendors that you are testing their product/system/application for suitability within your environment," says Weinstein. "The vendors need to understand that simply completing the pilot does not mean that the orders will begin to flow. This communication should be done in writing and well in advance of when the equipment arrives at your site."

Pilot projects usually take more time than one could reasonably expect. In addition to the extensive planning that needs to be done if a pilot is to produce useful results, there are many time-consuming aspects to these projects that might not be immediately apparent. These include: providing the necessary digital lines; arranging installation, setup, testing and training schedules that will not interfere with users' normal business; time-outs taken while vendors troubleshoot the inevitable snafus. Weinstein advises, "You should never underestimate the amount of time required to successfully complete a pilot project. For example, if your best guess says you will need twenty hours to conduct your tests, I would estimate fifty plus hours for the entire project."

It is also necessary to develop a list of questions that the pilot will help answer. According to Weinstein, "Before the start of the project, we create a list of the standard questions that we need to answer during the pilot. For example, there may be thirty-five technology questions, fifteen business case questions, and fifteen user questions. Clearly, these questions can and will be modified during the pilot program. However, starting off with a strong base is quite helpful." This kind of thorough preparation ensures that all key issues will be addressed and that there is a fair and relatively objective basis for comparison between competing solutions. It also reduces the amount of time required for a complete evaluation by helping users and technicians focus on the important issues.

The type of questions can also have a big impact on the usefulness of the data compiled during a pilot. Weinstein says, "In order to properly process user feedback, you need to ask very directed questions with very controllable answers. This will help avoid a subjective analysis of the answers. In asking users about video quality, a good question might be, How would you rate the video quality? Excellent [ ], Good [ ], Acceptable [ ], Poor [ ], Unusable [ ]. In contrast, the same question phrased as, How do you like the video quality? will produce less usable information."

Choosing suitable participants can also have a major impact on the usefulness of a pilot project. "One needs to select a user group that can somehow benefit from the technology yet will not attempt to dissect the solution," says Weinstein. "For example, when evaluating a desktop videoconferencing solution, one might avoid asking the IT department to participate in the pilot as the 'user' group."

It is a relatively common practice to use senior management as subjects for advanced pilot projects. While a successful pilot project can serve to enlist the enthusiastic support of influential members of management, the reverse can also be true.

In summary, a well-planned pilot project can produce a realistic evaluation of a particular solution, as long as a tight focus is maintained on the project's objectives and the substantial amount of time and technical resources required for a fair test can be allocated to the project.

The Request for Proposal (RFP)

The request for proposal (RFP) is possibly the most important document in the life cycle of a video communication system. If properly prepared, it will accomplish at least all of the following objectives:

1. Establish a complete set of technical requirements.
2. Provide a complete list of required system components and services.
3. Establish criteria of minimum acceptable performance for the completed system.
4. Create a clear statement of work and demarcation of responsibilities for the successful vendor/s.
5. Secure the training and technical support necessary for the proper functioning of the system.
6. Establish a baseline project schedule, with key mileposts that must be met by a successful bidder.
7. Allow for constructive feedback from prospective vendors that can point out flaws in the RFP or plan that require correction and suggest better methods of achieving the same objectives.
8. Assure that the products and services to be provided comply with all applicable laws and regulations (e.g., U.L. approvals) and all established company procedures, obligations, and regulations, such as insurance policies and employment practices.
9. Provide legal safeguards against liability related to safety, copyright, and other issues; and provide recourse and specific remedies for the failure of a vendor or system to perform as per agreement.

All too often, I have seen RFPs for critical systems that are seriously deficient in one or more of these important factors. This usually happens when people who are unfamiliar with the complex nature of VTC systems and telecommunication services write the RFP.

Taking the Necessary Time

A simple request for a quotation for a single set-top VTC unit can be prepared in a few hours, using your organization's standard procurement form or procedure. On the other hand, an effective RFP for a major videoconferencing system involving a variety of equipment, integration, and telecommunication services is a major undertaking, involving many days or weeks of effort. According to CSFB's Weinstein, "The time required to properly prepare and release an RFP is perhaps the most easily forgotten part of the process. The RFP needs to be clear, yet all encompassing. It needs to be fair to both the company and the vendor. It needs to include line-by-line detail about the service/product offering, yet cannot be so tactical that the relationship aspects of the contract are not emphasized."

It is important to involve both technical and business management in the preparation of an RFP in order to ensure that it reflects the widest possible range of relevant concerns and expertise. According to V-Span's Ingersol, "Potential new service offerings or technological advances are often overlooked in the preparation of RFPs. Frequently, RFP writers are procurement people who may not be up-to-speed with new technology, applications, or services." It is important that the technologists involved in the preparation of the RFP state their requirements in clear, unequivocal, nontechnical language. It is also important to include the quality of service expected from the system, not just the bare-bone technical requirements. Ingersol observes that, "Too many RFPs are clearly focused on price instead of getting the best service or value out of the use of the technology. In our world of multipoint conferencing, for example, cheap bridging usually produces inferior conference quality and reliability, and usage quickly starts to decline."

It is also a good idea to use the RFP process as a means for discovering new ideas and the latest technical information. "RFPs that ask for advice or help generally get proactive responses from vendors, and that will benefit the organization in the long term," notes Ingersol. In order to be in a position to take advantage of this expert advice, it is advisable to allow enough time for at least two full iterations of a major RFP.

But it isn't just purchasing managers who lack a complete understanding of the complexities of digital multimedia communication systems. There are usually many people involved in the creation of an RFP, and just as many involved in creating an effective response. The input of any of these "cooks" can cause serious snags in the successful deployment of the system. For this reason and others, the original draft must be extremely clear and complete if the project is to succeed. According to Diodato, who has prepared and reviewed countless RFPs for major corporate and governmental clients at Walsh-Lowe, "Many RFPs are poorly written, including some of those created by consultants. An RFP should not allow the bidder room for interpretation. In addition, the RFP and its accompanying drawings, documents, equipment lists, and other attachments should be developed as a set of instructions to build the desired system, especially if the systems will be integrated with the architecture, and more so if there are other vendors involved in the project. This set of instructions should be written in layman's terms, in addition to the technical jargon required to ensure compliance with good engineering practice. One thing that is often overlooked is that the RFP will end up in the hands of many people. The writer should know his audience. The audience may include young technicians with little experience, salespersons looking up part numbers, and clerks that have never worked on a similar project before. In other words, make the RFP a well-defined set of requirements. If an equipment list is included, it should accurately indicate the quantities involved. If a component is critical, substitutions should not be allowed. Conversely, substitutions should be allowed for noncritical equipment. This will allow the bidders to offer value-added recommendations that could improve the cost of the system."

Functional Controls

If you have selected specific hardware, software, or services to include in your RFP, vendors can usually provide precise descriptions of their products and services that will be helpful in ensuring that your needs are met. In cases where you are under the obligation to assure that competitive products are given a fair chance, you may have to modify the language slightly. For example, here is a functional description of the control system for a videoconferencing system prepared, some time ago, by VTEL:

- Near-end and far-end camera control (4 cameras each—P/T/Z/F/I with auto).
- User definable presets (8, with expandability up to 258).
- One-touch connect/disconnect.
- Easy audioconference. Add-on capability (to add audio-only participants).
- Saving, receiving, sending, and retrieving of slides and graphics (point-to-point or multipoint).

- VCR record/playback/voice-over/freeze-frame grabbing/both sides audio.
- Slide tray control and management.
- Audio-level control and muting.
- Electronic whiteboard and multicolor annotation (point-to-point or multipoint).
- In-band fax (no phone line required).
- Video mail (stored on hard disk or floppy).
- Full computer conferencing (template or keyboard control).

Note that the detailed description of some features can have a significant impact on other aspects of systems integration. If "in-band" and "no phone line required" was omitted from the requirement, a vendor might supply fax functionality that would require an additional analog phone port on a PBX and the installation of an additional wall-mounted RJ-11 jack. Though this omission might also create some compatibility issues, it would not, by itself, break the budget. A number of similar omissions or mistakes, spread across a twenty- or thirty-page RFP, could lead to major headaches for system managers, might cause significant delays, and could cost thousands of dollars to set right.

Request for Information (RFI)

It's usually a good idea to get input from reputable manufacturers, integrators, and service providers when preparing an RFP. A good starting point is to prepare a request for information (RFI). It can be as simple as a statement of your basic needs, that is, the type and size of meetings, general locations, and special requirement related to your way of doing business. The more detail you can put into an RFI, the more useful will be the responses you will receive. Even if you request written replies, you will still get a number of phone inquiries and lots of brochures and catalogs in the mail, so be prepared to screen sales calls and to organize a truckload of literature. Although the RFI process might seem more trouble than it is worth, the advice and information you will receive should be very helpful in identifying the most up-to-date solutions to meet your organization's conferencing needs. It will also alert you to specific issues that may need to be addressed in your RFP. For example, a feature that may be important to your application may be buried in the back of a spec sheet. However, if it included as a specific item in your RFI, it will surely be featured in the vendor's response.

Consulting with Experts

When should someone responsible for the rollout of a videoconferencing system or network employ a consultant or consulting firm, and what criteria should be applied to their selection?

Videoconferencing is a discipline that require access to expertise in a wide range of technologies and systems—video, audio, telecommunications, data networking, acoustics, lighting, meeting planning and management, reservation systems, codecs, ergonomics, control systems, and multimedia system integration, to name just a few. Not many user organizations possess high-level expertise in all or most of these areas. When that expertise is present it is usually overworked, underpaid, and not readily available for major additional responsibilities. To augment in-house expertise and to fill in the gaps that exist, many organizations hire consultants. On the simplest level these consultants may be temporary, freelance "employee substitutes," brought onboard to absorb the additional workload during the planning and deployment of a new system. At the highest level, some major organizations outsource the entire planning, design, deployment, and support of a worldwide network to one or more major consulting firms, such as Walsh-Lowe or Perot Systems.

According to Ira Weinstein, whose responsibilities at CSFB involve both the management of a large dedicated in-house technical staff and the company's relationship with wide range of consultants and contractors, there is no clear answer: "In the purest sense, a manager should employ a consultant whenever the project at hand requires specialized skills or experience that they don't have on their team. However, hiring a consultant is not necessarily the best path toward·a solution. "Sometimes in-house staff should be trained or hired to fill the need, particularly if the requirement is a long-term one. In other cases, contractor or integrator personnel possess the required expertise, and only need to be managed effectively by in-house staff. Weinstein offers the following advice for situations in which a consultant is the obvious choice: "When hiring a consultant, the expectations and roles must be clearly defined. If possible, a system for measuring the consultant's performance should be established. Finally, the consultant must be given a clear path to their manager/employer in order to avoid delays and possible diversions."

The decision to hire a consultant requires the examination of a number of key factors, according to V-Span's Warren Ingersol: "Considerations should be based upon the experience of the manager in charge of the project, the size of the rollout, the objectivity of the consultant, their experience in the industry, and their references. Videoconferencing technologies are moving at light speed, so specific industry experience is crucial these days."

Money-Saving Consultants

Though consultants are often seen as an expense, they often can save a client considerably more than they cost, both in the planning of a project and the day-to-day process of deployment and support.

Mike Diodato's duties at Walsh-Lowe include the management and supervision of design consultants, project managers, and technical specialists who work on major audio, video, and videoconferencing projects. He offers this insider's tip regarding the best way to investigate the potential values of consulting services for a particular project: "It is always beneficial to seek the advice of experts. With a few phone calls and a smart but brief RFP for consulting services, a manager can quickly tap the insights of several prospective consultants who are vying for the opportunity to work for that client. Frequently, a consultant will outline most of the necessary steps for the project within his proposal. If the RFP for consulting services is written smartly, the client could glean valuable information that will help to bring the entire project into a clearer focus, and will clarify the decision to hire or not to hire a consultant."

Though budgets are always an issue when considering consulting services, Diodato reports that the impact is often a positive one. "Many times it costs nothing to hire a consultant, based on the cost savings incurred by implementing a bid process for the vendors. For example, a design/build firm proposes $500,000 for a particular audiovisual/VTC project. However, a consultant might charge the client $50,000 for professional services, and develop a high quality RFP that nets at least one response priced at $450,000. The cost to the client is the same, but the quality of the design and final product should improve." When the project is a large one, and involves activities that may be subject to regulation or disclosure, there are other reasons to look outside your company for assistance. "Hiring a consultant is also imperative if the project will be audited," says Diodato.

Independence and objectivity are of great importance in the selection of a consultant. According to Diodato, "Once a consultant is onboard, he or she should have the client's best interest first and foremost. Hiring a design/build integrator or simply going to a distributor or manufacturer will not net the client the benefit of an unbiased viewpoint and objective expert advice." The opinions of an integrator or manufacturer's representative, no matter how professional or well meaning, will necessarily be colored by the self-interest of that organization.

The Buck Stops Here

The demarcation of responsibilities in the deployment of a videoconferencing system must be clearly defined and agreed upon in writing by all the major vendors. Specific responsibility should be assigned for every level of user hardware and software, communication interfaces, control and switch-room equipment, local area networks, and all telecommunication services. Telecommunication and VTC vendors have historically made an art out of passing the buck. This practice is deeply rooted in the differences that separate telephony and data communications, and the immutable tendencies for bureaucracies to avoid responsibility for problems at all costs. The impact of this problem is reduced if you have digital telephony engineering expertise on staff or on call, but the issues are complex, and your only real protection is a written contract that nails down the responsibility for every part of the signal path.

Ideally, a single organization should be responsible for getting your sound and picture from point A to point B, but this is rarely a practical solution. According to Ingersol: "At this time there does not exist a single-source solution available to the corporate user. While several of the carrier-class providers offer integration, service, and network, they are not generally considered best-of-breed providers. Videoconference network managers may also find their flexibility inhibited by choosing a single-source provider. With the rapid changes in the technology it is difficult to specify what the corporate standards for systems should be, particularly as the potential for H.323 conferencing becomes a reality." Total dependence on a 'phone company' can lead to other complications if and when corporate policy dictates a change in carriers. All in all, there are many good reasons to separate the responsibilities of your network, hardware and service solutions. That being said, it is crucial to develop a team with strong lines of communication and a good work-ing relationship to help facilitate an effective communications network. It is too often the case that vendors spend time pointing fingers rather than solving problems. Setting up lines of reporting and clarifying responsibilities ahead of time is strongly recommended."

V-Span and other high-level service providers sometimes take on additional respon-sibility to foster and maintain close client relationships. "Our greatest success," says Ingersol, "has been when we are granted agency authority to open trouble tickets on behalf of our client for both network and hardware vendors. This has allowed us to cut through the accusations and resolve problems most efficiently." CSFB's Weinstein sees the problem from a user's perspective: "In the ideal world, one would be able to draw a line on a chart and simply assign areas of responsibility. However, this is difficult to apply to videoconferencing because the lines tend to be very wide and fuzzy. For example, when a system is being installed, one uses both hardware vendors and system integrators. Furthermore, there are serious dependencies upon the networking teams both internal and external. Things can be further convoluted through the use of consultants."

Weinstein also stresses the importance of building a good "team" and clear definition of roles and responsibilities: "Typically, videoconferencing requires very strong interactivity between the various trades and skills. The hardware vendors need to accept full responsibility for the functionality and performance of their equipment. They need to be available to support the installation, and eventual use, of their gear. They are a critical part of the team and must behave as such. The system integrators are, in effect, the front line part of the project team. It is their responsibility to connect the kit and make everything work. When things don't proceed as planned, they take on the role of problem solvers and interface with all other parts of the project team (manufacturers, consultants, client, etc.).

Although service providers (specifically, video bridging companies) are an important part of videoconferencing, they do not typically take part in a project (integration) process. Instead, they provide a final "reality check"—by certifying the compatibility of the new installation with their equipment." According to Weinstein, "They can provide benchmarking information and often bring a great deal of experience to the table. However, one must remember that the service provider's role ends once the connection to their equipment is completed."

While this approach works well for larger organizations, users who are dependent on BRI (or even PRI) services may still find themselves trying to solve carrier-related problems without a high level of proactive support from their carriers.

Consultants can play an important part in clarifying the roles and responsibilities of the various players in a system deployment. Mike Diodato states that a good consultant should develop scope-of-work criteria for each group or person involved with a project. Just as "good fences make good neighbors," crystal clear delineation of roles and responsibilities helps turn vendors into cooperative and proactive project team members.

Outsourcing Integration and Support

When should users outsource integration and support, and what criteria should be used in the selection of partners for integration and support?

Few user organizations have the people resources or the expertise to provide integration for even the most basic videoconferencing system. Even fewer can provide anything more than a "first contact" or room-coordinator level of technical support for their VTC networks. Those that can contribute at least a basic level of expertise to an integration team have many reasons to leave the heavy lifting to experienced pros. According to CSFB's Weinstein, "For the most part, it makes sense to outsource both integration and support. In order to effectively perform system integration, an internal team must be both knowledgeable and experienced. Although knowledge can be obtained by reading magazines and books, experience requires time in the field. Until a team has installed a significant number of systems, many integration pitfalls may remain unknown to them. Outsourcing integration allows the user organizations to benefit from the experience that contractors and consultants have gained during other installations. This tends to improve the final product and help control both time lines and budgets. Finally, by outsourcing, the user organization has the option of changing their direction at any time. In other words, if the quality of the work does not meet expectations, the company can choose to cancel or simply not renew the contract with their outsourced vendor. When using internal staff, user organizations do not have the same hire and fire flexibility."

The element of consistency is of great importance to most network managers, and the business-critical nature of many video networks serves to turn that element from a virtue into a necessity. "Standardization and centralization are important factors in creating a successful communications network," says V-Span's Ingersol. "Whether integration and support are internal or outsourced, users are better served by a strong leadership team." Finding an integrator who will provide independent leadership is not always an easy task. According to Mike Diodato, "Integration of systems should be left to the experts that perform this work everyday. If the client does not have the talent in-house, they should seek out a professional integration team and get solid references. If possible, visit a previous client of the prospective integrator." Even if a user organization has some skilled VTC integration and support personnel on staff, there are other reasons to outsource this work. These include lack of sufficient human resources, personnel with insufficient training for the task at hand, high internal costs, and a temporary tenant situation.

Finding a Fit

When selecting vendors for videoconferencing hardware, software, and services, there are a number of factors that should be taken into consideration. Most experienced users agree that high-quality customer service is more important than many other factors. In the opinion of CSFB's Ira Weinstein, "The first and most critical point is that the vendor must have the customer-service mentality. They must clearly understand that the one and only priority has to be perfect customer service and support. In my experience, any company that does not understand this item cannot provide quality hardware, software, or services. It is important for the vendor, and specifically their support staff, to understand that customer service is not a job, it is an attitude. A good vendor realizes that customer service is the path to success—and therefore makes this their number one focus."

Perhaps the reason that VTC pros like Weinstein feel so strongly about the importance of customer service is that they are themselves in the customer-service business. Executives who rely on international videoconferencing to manage their enterprises expect perfect customer service, and the dedicated conferencing professionals who support their conferences are committed to provide just that. Is it any wonder that VTC pros have little patience with vendors who exhibit an offhand approach to customer service and support? When I served as a consultant to Senior Vice President Joyce Thompson and her Citicorp Global Information Network conferencing team, I witnessed this attitude at its best. Thompson thought nothing of coming in to work at 4 a.m. to assure that a major international multipoint conference would go off without a hitch. Her staff shared that dedication to customer service, taking a personal interest in the quality of every conference and the satisfaction of every user. While this kind of professionalism is not universal in the videoconferencing community, it is common enough to make subpar customer service from vendors and service providers the number one issue in the business.

Warren Ingersol, who works for a videoconferencing service provider known for its excellent customer service, agrees that this is the primary gating factor in the choice of a vendor, but notes, "The strategic plan and future direction of a manufacturer or service provider is also important. Users want to know that they will be able to upgrade their systems and services to meet their future needs. For this reason the reputation of a vendor is of great importance—in terms of customer service, in terms of a real commitment to a deploying advanced technologies, and in terms of their objectivity in recommending the proper system or service, based on price, application, and need."

Mike Diodato takes a very pragmatic approach to the selection of systems and vendors: "The proposed equipment must comply with the most popular industry standards. In addition, the equipment must be compatible with the connectivity that will be employed—for example, network versus dial-up lines. Of course, the equipment should perform to expectations in a demo, and should have received good reviews in industry publications." While the process of choosing the right equipment can be fairly straightforward, selecting a vendor is a very different story. Diodato advises: "After bids are leveled, selection of a vendor should be based on three criteria: cost, competence (by show of previous experience), and availability to perform within the client's schedule requirements. It's also a good idea to check with the other contractors and vendors to assure that there will not be any conflicts due to poor previous experiences with the prospective vendor." Reasonably priced support options beyond those required in the RFP (e.g., extended warranties and scheduled preventative maintenance) are also an indication of a vendor who has made customer satisfaction a high priority.

Time on Your Side

Given the complex and rapidly changing nature of videoconferencing systems and services, is it possible to create a realistic yet aggressive timetable for system rollout? Industry experts are divided on the subject. V-Span's Ingersol reports: "In today's environment it is very difficult to guarantee a timetable for system rollout. Several vendors have lost credibility in the marketplace because of flawed new product launches involving delays and unfulfilled promises. In addition, technical innovations have often made products obsolete before they were installed. With the advent of software-based products, it will be easier at least to maintain a network of systems with 'current' capabilities." Frequently, it is not the system or the integrator that is to blame for missed deadlines. "Network planning can often cause more problems than system integration," Ingersol says. "Delays in network installation can cause unacceptable delays in system rollouts. I believe that this will remain an issue with the advent of new broadband network access."

"In theory, it is possible," says Weinstein. "On paper, deployment plans and project time lines look wonderful. They demonstrate, quite clearly, the limited scope of the videoconferencing project. However, the reality in the field is quite another issue. Without exception, the deployment (testing, configuration/provisioning, call routing, etc.) of the ISDN lines continues to be the most challenging part of VC deployment. Many contractors, consultants, and networking staff lack the knowledge and expertise needed to deploy ISDN in a timely manner. They work hard, push the various vendors, but the ISDN service is still delayed." Construction and related tasks are also a source of scheduling snafus. Weinstein notes: "Fully integrated VC rooms require detailed millwork, electrical work, carpeting, custom furniture, and more. Each of these items has the potential to be delayed, and therefore can delay the project." Several years ago, a Citicorp VTC room system scheduled for installation in Albuquerque was delayed simply because Intel had already booked up every electrician in town to rush the completion of their new facility.

Sometimes the desire to optimize system performance is at odds with speedy deployment. Weinstein explains, "The best way to make complex systems easy to use is to use a touch control panel front-end [such as Crestron or AMX]. However, this means that the user interface must be programmed, staged, tested, and finally punched out. This never goes as smoothly as one might expect, and is another source of project delay/schedule-creep." He suggests that the answer here is to be extremely pessimistic when creating project plans. "Assume that a four-week lead time item will take six weeks to deliver—and then be happy when it arrives within two months. If your plans reflect this approach, you will meet your basic deliverable requirements."

Walsh-Lowe's Diodato feels pretty much the same way about the causes of rollout delays. "The answer depends on the project," he says. "If it involves network systems, construction, relocation, etc., then the construction manager will set the schedule, and it will be developed taking into consideration many factors." He is more optimistic for on-schedule rollout of simpler systems: "If the system rollout does not include construction and does not include other significant projects, then a realistic timetable can be based on a simplified task list for the evaluation, design, and selection process, and the lead-time for equipment and installation, based on the size of the project."

Project Management Considerations

The success or failure of a VTC system rollout often rests on the shoulders of the project manager (PM). For this reason, it is important that the person picked to handle this responsibility be knowledgeable about all aspects of the deployment process and is also a skilled PM with good conflict-resolution skills.

Diodato puts it this way: "A good project manager sets a rigid schedule. Decisions must be made in a timely manner to keep the project moving forward according to schedule. This is especially important for those decisions that will have an impact on other decisions involving different items and costs." Strong, focused, leadership is also required. "The project manager should not allow the project team to stray from the plan once it is approved," he says. "There is always a new gadget or new technique that will emerge during the course of the project, and someone will want to halt the project to investigate that alternative. The PM should not allow this to happen." For situations where a system absolutely must incorporate the latest and greatest technologies, Diodato offers the following advice: "Hiring a consultant to keep track of industry developments and incorporate these enhancements into a solid design will alleviate the client's desire to stray from the approved plan."

Weinstein advises project managers and planners to be very conservative in all time estimations. "A four-week lead time will take six," he predicts. "The network lines that you expect to be live on November 1st will not be live until December 5th." This safety buffer should be applied to all dependencies in your project. Furthermore, anytime a project requires global coordination, additional delays should be expected. According to Weinstein, "One critical part of system project management that is often forgotten is that videoconferncing systems are extremely modular in nature. This, in theory, allows modular testing and troubleshooting."

The modular systems are:
ISDN network—ISDN lines, network termination equipment, hub/switch/IMUX (if necessary).
Other networks/lines—LAN/WAN, analog lines, digital phone drops, etc.
Videoconferencing system—the AV/VTC equipment rack, including the codec.
Environmental/room—millwork, lighting, ceiling speakers, microphones, etc.

Weinstein advises: "An aggressive project manager will schedule each of the trades (electricians, carpenters, telecommunication technicians, etc.) appropriately, to allow full testing and handoff to the next trade. Unfortunately, many VTC projects are not coordinated in this manner, and therefore many trades are forced to troubleshoot at the same time. This results in wasted time, additional cost, schedule delays, and overall poor efficiency."

I have experienced this type of chaos firsthand, with electricians cutting power during network systems tests and carpenters banging away next door while a technician was trying to set up an echo canceller.

Addressing key issues in the optimal sequence can make a big difference in the effectiveness of any project-management effort. Warren Ingersol proposes this time-tested arrangement: "Start with budget and application before choosing a system, vendor, or protocol—a consultant can help to identify the issues and questions before starting the actual decision-making process. Carrier, system, and protocol decisions come next."

The Speed of Change

Upgrading and updating existing systems and services can be as great a challenge as creating an entire network from scratch. How can VTC managers keep their systems up to date while seamlessly supporting users existing applications? "With the speed of change continuing to be such a big issue this will be an important question going forward," says Ingersoll. "The days of hardware/board upgrades would seem to be coming to an end. With the advent of software solutions, upgrades can be handled in a more timely and cost-effective manner." In order for systems and applications to remain relevant to user needs, VTC managers need to stay closely in touch with both users and vendors. "You can't please everybody, but customer satisfaction surveys and user feedback can help with evaluation of services. Central to any effective ongoing evaluation and capabilities review will be strong lines of communications with your network, hardware, and service providers." Diodato advises VTC managers to subscribe to industry specific trade magazines and to join organizations that will provide this type of information (see Appendix B: General Resources). "There are also plenty of vendors who will give prospective clients opportunities to learn about their equipment. Several manufacturers offer training and certification for users of their VTC systems." Diodato notes: "Videoconferencing managers should take advantage of these sessions, and also make certain that others within their organizations are trained to operate and maintain the VTC systems."

The Changing Role of Integrators

Integrators function as a vital link between the raw technology offered by manufacturers and the fully functioning applications required by their customers. Their expertise is drawn from three sophisticated technologies—audio/video, computing, and telecommunications. Their goal is the seamless integration of hardware and software for the successful use of videoconferencing by end-users. But how do the multifaceted skills of the system integrator fit into the modern world of videoconferencing? It's a market dominated by low-cost boxes, tight budgets, and the hype of plug-and-play solutions. When can a user really benefit from the services of an integrator, and how will changes in the industry affect the relationship between integrator and user?

Innovative Applications

As end-users become more aware of the potential of conferencing technologies, integrators have risen to the challenge with innovative solutions. According to Carl Ceragno, president of Communications Research, who has been creating superior video solutions for more than fifteen years, "The role of the integrator is especially important in the design and development of systems where a cross-technology solution is necessary to meet a client's requirements. Since integrators interests often cross market boundaries, providing design, integration, and support in A/V, LAN, telecommunications and computing—they can 'cross-pollinate' technology from one area to another, providing cost-efficient solutions to client's needs."

As users become more experienced and sophisticated, they are often better able to appreciate the potential of these technologies, and the role that an experienced integrator can play in realizing that potential.

Tim Gilbert has been pushing the conferencing envelope since his days as one of Sony's first specialists in videoconferencing systems. Currently, he is the president of Worldroom Consulting, a company specializing in the delivery of just-in-time training via desktop videoconferencing and the Web. He says, "The good news is that integration services remain as valuable today as they have ever been because of the sophistication of the client base. From credit unions to public relations firms and the Fortune 500, multiple meeting objectives and needs keep integration service providers in business. These include the need for presenter support, the need to include multiple peripheral devices such as document camera, PC, VCR, and medical devices, and the need to include large numbers of participants in a conference." He cites the example of a north-east-based financial services company that has a 50 x 25 feet meeting/training room. The organization's president wanted to make presentations to employees in the room and to those at a remote site. In addition, the organization's training department wanted to be able to use computer-based presentations to train employees. Gilbert said, "The meeting objectives required multiple cameras, a 60-inch rear-screen display set into the wall, and an integrated audio system to allow pickup and output of audio without echo or feedback from all points of a very large room. The podium also needed to be wired for sound and computer inputs to facilitate the president's presentations and the training sessions." He points out that as feature-packed and low-priced as compact rollabouts and set-top units have become, these could not meet this client's needs: "Only a carefully designed and integrated room can meet user objectives for a high-class, high-efficiency, multipurpose meeting environment."

Teamwork Works

Integrators are often called upon to coordinate the efforts of many specialists to satisfy a client's needs. Wayne Williams, marketing director of video for AG Communications, explains, "We see three levels of integration partners: (1) room level, (2) staging level, and (3) network level. At the KSCADE [K-12 Schools/ College Alliance for Distance Education] distance learning network in Wisconsin, where thirty-two high schools had to be interconnected with a technical college, Midwest Visual did a great job handling the integration of all the room-based AV equipment—these are items such as cameras, microphones, room controllers, lighting, echo cancellers, etc. In fact, we have found that the audio portion of most installations has been much more challenging than the video portion, and expertise from an integrator in solving audio problems is indispensable. At the staging level, Anixter worked well to bring all of the equipment together—from the room-based equipment to the ATM switches, to our codecs—and ensured that it interconnected well and worked in harmony. This included such things as mapping the IP addresses of all the equipment so that the network could be managed properly once installed. And at the network level, Marcus FiberLink provided the end-to-end network management and ensured that all phases came together. It really was this team of integrators that made the overall solution a success."

Taking Control

Another area in which the services of an integrator are often required is for the creation of a customized control system that meets specialized requirements. Bob Maier, vice president of operations at EDR Systems, describes one such project: "We designed and installed the videoconferencing center for the Cleveland Clinic's new Minimally Invasive Surgery Center. As an integrator, we were able to design a rather sophisticated, customized system that controls a wide variety of cameras and telemedicine equipment. An integrator can offer exceptional functionality and flexibility to a customer by the way the video-conferencing system is designed. For example, these operating rooms each have eight video sources, including cameras inside the patient. Video and audio from multiple sources in several operating rooms can be fed through a single user interface at the clinic to receiving sites around the world. In addition, incoming signals from other centers can be routed directly into the operating rooms so that surgeons can see as well as hear the people asking the questions."

The issue of control systems is particularly important when complex tasks must be controlled by nontechnical personnel, as is often the case in distance learning applications. A critical difference between a system that works for users and one that works against them is the integrator's skill in creating and programming a user-friendly interface. Mike Albi, a systems consultant with CEAVCO Audio Visual Company in Denver, Colorado, illustrates this point: "We completed a contract with Central Wyoming College in Riverton, Wyoming, which included a fully integrated smart classroom for origination of program materials and distribution to a number of remote sites. After discussing the application with the end users, CEAVCO was able to design a sophisticated interface for acknowledging questions from remote classrooms, which utilize the AMX control system. The technical effect of switching the video and audio signals is quite complex in that the audio mix minus requirements are met specifically for each remote request and then released. Even so, the use of the system is intuitive and simple for the instructors."

Up Against the Video-Wall

The challenges most often cited by integrators today include keeping up with rapidly evolving technologies, educating the public, managing user expectations, and maintaining profitability in the face of the proliferation of packaged systems.

According to Ceragno, "The VAR/integrator is faced with the ongoing requirement to educate and train staff so that they remain current on technology development and applications. Twenty years ago in the A/V business, your basic toolkit of knowledge was strong ability in analog audio, video, and digital-control technology. Today, application development specialists must understand all of these as well as be knowledgeable in data transmission, computing, software, digital signal processing, transmission, and network interfaces."

A lack of understanding of the role and importance of effective system integration, particularly on the part of new users, is also a significant factor. CEAVCO's Albi sees it this way: "Keeping up with the technology is always a challenge. However, to stay successful we must continue to provide end users with a clear understanding of our function and what benefits we can bring to the table when deploying a complex, multipurpose communications facility."

139

Kirk Muffley, director of videoconferencing solutions for The Whitlock Group, agrees and sees additional educational responsibilities for integrators: "It is easy to be successful if you listen to your customers and provide a wide array of products and services. The biggest challenge is educating customers on the solutions that are available and helping them choose the right long-term strategy."

More Than Just a Box

The proliferation of low-cost packaged systems is seen by many as a key challenge to the continued economic health of the videoconferencing integration business. These "boxes" are sometimes promoted as plug-and-play solutions for every conferencing need by manufacturers, service providers, and by mail order retailers. Gilbert explains, "The future relationship between integrator/VARs and end-users will definitely be affected by lower profit-per-system sold. There will be less time available for needs assessment and user training, and integrators will be under pressure to get the deal done with a lower cost of sale. In this sales environment, end users will need to be better prepared to ensure they get the right room at the right price."

According to Maier, "Our primary challenge these days comes from service providers who are becoming product providers. A lot of what I call 'rollaround' portable systems are on the market now from service providers, and these systems simply aren't designed for the customer's unique needs. For example, Parker-Hannifin Corporation here in Cleveland had a portable system that simply didn't meet its needs. We designed a videoconferencing interface around an AMX control system that allows Parker executives to control all aspects of a videoconference on a more efficient basis."

The decreasing cost of systems is not entirely bad news. "Decreasing hardware prices will help open new videoconferencing markets, including retailers and small businesses," says Maier. Gilbert notes that lower-priced/higher-functioning solutions are presenting integrators with both a great challenge and an opportunity. "The challenge to integrators and end users alike is to embrace new models for design, implementation, and support of their applications that keep pace with the efficiency gains of the hardware itself," he explains.

Ceragno sees "evolution" as an answer to the decreasing profit-per-sale from commoditized systems: "At the low end of system integration, some business may slip away, in the form of prepackaged systems, to manufacturer's providing total solutions. That is progress; it will continue in the future and in any technology. It is not the death of the VAR/integrator, it only means they have done their job and must continue to the next plateau of technology implementation. Hopefully, integrators/VARs will keep an ever-watchful eye on new technologies and emerging industries. They must be prepared to migrate when margins shrink due to the commercialization or deployment of 'box' solutions from manufacturers and, most important, to be ready when their long faithful clients require these unbundled new solutions."

Are You Being Served?

The commoditization of conferencing also presents service opportunities for savvy system suppliers. Wayne Williams says, "One of the biggest challenges for integrators will be to focus on the service and consulting aspects of their role, particularly as equipment becomes much more of a commodity. Integrators must learn to leverage their experience and confidence and trust that they have earned to add value based upon the additional services they can offer. The core asset of an integrator will be this trust and the relationship built with the end user.

In the coming years, there is tremendous opportunity for integrators to sell their service expertise in engineering, installation, and maintenance. The integrator's challenge is to completely understand the technical and equipment choices available in the market and make the best recommendations to customers to solve their problems. This means that human skills are critical, that is, real-life experience with what works and doesn't work, and the ability to apply that knowledge in different situations."

Expert moral support also has its value. According to Mufffley, "Regardless of how easy a product is to use, which H.3xx standard it complies with, or how well the manufacturer markets the product, customers still want to feel comfortable that they have made the right decision."

Future Integration Trends

As to the future of the relationship between users and integrators, it appears that two divergent trends will shape the market. On the one hand there will be an increased need for technical services, and for customization of hybrid systems that meet the needs of an informed user-base. On the other hand, integrators face a belt-tightening in every aspect of the process of system supply, brought about by lower costs per location, lower profit per sale, increased competition, and other factors.

Users that understand the true value of system integration services, as well as the economic realities of the integration business, are in an excellent position to form durable, mutually advantageous relationships with these highly skilled and professional teams. To locate experienced video communications integrators in your area, can contact the International Communications Industries Association (*see* Appendix B: General Resources).

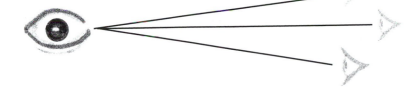

Managing the Conferencing Process

7

Executive Summary

Several factors contribute to the success of a network of videoconference systems. Among the most important of these are proper design, support from management and users, competent and timely technical support, and effective user training. This chapter provides practical guidelines and tips on marketing your system internally to foster demand and support, training your users, and providing them with the support they need to make productive use of the system.

Common Reasons for System Failure

There are several reasons why videoconferencing systems fail:

1. Design Flaws: Many systems have design flaws in a critical area (hardware, software, connectivity, ergonomics, or technical support), and cannot possibly meet the communications needs of users without a significant overhaul. A comprehensive design and integration process (such as the one described in the earlier chapters of this book) will help ensure that your system will work the way you want it to.

2. Lack of management support and user acceptance: In most organizations, the success of a videoconferencing network will depend on the cooperation of many individuals. This cooperation can be assured by strong support from upper management, and by ensuring that users feel that the system addresses their needs. If the use of the system receives encouragement and support from senior management, then people throughout the organization will be more likely to integrate its use into their work processes. By involving sales, accounting, manufacturing and other major functional groups in system planning and rollout, you will ensure that the system will meet real users' needs and will be accepted as an integral part of your corporation's or institution's communications culture.

3. Lack of proper user training: Sometimes, good systems stay dark (never get turned on) because users have not been properly trained. Procedures for system use and operation that are unwieldy, or have been created without the proper attention to the real needs of users, can create additional barriers to usage.

4. Lack of technical and meeting support: Both technical and room/meeting support staff are critical to the success of any videoconferencing network. It does not matter whether these functions are carried out by your staff or those working for a vendor or service provider. What is critical is that conferees have all the help they need to conduct successful meetings.

If you have followed the guidelines for conducting a comprehensive needs analysis and ensuring good system design and integration described in the earlier chapters of this book, you should be well on the path toward implementing an effective and appropriate video communication network. Here is some practical information to help you manage your systems in a way that will produce good, long-term results.

Internal Marketing

What if you built a system and nobody came?

In many organizations, people need to be motivated to incorporate new technologies into the way they work. In these cases, it is often the responsibility of the VTC system manager to "market" the technology to potential users throughout the organization. While most people can benefit from the use of videoconferencing, they first need to understand the potential advantages (and overcome their fears and misconceptions) before they will be willing to give it a try.

You can use your knowledge of your own organization to identify the kind of leverage you will need to get the ball rolling. Sometimes, all it takes is a small push from senior management.

Example: A letter from a group controller at Sony, urging managers to use the system to cut travel time and expenses (and thereby improve productivity) was very effective in getting people to give the system a try.

In some organizations, an organized outreach program may be required. For maximum impact, this program usually combines elements of both conventional marketing and training programs. In a traditional marketing program, you first consider the identity, needs, and unique concerns of your target audience through market research. Only after you have a clear picture of your "market" can you effectively integrate your objectives and resources, and develop a marketing plan to achieve those objectives. In the deployment of a VTC network, the needs analysis is the basis for your market research, and the process deploying your system is the equivalent of a "product launch."

Taskforce Is a Nine-Letter Word

One of the best means of ensuring the successful development and deployment of a VTC system is to involve your major constituencies in the entire process, from planning to ongoing support. Depending on the size of your organization and the degree of collaboration that exists between its major functional and business groups, a taskforce (committee, change group, etc.) can ensure that your system is truly responsive to both users' needs and management's strategic imperatives. This type of involvement also goes a long way toward providing a sense of "ownership" and securing active support for your training and room coordination initiatives. Of course, this kind of preparation may be overkill if you are just planning to put a couple of set-tops in branch offices. And in some organizations, "the boss says so," can provide all the necessary motivation. But for larger organizations, user-driven "marketing" is often an essential component in a successful system rollout.

Example 1: One major financial institution organized a taskforce to plan a coordinated rollout of desktop videoconferencing. One objective was to moderate the urge of various business units to deploy untested, and possibly unsupportable, systems. Another effect was to gather the support of all concerned functional groups (IS, PC support, telecommunication, etc.) for a supportable, effective, long-term plan. The task force participated in user surveys, equipment tests, and pilot projects, eventually developing a list of acceptable equipment and procedures.

Example 2: A large aerospace company created a "change board" to monitor the deployment of desktop conferencing. It was composed of representatives from major business divisions, operations groups, and technical specialists. In addition to developing overall goals and equipment standards, the group meets regularly to address users' problems and the effects of system growth.

Note: One word of caution: before suggesting the formation of such a group, be sure that effective control remains with those who are able to exercise it intelligently (namely, you). It is said that a camel is a horse designed by a committee, but the family nature of this book prohibits me from printing the nickname of a VTC network designed by a nontechnical working group.

Marketing Nuts and Bolts

Here are some practical tips for marketing a VTC system to potential users.

A good internal marketing program has at least four key objectives:
- Create an atmosphere of acceptance for the system and the use of videoconferencing in general.
- Get potential users to try the system.
- Provide users with a positive first impression of the system.
- Gather feedback from users to help you improve the system.

These objectives can be achieved through the use of a variety of media and marketing strategies:

1. Presentations and Demonstrations

a. Presentations: Perhaps the most effective way of marketing the use of VTC is with a carefully designed presentation, whether delivered in person, on disc, or via videoconferencing. This presentation should high light the advantages of using the system, the ease of using it, and success stories. Go light on the technical aspects at this early stage—your objective should be to simply get users to ask for a demonstration.

b. Demonstrations: These can be similar to user training sessions, but should be less technical, with content related more to users' interests and enjoyment than to teaching them how to use the system. Demonstrations are most effective when they draw participants into the system and encourage interaction with a remote site through the system. To this end, it is often useful to have someone at the distant end deliver an informal (interactive) presentation about the advantages of the system, and to engage potential users in conversations about their communication needs.

Note: It's a good idea to prepare usefull handouts for these presentations and demonstrations, such as rollodex cards or laminated sheets with simplified instructions for reservations and system use.

2. Conventional Media

Use newsletters, bulletin boards, memos, and videotape to increase user awareness and to provide opportunities for potential users to try out the system.

> a. Direct mail: Whether this takes the form of memos, flyers, or some thing more elaborate will depend on your budget and organizational culture. Multiple "drops" of mailings is a basic principal of direct mail. Typically at least three would be required: one or two before the system rollout to peak interest, one to announce the "grand opening," and one or more to elicit direct participation ("Have you used it yet?").

> b. Newsletter: If you have even a minimal budget or desktop publishing skills, a newsletter touting the successful use of your system can keep it on everybody's radar screens. Whenever possible, feature people, such as room coordinators, key users, and unusual events—multipoints, high-profile meetings, and so forth.

> c. Contests/incentives: Get people excited about the system by running contests and offering incentives. To "compensate" users for lost travel perks, one service provider offered "frequent conferencing miles." You could offer the same to users or departments that save travel miles by using VTC. Targeting rewards or recognition to administrative personnel can be particularly effective.

Note: Every marketing communication should have a "call to action," such as "to arrange a conference call 555-123-1234" or "to find out how the Banco Binkara VTC Network can increase your productivity, e-mail VTC@bancobinkara.com."

3. Intranets and the Internet

If you have access to your organization's Web site or intranet, you can use them to great advantage in the marketing of your conferencing system. A Web site can put all your presentations, newsletters, and other information just a click away from your potential users. You can also post training materials, help desk information, frequently asked questions (FAQs), and even your reservation form. Be sure to organize your pages in a simple and accessible way, and place links to your videoconferencing pages wherever potential users might look (travel pages, meeting planner pages, newsletters, etc.). This can also be a great place to put all that information about your sites and your network.

Advanced reservation systems, mentioned later in this chapter, can even book conferences directly from a user's desktop. In the near future, your website or pages could even be users' direct portal to their videoconferencing experience.

Note: These critical educational, image-building, and branding activities also present an important opportunity for creating reasonable and sustainable user expectations as to the capabilities and quality they can expect from their VTC systems.

The preceding suggestions are just few of the ways in which you can "market" your VTC network. Other methods will also succeed if they communicate your own enthusiasm for the network in a way that relates to the everyday concerns of your potential users.

User Training

User training can be relatively painless if you are fortunate enough to have one or more people in each location assigned to coordinate and support conferences. One of the best training methods is to have a specialist visit each location and hold two or more training sessions, depending on the complexity of your system. If your expert resources are spread too thinly for this course of action, training sessions can also be conducted via videoconference!

Training of Support Personnel

The first training session should include all support personnel—technical or administrative—who may be expected to assist in meetings at that location. A second session can be conducted solely for on-site technical support personnel, if you are fortunate enough to have any. The primary objective of the first session should be to imbue trainees with a relaxed confidence in the system, and in your team's ability to solve any problems these support personnel might encounter in the course of their duties.

Typical Support Personnel Training Agenda—First Session:
1. Brief introduction to the system.
2. First call (a quick and easy way to demystify the system and to relax the group).

3. Demonstration of key system features (pan/tilt cameras, copy-stand camera, whiteboard, etc.).
4. Handout and discussion of simplified instruction sheet.
5. Have two or more members make calls and use key system functions. This call should be made to another support person who has already been trained. If possible, at least one of these calls should have, at the far end, coworkers who (up till now) may have been just voices on a phone.

Example: After installing the first system for a credit management group, we conducted a conventional on-site training session at that initial location. As we rolled out systems at new locations, the training sessions always involved a conference with the staff of a previously installed location. In this way, training sessions took on the characteristics of a reunion with distant coworkers, and a strong positive relationship with the system was established.

6. Present and discuss the procedures that have been established for scheduling, setting up, and conducting meetings. In addition, if you have procedures established for reservations, accounting, or other processes, they should be covered in this session, and appropriate documentation provided. A nice touch is a three-ring binder labeled "XYZ Inc. Videoconferencing Coordinator's Manual." While PDFs and CD-ROMs are cool, a solid three-ring binder is more reassuring and useful in an apparent emergency.
7. Discuss your help desk procedures and describe typical scenarios for dealing with common technical problems (e.g., dropped lines, audio echoes, etc).

Tip: If you don't have a formal help desk, you should at least have a beeper that is always in the possession of someone who can help a room coordinator in panic to troubleshoot a botched videoconference. People can accept occasional disruptions due to computer or network failure, but nothing can ruin the reputation of a VTC network more quickly than an important meeting that stays disrupted to the point of cancellation.

8. Summarize the key points, including:
   • Plan ahead.
   • Don't panic if your plan fails.
   • Get help ASAP.

You should have already prepared simple, large-type-face, customized instructions. These instructions should include step-by-step procedures for making a basic video call and your help desk number. Figure 7-1 shows a sample instruction sheet for VTC room use.

Provide three-hole punched, laminated copies of these instructions for all support personnel, and mount, frame, or glue a copy permanently somewhere near the system itself.

By all means provide instruction manuals, technical information, and backup documentation to your heart's content—but make sure everyone is familiar with the above mentioned simple instructions before you move on.

Try to keep your instruction sheet free of extraneous information. I'm sure that your network architecture and room design belong in the hall of fame. Unfortunately, the presence of jargon and complicated diagrams has been known to precipitate panic attacks (or worse) in room coordinators whose VTC system stopped working five minutes before the boss's big meeting.

Banco Binkara Maui Videoconferencing Room #1
Voice Phone Number: 555-555-5555
Video Phone Number: 777-777-7777
Instructions for Placing or Receiving a Video Call
Your videoconferencing connection should be established at least 20 minutes before your scheduled meeting time.

1. Turn on the system by pressing the On button on the touch-panel control on the conference table.
2. If you will be receiving the video call, wait for the connection to be completed.
3. If you are initiating the videoconference, press the Phone Book button on the touch screen.
4. To place the call, press the name of the location you wish to call (e.g. New York) and then press the Call button (lower left corner of the touch screen).
5. If your video call cannot be completed, make a voice call to the distant location to confirm that their system is turned on. Then try the call again (repeat steps 3 and 4). A list of voice phone numbers for all locations is located on the back of this sheet.
6. If it is 10-minutes before your scheduled conference, and you still cannot see and hear the remote site, call: **888-123-HELP.**

Figure 7-1 Example of simple VTC room-use instruction sheet.

Stress that "there are no stupid questions," and that support personnel should not hesitate to call your "help desk" immediately if they run into any problems. Many VTC disasters have been caused by local support personnel trying to "troubleshoot" just before a meeting.

Example: One rollabout system belonging to a major entertainment and theme-park company was located at their advanced engineering facility. After numerous on-site service calls in the first months of operation, the system was permanently "repaired" by installing a lock on the equipment cabinet door. It seems that everytime there was a small problem with the system, such as a busy number, low picture contrast, or improper audio level, the local "doctors of engineering," could not resist the urge to "operate."

End-User Training

Depending on the organizational level and technical expertise of end users, you may want to conduct on-site or remote training for them using the system. These sessions should be short (under one hour), and should focus on the ways the system can be used to conduct more effective meetings. A "get acquainted" call to someone the users know (e.g., a manager in another region), is a great way to break the ice and get them past the technology—and into the system.

The Power of Presentations

One of the best ways to introduce nontechnical managers to videoconferencing is to deliver an electronic presentation using MS PowerPoint, Astound, or some similar presentation program. Not only is this a familiar and comfortable milieu for most managers, it provides you with an opportunity to introduce them to your system—painlessly.

As mentioned earlier, after connecting with a distant site, you might want to have the person you have called "present" the basic concepts and processes with an electronic slide show. If he or she does a good job, you will achieve the following objectives:
1. Your "students" will understand the basic principles of conducting an effective and productive videoconference.
2. They will experience and understand the capabilities of their system.
3. They will have participated in a lively, informative, and productive videoconference.
4. They will have some good ideas as to the ways in which they can use the system to achieve their objectives.

5. They will have a realistic expectation as to what the system can and cannot do.

The basic goal is to immerse them in the process of communicating through the system. So be sure to include plenty of opportunities for interaction in your presentation. Asking routine questions is a good way to do this (for example, "Bob, you've had to change planes in Chicago during a snow storm, haven't you?"). It is also important to leave plenty of time (and space) for student questions.

Getting Help

If you have the budget, or many users and support staff to train, you might want to enlist the services of a professional instructional designer and a creative presentation producer. You have only one shot to get the users on your side, and you owe it to them (and yourself) to give it your best shot. In any case, the presentation should be rehearsed several times with a simulated audience before it goes "live."

For systems involving a large number of desktop systems, a canned presentation is the very least that you should offer. If you have the capabilities or the budget, consider developing a well-designed interactive tutorial. Whether this tutorial is delivered via disc or network, it will save you many hours of support time per user.

Scheduling, Planning, and Conducting Meetings

While the needs, procedures and meeting styles of organizations vary as widely as taste in food, there are some basic principles that are helpful in the planning, scheduling, and conduct of distant meetings.

Scheduling

It may seem obvious, but in order to schedule a successful videoconfereence, all of the following information must be available:
- Room: availability and capacity.
- People: availability and contact information.
- Connectivity: cost, availability, and responsibility.
- Equipment: condition, availability, and special needs.

Room availability is particularly important when VTC rooms are also used for normal conferences, training sessions, and other purposes. Conflicts often arise if the room's use is scheduled in an informal manner. If a room is to be used for videoconferencing, it is imperative that some sort of formal scheduling procedure be established. This can be as simple as a sheet of paper taped to the door, with a schedule and the phone extension of the person responsible for scheduling the room.

Computerized VTC scheduling systems have many useful features, some of them designed to prevent common miscues from interfering with your meeting. Look for a scheduling system that reflects the way that your conferences are planned and conducted. In many organizations, for example, the number of participants tends to increase after a videoconference is announced. This suggests the need for a system (or procedures) that will alert the meeting planner when a conference grows too large for the scheduled room so that remedial action can be taken.

Scheduling Systems

Several powerful computerized reservations systems are commercially available that have been designed specifically for videoconferencing use. Many successful VTC networks, however, have been managed with nothing more complicated than a central reservation book. As long as procedures are in place that assure that all required information has been confirmed and kept up-to-date, that all participants have been notified, and that rooms are never double-booked, the medium can be whatever is appropriate to the size and nature of your network.

Most multipoint bridging service providers will schedule and manage your meetings at a small additional cost (more about this later in this chapter, under "Outsourcing Support and Management Services"). For larger or more complex networks, or for those that frequently host multipoint conferences, a computerized reservation system can be a real life saver.

Scheduling Software

There are two basic classes of software suitable for scheduling videoconferences: general-purpose facilities scheduling programs and those applications designed specifically for videoconferencing. Figure 7-2 shows a sample screen of VC Wizard scheduling software.

The first category includes general purpose meeting management programs such as Facility Master II Scheduling Software, from Comsec; Synchronize, from CrossWind; Office Tracker Scheduler, from Milum Software; FASTbook, from Event Software; Scheduler Plus, from CEO Software; and ResSched 4.0, from Madrigal Software. These programs are designed to handle a wide range of scheduling tasks, will operate over LANs, and WANs, and offer some Web-based access capabilities. Each one has features (and costs) that make it more or less suitable for VTC networks of different sizes and types.

To handle the technical and logistical challenges of frequent multipoint conferences or the general complexities of a busy far-flung network, you may need a program such as VC Wizard Merlin, from AC&E, Ltd. It is a comprehensive, client-server scheduling system application, built on an Oracle database, which performs room scheduling, user notification, multipoint bridge and network resource scheduling and control, internal billing, and other functions. The relatively high cost of this scheduling system may be a sound investment for the manager of a large or rapidly growing VTC network.

PictureTel delivers a program called Live Scheduler, which provides many of the same functions as VC Wizard, including interface with common multipoint control units (MCUs) and user notification via e-mail or fax.

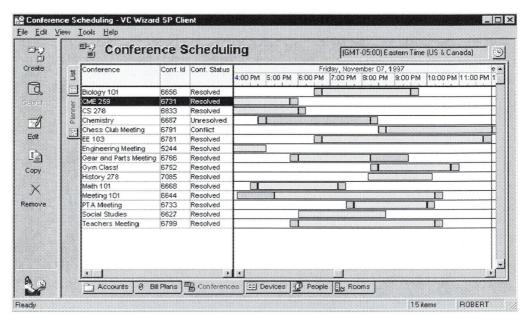

Figure 7-2 Sample screen of scheduling software. (Screenshot: AC&E)

Most reservation systems will allow users to make reservations and/or check conference schedules via the Web. This not only makes the system more user friendly, it helps keep the schedule up-to-date and minimizes overbooking of limited resources. Systems that can be Web-enabled include VC Wizard, Facility Master II, Scheduler 2001 Plus, and most of the reservation systems used by V-Span, MCI, and other videoconference service providers.

There are also a number of powerful, interesting Web conferencing and e-conferencing applications, like Latitude Communication's MeetingPlace. Although most of these do not yet offer video capability, they manage the conferencing process on the basis of content, interaction, and productivity, instead of focusing on schedules and facilities.

Content Creation

In much the same way as people plan for the productivity and success of an in-person business meeting, the effectiveness of a videoconference depends on the proper planning and production of the key content to be discussed. What can you do to help your users prepare for their distance meetings?

Let us first consider the elements that make for success. Among the critical components to a successful meeting are:
1. Presentation materials
2. Communication skills

Both components can be improved with training and practice. However, you may not be in a position to ensure that users of the VTC systems get formal training in presentation skills. But you should be able to make recommendations as to where one can train or when it is best to outsource production of materials to a media design and services company. In addition, you can develop guidelines to assist videoconference users in the preparation of their materials and their on-camera presentations. Below are factors that should be included.

Presentation Materials

Print: From the agenda to the handouts, a consistent look can be achieved by repeating a graphic element (such as a logo) on all printed pieces and by using the same set of fonts.

On-Screen Type and Graphics

Be it PowerPoint or another presentation program in which the electronic presentation is assembled, use large fonts. Design consultants recommend 44-point type and not more than five lines on each slide. Anything smaller than 28-point type requires special transmission and display considerations. Wherever possible, spreadsheet data should be converted for display as smaller tables or sheets with large (28- to 4-point) type. Graphics should also be kept simple and large to compensate for the loss of detail and quality caused by video compression.

If you must transmit and receive high-resolution graphics, your system should use 4CIF graphics or direct computer-to-computer transmission of slides. A large-screen video data projector or plasma display may also be required to make it possible for the entire group to view the graphic details.

When presenting to sites outside your network, advise users to assume the worst. Large, simple slides may not win any design awards, but they will get the point across without eyestrain.

3-D Objects

The document camera is a good tool to display a close-up of anything from a new product to a part that needs repair. Document cameras are also favored by users who are accustomed to overhead projectors, providing them with the same type of pointing and annotation capabilities. Some newer document cameras will also store multiple shots of products or charts, which can then be played back as a slide show.

Video

While prerecorded video is a good way to show a location, plant, or demonstrate the use of equipment, even the best-produced videotape can look awful when transmitted via a videoconference system. If the video segment is a fast-moving, attention-grabbing clip that is intended as an opener, it is best to mail the tape to the remote sites ahead of time.

Video shot for transmission over a VTC system should be simple, slow moving, and have as plain a background as is possible. This will enable the codec to encode and compress the picture information with a minimum of distortion and distracting motion-blur.

If recorded video content is an essential part of your business communications, consider the use of a MPEG-2-based system. These use more bandwidth (typically 1.54 to 10 Mbps), but can provide the high-quality video transmission viewers associate with videotape or broadcast television.

Communication Skills

Good communication skills and practices are particularly important in a videoconference, where the unfamiliar technology can sometimes create barriers to achieving effective communications.

Opening

A good way to connect with the participants at remote sites is to establish a connection with them before the meeting formally begins. Use the remote site facilitators to help establish a personal touch.

It is also a good idea to send the agenda and other support materials for distribution before the meeting. This allows the critical first few minutes of a videoconference to be used to establish real person-to-person communications.

Videoconferencing technology can sometimes create a sense of distance or separation. For this reason, it is even more important to introduce all of the participants in a remote meeting. The presenter should also be encouraged to interact with the "audience" early in the meeting to break the "digital ice."

Collaboration

Your user training should cover the various collaborative tools that are available on your system. Work with your IS or training departments to ensure that users are able to use NetMeeting and similar tools to increase the effectiveness of their meetings.

If your organization does not offer training in the use of collaborative software and hardware (e.g., whiteboards), consider adding such sessions to your user training program. Effective use of collaborative computing can produce a great increase in VTC productivity—and user satisfaction.

Formal Closing

The meeting host should plan for a formal sign-off. While this is an item on all good presenters' list of "to dos," it is particularly important in a videoconference, as it is a signal to all sites to turn off their microphones or disconnect, and thereby avoid embarrassing transmission of after-meeting chatter.

Help! They Need Somebody

We have repeatedly referred to two types of support personnel—technical support and room coordinators. They are both critical to the success of your VTC network, and can be supplied by members of your organization or employees of your service provider.

A realistic assessment of your organizational situation and your resources is necessary if you are to provide effective support in the two key areas of room coordination and technical support.

Room Coordination and Meeting Support Services

In an ideal world, you would have two dedicated, trained, full-time employees assigned to coordinate the activities of each VTC system location. This would assure that conferences would be properly scheduled and that conference rooms would be properly prepared (and up and running) for every scheduled conference. It would also assure that users would have the kind of skilled and courteous assistance they required—whether in operating a copy-stand camera or preparing handouts for presentations.

In today's lean and mean business environment, it is unlikely that even one employee can be dedicated to coordinating every VTC room. But this does not mean that you cannot have skilled room coordinators for your facilities. Each organization has different ways of handling shared responsibilities, but here are a few tips that could improve your results in this area:

1. Ask that two people be assigned and made available for training as room coordinators—with the rationale that coverage cannot lapse because of vacations, sick days, and other reasons. One person could be the one already responsible for scheduling that conference room.
2. Provide formal, ongoing training for those coordinators, including certificates (suitable for framing). This can be at low cost—via videoconference.
3. Encourage esprit d'corps, with newsletters and career development activities, even if coordinators do not report to you.
4. As your network grows, build a case for full-time coverage at key sites (e.g., regional HQs).

Technical Support

This area is somewhat more complex than room coordination, though sometimes local front-line technical support personnel are asked to double as conference coordinators.

Videoconferencing technical support is, by its very nature, multilayered, and the success of any VTC technical support program is determined to a large extent by how well it handles escalation procedures. Because VTC systems are highly automated, a well-informed junior IT telecommunications technician (with a few days of special training) can solve at least 80 percent of the common problems that might arise during a videoconference. Most of the remaining snafus can be solved quickly by an engineer or senior technician who has a few years experience with codecs, Imux, and switched digital circuits. The remaining few percent require the expertise of the high-priced talent squirreled away at service providers and system vendors.

The trick is to provide access to the right level of support quickly enough so that users will not be seriously inconvenienced. Even the best (and most expensive) support systems cannot assure that every conference will procede without a hitch. But it is possible to solve 95 percent of VTC problems within fifteen minutes of occurrence. The remaining 5 percent usually involve either a hardware breakdown or the failure of a telecommunications link. The former can be resolved quickly only if spare equipment or components are available on-site. The latter problem can be avoided through the use of backup or redundant circuits or services. Both are practical (though costly) solutions for mission-critical systems.

A Reasonable Strategy

For everyday business conferencing, a feasible support strategy might look something like this:

On-Site
The local PC or LAN technician(s) receives basic training (one day) in system operation and troubleshooting. Periodic training (e.g., two hours via video-conferencing every two months) keeps them involved and up-to-date.

At Headquarters
At all times during business hours, at least one IT/telecommunications technician should be available for phone and online support (remote diagnostics). This technician should attend "factory" training for every major piece of equipment in the system (typically a total of five to ten days per year). Patience and grace

under pressure are also requirements for this position.

Under Contract

Unlimited technical support should be provided under service contract from a single source, or a combination of telecommunications and system service providers. Without rapid escalation access to high-level engineering support, a small problem can sometimes become a meeting killer, and a big problem can shut down an important system for days or weeks.

Key Support Concerns

One key aspect of this high-level support is accountability. Even if you cannot secure a single point of responsibility for technical problems, you can have the kind of expertise on your side that will prevent the buck from being passed from phone company, to codec manufacturer, to integrator, and so on.

All the previously mentioned levels of support can be provided by either vendors or in-house staff. However you plan to secure this help, it is critical for the success of your system that you build the related costs into your basic budget for system operation.

Outsourcing Support and Management Services

There are many videoconferencing functions that can easily be outsourced. These include: technical support, telecommunication services, meeting planning, scheduling and support, and room coordination.

Outsourcing Criteria

The degree to which you outsource your VTC management functions will be determined by the relationship of your needs to your resources. If your requirements involve a light load of point-to-point conferences between your own sites over dial-up ISDN lines, you can probably manage this type of activity yourself. Easy-to-use tools such as SNMP and the Polycom Global Management System will allow you and a minimal staff to effectively support most user needs. Occasional requirements for large or complex multipoint conferences can be handed over to providers such as V-Span or Vialog.

If, on the other hand, your conferencing needs are large, complex, or formal, you will need a deep and reliable support structure. Your resources and organizational structure will determine how much of that support comes from staff and how much from vendors. Inadequate support inevitably leads to disaster, so plan way ahead.

Common Mistakes

The most common mistake among newer VTC managers is to try to do too much with too little support staff. This either results in burned out staff, disgruntled users, or both. Even the top VTC managers regularly call on service providers and consulting firms to provide support for major events or system expansion. As a matter of fact, the trend among large networks is to outsource more support services as time goes on. There are two reasons for this:

1. Cost and scarcity of trained personnel: It is virtually impossible for a small or medium-size organization to keep up with all the skills required to support rapidly changing VTC technologies. Even if you could hire and train the high-level technicians needed to keep things running smoothly for every meeting at every location—you probably won't be able to hold on to them for long. The job market for those skills is just too competitive. The path chosen by many companies is to build a core group of technocrats that can manage the performance of these duties by vendors. Instead of competing for the services of technical support personnel, technical support service providers will compete to capture and keep your business.

2. Improved service offerings by vendors: As videoconferencing has grown into a mainstream application, a wide range of support services have become available. Service providers have been able to leverage their efficient use of expensive skilled personnel and to take advantage of the revenue streams available to them as resellers of bandwidth, to provide users with multipoint bridging, scheduling, and meeting support services at very low cost.

If you wish, you can call on these vendors to plan your meetings, provide facilities and equipment, train your presenters, connect your users, monitor and support conferences, and provide you with billing and usage reports afterward.

V-Span, Vialog, MCI Conferencing, Global Crossing, and others provide everything from assistance with planning of meetings to operator support of conferences in progress.

In "Appendix B: General Resources" you will find a list of vendors and consulting firms that provide technical support services for VTC.

And the Answer Is

Given enough time and money, you can achieve virtually any conferencing objective. Satisfying your users' conferencing needs in a cost-effective way requires careful planning and an intelligent balancing of in-house and vendor-provided services. For several other perspectives on this issue, including those from a system manager, a service provider, and a consultant, you can refer to Chapter 6, "Putting It All Together—The Challenges of Integration."

Perhaps the most difficult part of successfully managing a videoconferencing network is managing user expectations. This requires a consistent effort to train users in the use and capabilities of your system, and a continuous effort to involve your user community in the creation and evolution of your multimedia communication network.

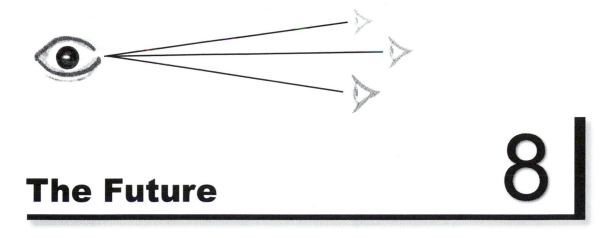

The Future

8

Executive Summary

"How can you be in two places at once when you're nowhere at all to begin with?"—The Firesign Theater

The rate of technical development in videoconferencing continues along a high-speed, zigzag trail. Over the past year, there have been twists and turns in the progress of video technology that few would have expected. The spread of wide area Ethernet, bandwidth logjams on cable modem networks, and interconnection logjams on digital subscriber lines (DSL) are just few of the business twists that the trail has taken in the past few months. The cliff-hanging saga of G3 wireless has shown clearly how the fate of major technological innovations are often held captive by a tangled web of politics, money, and business strategy.

Perhaps the most dramatic development has been a quiet one that has slipped under the radar of many business publications—the growing integration of videoconferencing into the Web-based trend to e-business and e-commerce. When I am asked to predict the future of videoconferencing, usually by analysts and children, I usually say that it will soon become as commonplace as the telephone and the expense report. Unfortunately, I have been saying that since the dot matrix printer was considered hot stuff. To accurately predict the course of visual communications technology over the next few years may be impossible, particularly in the consumer realm. In that area it depends on too many nonlinear variables, such as the ability of carrier management to continue to invest heavily and effectively in universal broadband access.

In the business and institutional sector, the future is much clearer. The same advantages that VTC has provided over its short lifespan will continue to fuel expanded use. These include increased productivity, reduction in travel, and generally improved communications. As I mentioned in Chapter 5, developing a future-proof strategy for video communications is mostly a matter of using Occam's Razor, that is, finding the simplest, most cost-effective way to gain the benefits of a new technology. This usually involves avoiding a premature commitment of human and financial resources. Here (again) is my five-point test for that shiny new technology:

1. Does the new-technology component of the solution answer a specific, substantial, demonstrable user need?
2. Is there an older, better-tested, or more widely accepted technology that will address this need as well as the shiny new one?
3. Is there more than one source for this new technology, or will I be dependent on the continued ability of a single vendor to supply and support it?
4. Where in its development or deployment life cycle is this technology, and is my organization the appropriate user for it at this time vis-a-vis technical support, mission-critical applications, and other purposes?
5. Is there a way that I can implement a phased rollout of this technology, one which will not interfere with or endanger existing mission-critical applications? Alternately, is there a way to outsource the deployment of this technology that will answer short-term users' needs in a cost-effective and flexible manner (e.g., to an application service provider)?

Safety Nets

The trend in VTC is toward better, cheaper, and easier-to-use systems and services. Combining these advantages and trends will inevitably lead to greatly increased usage. The only fly in the ointment could be the ability of service providers and VTC managers to maintain a high quality of service (personal, not QoS) in the face of skyrocketing demand and strong competitive pricing pressure. On the user side, many organizations recognize the scope of this potential challenge and are reconfiguring their plans to adapt to the overabundance of demand. They are doing this by forming multidisciplinary groups to develop realistic plans that will result in supportable and sustainable solutions for the foreseeable future. One advantage of this multidisciplinary approach is that it is relatively "BS" and techno-evangelist proof. Very few organizations have individuals on staff that are expert in all the technologies that are converging to create the multimedia communication applications of the future. I have seen the senior IS staff of a major international bank "snowed" into buying a suboptimal solution VTC that any competent audio engineer would have given a thumbs down. They were so enamoured of the elegance of the software and the tele-communications interface that they overlooked serious shortcomings in audio system performance. Others have accepted assurances that "minor" glitches would be fixed in the production model. It seems that every technical discipline tends to underestimate the complexity and importance of other fields. "It's only audio," could just as easily have been, "it's only software," or video, or telephony.

Perhaps the most important component in a good multidisciplinary VTC group, and the least comfortable for technocrats, is the participation of actual users. Nevertheless, the input of front-line human resources, sales, facilities, and other operational units appears to be critical to the timely and effective deployment of a workable multimedia communication system. As long as roles are clearly defined (e.g., as an advisory panel), the presence of nontechnoids should not be too disruptive to the process, and it will provide invaluable and timesaving insights into the real-life advantages and problems hiding inside every shiny new technology.

ASPs to the Rescue

New, complex, multidisciplinary video applications may present a difficult challenge for most user organizations, but they offer a great opportunity for service providers flexible enough to stay ahead of the curve. Multipoint bridging services and conference savvy carriers have been providing remote computerized support since before the WWW was born. These companies have adopted the application service provider (ASP) model so successfully deployed by dot-coms, by emphasizing and expanding their already strong Web-based reservation and H.323 services. According to a recently released study by Frost & Sullivan, *U.S. Videoconferencing Services Market*, "Application service providers (ASPs) are leading the way for turnkey video services at affordable prices. They are going to drive the migration from traditional transport services to value-added, Web-based, comprehensive managed services." Frost's research shows that "video-conferencing transport and managed services generated revenues of $1.55 billion in 1999. It is projected to reach $3.26 billion by 2006." Frost & Sullivan expects "considerable migration of revenues from traditional transport-only videoconferencing service model to comprehensive managed services, or ASP offerings delivered via Web-based portals." This paradigm shift is taking place with established bridging and conference services companies such as V-Span, ACT, and WorldCom as well as with newer, dot-com entries into the field such as eVDO, Evoke, and WebEx.

Not all the outsourcing activity has been a reaction to potential problems. In many cases, service providers are gearing up to deliver new and innovative solutions to business needs created by the success of e-commerce and e-business. The increased speed of business conducted on the Internet or multi-organization extranets has brought with it a need for a more personal way to communicate over the Web. Whether this dizzying pace has been made possible by supply-chain automation or plain old e-commerce, the need for high-touch customer/vendor communication is widely recognized as a major factor in the achievement of sustainable business success. As the new millennium gets into gear, expect to see major e-commerce and e-business service providers (e.g., Siebel and IBM) integrate videoconferencing and multimedia collaboration into their Internet tool sets and service offerings to satisfy these needs.

Integrated IP Multimedia

For several years now, it seems that fully interactive remote collaboration has been just around the corner. All the ingredients for fully integrated, networked collaborative multimedia communication have existed for some time. But except for highly motivated and skilled users, such as engineers and doctors, few have had the patience or resources to take full advantage of remote collaboration. Deployment of these powerful tools seems to be dependent on finding the appropriate mix of tools and services for a particular organization or group of users. Fortunately, this is becoming easier every month, as new user- and network-friendly tools become available at a reasonable cost. Most users still require some assistance with collaborative tools, and service providers like WebEx and V-Span are eager to provide this support.

On the systems side we can expect several manufacturers to play catch-up with Polycom and Zydacron in the area of packaged collaborative conferencing systems. VCON and VTEL have moved strongly to integrate multicasting capabilities into their VTC systems, as has Lucent with their ICOSM products. The next few years should see lower-cost multipurpose hardware add-ons that will support a variety of standards and applications. Array Microsystems and other PC-board suppliers will offer better and cheaper hardware solutions to the need for higher-quality video for collaborative applications. At the high-end, expect Tandberg and others to continue to push the envelope with better, high-res graphics, and multistream video solutions. Who knows, the next few years might even see an economical motion-tracking camera that really works!

Back to the Future

In many cases, bandwidth- and QoS-hungry two-way video is not required for optimal communications. Many training and presentation-related applications need only one-way video, combined with voice bridging, graphics, and lighter forms of interactivity such as polling and text-based chat. For these uses, new services like One Touch Front Row, introduced in partnership with Hughes Network Systems, will do the job. Front Row combines DirecPC (satellite-based Internet access) and other existing tools in a turnkey application to deliver verifiable distance learning to remote locations. Somewhat similar, terrestrial services are offered by VTEL, Akamai, and others.

ISDN Forever

There is a general expectation among videoconferencing professionals that, by the end of the decade, virtually all video communications will travel via some sort of packet-switched IP network. However, there are still many technical, social, financial, and regulatory hurdles to be cleared before that time arrives. Providing reliable, economical communications will still be the responsibility of VTC and network managers, and they will need to employ the same careful, failsafe strategies that have helped their organizations grow and prosper. It seems that ISDN will still be a part of that strategy well into the twenty-first century.

Initially, ISDN will remain the wide area transport of choice for room-based conferences and desktop systems, with local traffic migrating rapidly to the LAN. A variety of shared H.320 codecs and H.323 gateways will emerge to ease the transition. Network managers will gradually become confident enough in the reliability of IP-WAN services to move more of their conferencing traffic via that route. Two other emerging technologies should help to accelerate that transition— Web conferencing and the local use of low-cost H.323 multipoint bridges. Web conferencing is a natural extension of the ubiquitous PowerPoint meeting, and popular services like PlaceWare and WebEx are already developing distributed networks to assure that their customers can seamlessly add high-quality video to the mix whenever they want. The availability of low-cost, powerful H.323 multipoint bridges, like the sub-$4,000 Encounter 1000 from Ezenia!, will facilitate the use of collaborative video by more users—first on a local scale and then in the wide area. As pressures build to add distant colleagues to these meetings, more network managers will test the H.323 WAN waters, if only to avoid big H.320 bridging costs. And so it goes—each user-friendly advance in one application area driving increased demand in another.

Videophones

When asked to pick the best example of a technology that is still looking for an application (or market), pundits often point to the videophone. The poor thing has been a perpetual bridesmaid since the 1963 World's Fair, patiently waiting while upstarts like the PC, the Microwave oven, and the Internet became part of the cultural substrate. While ISDN videophones have had some success in vertical markets such as telemedicine, their widespread acceptance has been limited by the rapidly falling cost of PCs and PC-based systems. With a VTC capable PC on every desk in the developed world, who needed a videophone? The recent emergence of serious, CTI-based, IP telephony may finally give the videophone its chance to shine. I expect several kinds of IP videophones to become a common sight over the next few years. To take advantage of the spread of IPBX and H.323 MCUs, at least one type will combine a full function IP speakerphone and a tidy (6-inch) screen for video calls, TV programming, and call data. Some of these videophones will connect directly to the network via an RJ-45, while less expensive models will hitch a ride on the user's PC with a USB connection. Both will keep the PC screen clear of extra windows and provide a comfortably sized, high-quality picture, while maintaining tight integration with their collaborative applications.

Wireless Wonders

Currently planned third-generation (3G) wireless services will offer data transmission at speeds from 384 kbps up to 2 Mbps within the next several years. This will enable mobile videoconferencing and collaborative computing applications that would have made Dick Tracy jealous. Golf cart-based branch offices are just one of the brave new businesses we can expect before the end of the decade. Nokia, Erickson and other manufacturers have already demonstrated prototypes of exciting mobile video communication devices, but the picture may be brighter overseas than in the United States. In the States, bandwidth (or spectrum) has become a major political and economic hot potatoe. The Federal Communications Commission (FCC) is scheduled to begin auctioning off rights to use spectrum in the 700 MHz band, starting in March 2001. Though this is not the band originally envisioned for these 3G services, it is the only one that we are likely to have in this decade.

There are at least two problems that may delay a quick rollout of pocket videophones. First, TV broadcasters are already using these frequencies and won't be forced to vacate them until 2006. There is some indication that they will move out early if the new tenants (AT&T, MCI, and others) make it worth their while. The strength of the mobile carriers' motivation in this area is uncertain due to a second technological roadblock—the lack of 3G-compliant hardware for operation on the 700 MHz band. I guess that users will just have to wait and see which side of this chicken-or-the-egg puzzle cooks up first.

We may have to wait a few years to hold videoconferences from the beach or golf course but, politics allowing, I plan to have a real Dick Tracy video wristwatch before the decade is out.

Technoshock

Some managers and organizations seem to be so overwhelmed by the rapid pace of technological development that they are unable to decide which new communication tools will help them. By the time they have identified a likely new solution, ten more have hit the market claiming to be the next greatest thing. Conversely, some users rush to adopt every latest twist in the videocom pantheon so as not to be left behind by the competition. Both of these behaviors are symptoms of what I like to call technoshock. Applying my fivefold criteria is helpful, but generating realistic answers to these questions requires some real expertise and insight in a wide range of disciplines.

It is virtually impossible for any one person to be enough of an expert in every aspect of video communications to answer all these questions without some help. My twenty-plus years of experience in the field have taught me that careful listening to both experts and users usually produces the best results. The advice of real experts and experienced specialists is essential in the development of coherent solutions that will really work, but only users can keep you ahead of the curve of rapidly changing needs. Solutions that address real user needs in a sustainable way are almost always a better choice than new, elegant, high-tech applications that require users to reshape the way they communicate. I hope this book will help you formulate and implement a sound video communications strategy. In the appendices that follow, you will find some helpful information and access to resources both more and less technical than this book.

May all your systems run smoothly, and may all your vendors be truly user friendly.

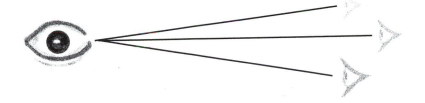

Appendix A: Case Studies and a Research Summary

Case Study 1: Corporate Customer Service Training Program

Organization

USWEST Media Group Shared Technologies
USWEST Dex Client Services

Program Directors

Peggy Kaye, USWEST Media Group Shared Technologies
Mark Mongar, USWEST Dex Client Services

History

The Client Services and Shared Technologies entities were one group until they were separated in a reorganization. Both provide information services systems support to USWEST Dex and USWEST Media Group internal customers. Shared Technologies provides the network and its management. Client Services provides and maintains the hardware and software. Typically in an IS organization, the skill set emphasized is always technical competence. The most important job for technicians is to fix the problem. Management had few problems with its employees' ability to fix the software problems or equipment, but saw a need for better handling of customers' requests and to more efficiently meet their needs. In today's business environment, customers expect not only functional expertise, but for their needs to be handled individually, personably, quickly, and with the least inconvenience to them. However, the interpersonal skill set of the IS employees lagged behind their technical skills. Reasons for this were that interpersonal skills typically were not emphasized during job interviews and performance evaluation experience with technology was valued, and technicians were provided extensive technological training. Customer service skills were not part of the appraisal nor the interview process. Client Services and Shared Technologies did not have a high number of customer complaints, but recognized that this was an area that they could pursue to improve customer satisfaction.

Target Population

The target group consisted of two hundred employees that are part of Client Services and Shared Technologies. The group included the help desk personnel, service technicians, strategic planners, and network administrators. They plan, install, rearrange, and maintain the network and equipment systems within USWEST Media Group and USWEST Dex.

Background Information

Client satisfaction level in 1996 averaged 3.7 out of 4.0. The performance standard set was to resolve out-of-service problems within four hours. An overall satisfaction survey that rates professional courtesy, resolution of problems, and demonstrated technical expertise is conducted routinely.

Linking the Need to Management Goals

USWEST Dex Client Services' director's vision is to "provide outstanding value-added service by being the one-stop solution." A goal is to be more effective as an overall team in servicing the customer. The group wants to serve customers professionally in handling out-of-service problems. However, problems are often not technical in nature. Frequently, the problem lies in how the customer operates the equipment or uses the software. To more efficiently handle the customer's request, the employee needs to improve communication skills to do a better job of analyzing the problem. Identifying the customer's difficulty and clearly defining the problem would improve the proper routing of the job ticket.

Why Now?

Leadership recognized that customers' overall expectations would continue to grow and that the company would have to keep pace. Technical expertise was up-to-date, therefore only marginal improvement could be realized in that area. However, little emphasis had been placed on customer service skills, so training in this area had the potential to produce good yields. Also, the directors of the two groups saw a need to strengthen the relationship between their groups since they often worked together on customer needs and problems. Training together would be a team-building experience and make for consistency in the training they received.

Objectives

The overall objective was to provide employees an opportunity to learn customer service skills to increase customer satisfaction. Employees' objectives included: to make every contact a customer service opportunity, to work as a customer service team, to become better listeners, to make encounters with difficult customers produce positive results, to communicate effectively on the telephone, and to manage projects and time efficiently.

Solutions

Why external rather than internal? Customer service training is available off the shelf at USWEST Dex, but with the internal resources to customize and deliver it. Management also wanted a certification process so employees would recognize that the skills learned and knowledge gained were important.

Customized Product

In meeting with a NSG representative and USWEST Dex in October 1996, USWEST Dex discussed the need for team building training as part of the overall program. To meet this need, NSG substituted "How to Work Together As a Team" for one of the standard modules. The two groups jointly identified specific needs of the employees and program objectives. They made sure the program supported management goals and complemented job performance expectations. Individual modules were customized to fit the specific situations of Client Services and Shared Technologies.

Program Implementation

Faced with the challenge of training two hundred people scattered over a fourteen-state area, the decision was made to train at six sites. Four of the sites would have less than twenty people each. The decision was made to have the trainer conduct most of the training at two major sites in Omaha, Nebraska, and Aurora,

Colorado. The other sites would participate through videoconference. However, managers knew it was important for employees at remote sites to be fully involved in the training from the start. They felt it was critical that initially they participate face-to-face with the trainer. For the first day of training, most employees attended in Omaha or Aurora. For the remainder, the trainer traveled to two of the remote sites to present the first day of training. The training program was conducted in six sessions, beginning March 5, 1997 and ending August 21, 1997.

The Technology

Since the audience was dispersed in six locations over a fourteen-state area with a 20 percent turnover, portability of the content would be necessary. Additionally, all six sessions would have to be documented. Since some employees would not be able to attend scheduled training due to vacations or sickness, each session was videotaped. The tapes would also provide a reinforcement tool for managers if they wanted to schedule refresher training. Using videoconferencing, the instructor-led training could be delivered simultaneously to all six locations. In addition, workgroup activity at remote sites was designed for small, interactive, and collaborative groups.

Results

Customer satisfaction has increased from 3.7 to 3.8 on a scale of 1 to 4. The cost of travel and facilitators' fees decreased and resulted in savings of about $50,000. Individual feedback from participants has been very positive. Employees feel motivated to use the techniques and ideas that they learned in the classroom. They feel confident that they have the tools and information necessary for situations encountered on the job. In addition, supervisors now have assessment tools for evaluating and rating the employees' customer service skills. They use this information in coaching and reinforcement discussions with individual employees.

Case Study 2: Government—The U.S. Navy's Video TeleTraining Project

Organization
CESN, U.S. Navy

Program Manager
Jean C. Jones

History

The CNET Electronic Schoolhouse Network (CESN) is the U.S. Navy's Video Teletraining (VTT) network that has provided quality training to 82,000 students and conference attendees since 1989. The CESN was first proposed for the navy in 1988 as a way to provide effective training to a greater number of students, with fewer instructors, while simultaneously reducing training costs. After an extensive feasibility study identifying training requirements for VTT, network implementation began in 1989 with four East Coast sites and one network hub in Virginia Beach, Virginia. By 1993, VTT had proven to be a viable, cost-effective method of training that was also required on the West Coast to link training commands coast-to-coast. The West Coast hub was established in San Diego, California, with three remote sites in California and Washington state. Today, there are thirty CESN classrooms nationwide.

Shore-to-ship training on VTT was demonstrated in 1993 using INMARSAT satellite communications on the USS Theodore Roosevelt. Although the concept of shipboard VTT training was proven successful, INMARSAT rates were too costly to continue beyond the demonstration phase. During this time, the chief navy officer's special project, Challenge Athena, began to offer expanded communications to deployed ships by using commercial satellites as a supplement to military satellites providing a high-data-rate T1 duplex link to a 2.4 meter shipboard antenna. The USS George Washington and the USS Carl Vinson were the first ships to receive Challenge Athena communications, and VTT was implemented on the ships as one of the uses of the new communications system. The ships are scheduled on the CESN as any other remote site, providing training and conferencing opportunities to the deployed sailor.

Network Description
The hubs and remote sites are linked by dedicated FTS-2000 land lines at a

fractional T1 data rate of 384 kbps. Each hub uses a VTEL multipoint control unit (MCU) to connect sites in any desired combination simultaneously. The MCU also switches between the sites at a selectable interval for continuous monitoring by the instructor, and will automatically display a site that is speaking or asking a question, thereby creating virtual eye-to-eye contact. The CESN is interoperable with commercial and military network sites globally, via ISDN access.

Classrooms

Each classroom has a seating capacity for twenty-four students at tables installed with push-to-talk microphones. A ParkerVision student camera in front of the classroom is keyed to the student's microphone and zooms-in focusing on the student that has pushed the button, thereby opening the microphone. Once the microphone is open, all sites involved in the course or conference will automatically (in less than one second) see and hear the remote site student. Since this voice-activated site-switching feature is an automatic function of the MCU, it does not require the instructor to manually select sites.

VTT classrooms have two 40-inch monitors in front of the classroom for the students to view the instructor, graphics, or other sites. A 40-inch monitor in the back of the classroom enables the instructor to see the remote sites, and an adjacent 25-inch monitor is used to preview graphics.

Training Aids

Instructors have a wide variety of graphics equipment in the VTT classroom to enhance their training. Most instructors present graphics using PowerPoint software on the classroom computer, which is connected to a VGA-to-video converter. The instructor can illustrate on a Microfield Softboard that replaces the chalkboard and stores the created illustrations on disk. The instructor can also use a VCR, Elmo copy-stand/overhead projector, slide chain, PEN PAL electronic annotation pad, and a still-image recorder that can record up to fifty transparencies (or hardcopies) on a standard floppy disk. All the graphics components can easily be selected by touching the icons on the AMX controller touch-screen installed on the podium.

As the instructor is teaching in-house students, a ParkerVision camera in the back of the room is automatically focused on and tracks the movement of the instructor. Thus, remote site students are able to see the instructor at all times from any position in the classroom. Under the instructor camera in the back of the classroom is a 40-inch monitor automatically scrolling through (in twenty-second intervals) and showing the instructor all of the remote sites involved in the convening course. When a student asks a question, auto scroll is immediately overridden and the student is seen and heard by all sites.

Instructor Training

All instructors must complete a one-day VTT instructor training course prior to teaching on the network. The goal of this training is not to change the way the instructor teaches, but to support the instructor with the necessary technology so as to enhance instruction. The course provides the qualified military (or civilian) instructor with the basic knowledge and skills required to conduct training in a distance learning environment. The training focuses on the methodology and technology of distance learning, which differs from the standard group dynamics of a confined traditional classroom environment. The course familiarizes the instructor with the equipment in the classroom and provides skills for modifying graphics, interactive teaching, management of the classrooms, and other facilitator duties.

Course Selection Criteria

Most of the courses taught on the CESN are soft-skill lecture-based courses, such as Ammunition Administration, Operation Security, and HAZMAT Recertification, which do not require a "hands-on" lab or the manipulation of equipment. These courses most readily lend themselves to VTT and are usually one week or less in duration. Historically, short courses of one to two weeks in length that have a high demand and are well attended are the best choice for VTT. Courses, convening dates, times, and locations are advertised through a quarterly message and are published in the *Catalog of Navy Training*, available to every training officer Navy-wide. Reservations for VTT courses are processed the same way as traditional courses through the Quota Control Office at the training command.

Future Initiatives

Future plans for the CESN include the implementation of additional shore-based and shipboard classrooms and increased interoperability with other networks to share classroom resources. Projects expanding the capabilities of VTT that are currently being conducted include:

1. The implementation of interactive instructor/student computers in VTT classrooms.

2. Collaboration with universities to offer off-duty college degree/certificate programs specifically tailored for navy personnel at CESN shipboard and land-based sites.

Lessons Learned

Video Teletraining offers the opportunity to expand the horizons of military training, conveniently reaching students in or close to their workplace, without the disruption of travel away from home. The effectiveness of VTT, however, depends on a multitude of factors that can be divided into two categories:

1. Instructor Responsibilities:
   a. The instructor must be an expert on the subject matter and establish credibility with the students.
   b. The instructor must complete the VTT instructor training course.
   c. The instructor must coordinate with the site facilitator to provide course materials prior to convening the course.

2. Network Efficiency:
   a. Standard operating procedures for the daily operation of the network must be complied with by all remote sites.
   b. Scheduling and data collection must be centralized.
   c. Network use needs to be promoted through continuous marketing of its capabilities and cost-savings for distance learning and conferencing.

As the success of the CNET Electronic Schoolhouse Network has clearly demonstrated, interactive Video TeleTraining can be a powerful tool for the cost-effective dissemination of mission-critical job-related information within a large, geographically dispersed organization.

Research Summary: Educational Telecommunications and Distance Learning—The State-by-State Analysis, 1998–99

An Overview of Educational Telecommunications and Distance Learning in the United States

HezelAssociates
www.hezel.com

Introduction

As the dawn of a new century approaches, education institutions at all levels are embracing technology for administrative and instructional uses. Several years ago, a school or university with sufficient equipment and a well-developed plan for technology implementation served as a model for others to emulate. Today, it is rare to find any educational setting without a short- and long-term technology plan and at least one computer center or other technology initiative in place.

What has fueled developments in educational technology and telecommunications? A combination of state- and local-level efforts contribute to the growing presence of technology in education settings. Since the early and mid-1990s, states have devoted time and energy to create statewide telecommunications networks. Perhaps more than any other factor, these statewide networks have enabled educators to experience tremendous technological maturation. Certainly, the physical connections among K-12 schools, postsecondary institutions, and state network backbones have made diverse technology projects possible. Just as important, however, is the fact that the development of statewide telecommunications infrastructures has required that educators participate in collaborative discussions with representatives from other sectors, including state agencies, private industry, public safety, and the military. As educators take part in such broad-based deliberations, they have been able to make important contacts and embark on creative partnerships.

Simultaneous with the development of statewide infrastructures for educational technology has been a fundamental shift at the local level in the acknowledgment of technology's right and proper role in education. In the past, many teachers, faculty members, and administrators have voiced doubts about the benefits of using technology. Equipment, local networks, and other capital and operating costs were perceived as expensive bells and whistles that detracted from the "real" resources educators and students needed. Although healthy skepticism still exists today, it takes place against a larger context where technology is identified as a key aspect of a state's strategic education plan and as a critical tool to facilitate an institution's ability to reach more students.

What new directions and common concerns have emerged amidst the growth in educational telecommunications and technology? This overview section of Educational Telecommunications and Distance Learning—The State-by-State Analysis, 1998–99, focuses on the key trends in education technology planning and implementation that have taken place at K-12 and postsecondary levels.

Leadership and Governance in Telecommunications Development

This report was initially prepared in 1987 to examine the leadership, collaboration, governance, and coordination of telecommunications at the state level. Underlying the first report was the hypothesis that the better the coordination taking place, the more likely the development of useful telecommunications infrastructures for education. Again and again, this hypothesis has been supported: better planning, coordination, and management lead to better, longer-lasting educational technology-based solutions.

Why has Hezel Associates taken the state level as the unit of analysis? Statewide telecommunications planning and development have been at the heart of this and prior reports for several sound reasons. First, most network development takes place in and is coordinated by state agencies. Second, education generally operates within state boundaries and is subject to state agencies. Educational technology and telecommunications efforts tend to serve the mission and needs of state agencies and the institutions they represent. Third, educational technology projects that have exerted the most impact typically are observed at the state level. Fourth, investment in the development of telecommunications infrastructure is a state-subsidized concern, not a federal government matter. Finally, states have become major supporters of the use of technology and telecommunications in schools.

Based on data from its 1987 report, one of Hezel Associates's first observations was that leadership from state governors was critical to the development of telecommunications infrastructures for state agencies and education. This assertion is no less true today. Most governors have recognized the inherent link between telecommunications and information technology and a state's competitiveness and economic well-being. The thriving educational technology initiatives in state, including North Carolina and New Jersey, can be attributed in a large part to strong gubernatorial leadership. Today, only a few governors have failed to prioritize telecommunications development.

Legislative support travels hand-in-hand with the development of educational technology and telecommunications, as Hezel Associates' series of reports have documented. In 1987, when Hezel Associates began tracking funding and policy leadership, only a few states, such as Indiana, Virginia, California and North Dakota, offered information technology initiatives for education. Today, California continues to set the pace for legislative support, and Texas offers another fine example of the tremendous difference exerted by the policies identified and funding provided by state legislatures. Without exception, state legislatures across the country have deliberated technology-related issues, ranging from the definition of distance education to strategic planning for information technology.

To aid governors and state legislatures in assembling resources for educators, a variety of state agencies have assumed the responsibility for coordinating statewide technology planning and implementation. Over the past two years, states including Utah and Wyoming have created the new position of chief information officer (CIO) to oversee technology planning. In general, CIO positions exist in states where information technology boards and commissions take the lead in supervising the planning and design of information systems. Alternatively, states such as Louisiana and Georgia have charged the administrative division of telecommunications departments with facilitating statewide technology planning. These organizations usually assist in the collaborative planning and, development of high-speed, high-bandwidth digital networks for intrastate and interstate communication. In several states, including South Dakota, information technology and telecommunications planning occur under the guidance of a single state agency. On occasion, despite the presence of state agencies invested with the responsibility of statewide information technology planning, a dominant university system has established its own network independent from the coordinating authority.

To summarize, statewide educational technology initiatives thrive or flounder for very real reasons. A state's educational technology planning usually takes place against the larger framework for statewide telecommunications and technology. When educational technology initiatives succeed, it is usually because governors and state legislatures have provided the leadership and resources necessary to foster growth, while centralized planning agencies have created a system for the overall coordination of efforts. The converse is also true: when statewide educational technology initiatives fail, it is often because no one entity, agency, or office (the governor, office of information technology, department of administrative services, etc.) has identified technology and telecommunications as a priority issue for the state. Without a supportive environment, even the most well-conceived educational technology projects have to struggle.

Changing Models of Coordination

With great interest, Hezel Associates has followed trends in the statewide coordination of planning for educational technology and telecommunications. When Hezel Associates began its study of statewide coordination in 1987, the delineators were readily evident: it was easy to detect which states "had" or "did not have" statewide planning efforts underway. Moreover, characterizing from which direction planning originated, either from the "top down" or the "bottom up," was also relatively simple.

Today, however, these distinctions are less clear and not as useful. To some degree, all states today house "statewide" planning efforts which center around educational technology and telecommunications. In a few cases, such as Iowa and Utah, specific agencies have been charged with developing statewide educational applications. But "statewide" initiatives may also emerge as the sum of planning efforts stemming from a number of locales—within a university system, among all the regional educational agencies, or in all school districts. Further, the "top down" versus "bottom up" distinction has limited meaning in places where a dual approach is under way. States like Maine and Pennsylvania, for example, are among those that have worked diligently to combine state oversight with local control.

Today, a more accurate representation of statewide planning for educational technology and telecommunications is as a continuum, which ranges from "tightly organized" to "highly decentralized." This model acknowledges that even the most underfunded state that lacks critical personnel is nonetheless engaged in planning. Moreover, it reflects the fact that the combined efforts of grassroots organizations and state level leadership can lead to a supportive environment for educational technology and telecommunications.

Technology as a Tool

The use of technology in education settings, especially in K-12 schools, has typically involved limited interpretations. Technology has been portrayed as an end unto itself, as evident in the scrupulous attention paid to statistics such as computer-to-student ratios and percentage of schools connected to the Internet. Discussions of "technology in schools" have usually focused on purely instructional applications. Into the late 1990s, however, increased emphasis has been directed at technology's other roles in education settings. More and more, technology is being characterized as a tool to assist educators in three important ways: as a means to redress inequities, to support statewide subject-area standards, and as a way to facilitate administration and disseminate public information.

Technology was first seen as a means to address educational inequities in 1990, when Kentucky recognized that technology could be used to deliver quality education to all children in the state. Kentucky's efforts to integrate technology into its education reform efforts led to the inception of a fine statewide system for educational technology and telecommunications. A more recent spate of equity-related lawsuits and judgments facing K-12 education systems throughout the country also point to technology's preeminence in assisting reform. States, including Illinois and Wyoming, have determined that the funding mechanisms for K-12 education are unconstitutional and lead to inequitable access to technologies across school districts, exacerbating the gap between technology "have" and "have nots." In response, states have developed long-range technology plans and grants targeting the needs of poor school districts. For many states, access to technology has become synonymous with access to greater educational opportunities for traditionally disenfranchised students.

Technology now appears as a tool in state standards initiatives. Today, it is the rare state that has not articulated standards of learning in content areas such as math, science, and history. In states like Virginia, there are specific technology standards that students must master in order to graduate. In other states, technology per se is not a content area for students to learn, but rather is used to facilitate student learning in the content areas. Students are not the only educational audience that must concern themselves with technology knowledge. States such as Idaho and North Dakota have identified a number of technology competencies teachers must display as part of certification and recertification. It appears, then, that states are becoming more concerned with establishing minimum requirements to prepare both students and teachers to interact in today's technological settings.

Many states have prioritized administrative applications for technology. Two broad patterns of administrative use can be detected. First, technology helps schools, school districts, state agencies, and institutions of higher education in states like Ohio share information more easily. Electronic student records, financial information, and test results lead to streamlined and cost-efficient communication. Second, the schoolwide data collection can be shared with parents and other concerned citizens as a means to assess school performance. States including Delaware and Michigan have invested in developing databases that enable statewide comparisons of schools and school districts. Technology in this situation exists as a means to support school accountability.

The Integration of Technology in Education

More than ever before, good planning is leading to a true integration of technology in learning; technology is not just an add-on to education. Not only can this phenomenon be observed in state plans tying technology to curriculum and standards, but also in colleges' and universities' plans for technology. Many postsecondary institutions have reorganized their electronic resources under an information office, which combines academic and administrative computing, network services, and media services. At the same time, those universities are developing distance learning offices that coordinate all distance learning efforts of the university and market the programs.

Most important in the reorganization is the recognition that the programmatic development remains with the faculty, wherever they might be located, and that technology serves learners wherever they might be located—whether in the classroom with the teacher, in the dorm rooms on campus, at home or work in the local community, on another campus, or anywhere in the United States of America or in the world. As a result, *distance learning* is becoming more difficult to distinguish from *technology-based learning*.

Growing Federal Influence

In the past, the federal government has maintained a relatively low profile in encouraging the development of educational technology and telecommunications. Over the past three years, however, its influence on statewide initiatives has become more tangible, especially within K-12 settings. The incentive for schools and institutions to attend to federal technology and telecommunications directives can be summarized in one word: funding.

The most revolutionary system for funding school technology, especially telecommunications, has come in the form of the E-rate. The E-rate permits schools and libraries to obtain discounts on telecommunications services and some equipment, and the level of the discount for any school or consortium depends on the poverty or affluence of the district, as measured by the percentage of aidable students. A special provision of the Telecommunications Act of 1996, the E-rate stems from the Federal Communications Commission's long-standing universal service rules, which have provided a fund to support telecommunications services at reasonable rates for senior citizens and rural residents. Although there have been challenges to the E-rate, notably by SBC (formerly Southwestern Bell), and although the management of the application process has experienced first-time glitches, it appears that the nearly $2 billion fund is ready for disbursement to states, consortia, and individual schools.

The E-rate will have produced other salutary effects on school technology development in addition to the windfall funding for educational telecommunications. In their applications for the E-rate, schools are required to demonstrate their technology plans, and for the first time many schools, districts, and even states have developed strategies and committed them to writing.

Several initiatives of the U.S. Department of Education have stimulated the perfusion of technology in schools. Goals 2000 funding is designed, in part, to enable the integration of technology into the establishment and attainment of content standards. Technology Literacy Challenge Fund (TLCF) grants have enabled states to create their own coordinated technology plans and to oversee the development of school district and school technology plans. Requiring schools to have their own technology plans in place in order to qualify for sub-grants can be tricky, however. Schools that have the least resources are the ones least likely to be able to devote time and effort to putting together a technology plan. Some states have addressed this by making technology planning funds available to schools in poor school districts. Professional development and Internet access are the most widely supported applications of TLCF grants.

The U.S. Department of Education also funds the Star Schools program. Now ten years old, the Star Schools program has supported the development of educational programs in math, science, and foreign language for delivery via telecommunications, initially satellite and later fiber optics. In the 1997 funding, however, the Star Schools program funded the development of instructional resources to be delivered by the Internet and CD-ROM.

At the higher-education level, one of the most crucial funding mechanisms comes through the Higher Education Reauthorization Act, through which funds are allocated for subsidized student loans and grants. Congress continues to withhold full support for college students who obtain courses and degrees via distance education.

The Web and Distance Education

Without doubt, over the last three years, the availability of the World Wide Web has fundamentally changed thinking about distance learning. The Internet has not only offered a new technology of distribution, it has also changed the potential market, content, and even the pedagogical framework for the delivery of instruction. The issue on the collective planning agendas of postsecondary institutions is the use of the Internet and World Wide Web to reach more students. In community college systems, private colleges and universities, and state university settings, administrators and faculty members are working to integrate the Internet into their distance education efforts. Almost all institutions of higher education are using the Internet and World Wide Web as a means to supplement campus-based instruction to some extent. In many cases, faculty members have developed modules or courses that rely entirely on the Internet. A still more limited number of institutions have offered entire degree programs through the Internet.

"Virtual universities" epitomize the potential of the Internet for higher education. An institutionalized means of bringing instruction to learners at anytime and anyplace, virtual universities have changed the face of higher-education marketing. In an attempt to keep up with the competition, many universities have put courses on the Web. Many others are developing full-scale virtual universities, which are simply outreach or distance learning divisions of the university.

In a few states, like California, Kentucky, Pennsylvania, and Texas, statewide virtual universities are emerging. California is noteworthy, not only because the state snubbed its neighbor states by not joining the Western Governors University, but also because the California Virtual University offers courses from the University of California, California State University, and the California Community Colleges. On the other coast, in New York the SUNY Learning Network, whose administrators avoid the term virtual, has grown to thirty-seven campuses and 6,000 students participating annually in just three years.

On the broadest level, regional virtual universities like the Western Governors University (WGU) have made a significant impact on higher education. The goal of the WGU is to meet the needs for easy access to affordable, practical education in the fields of study that are in demand. The WGU offers distance learning courses from dozens of universities and corporations to the learners, wherever they are located. These courses use technology from the Internet, to satellite, to the postal service to provide different options for receiving an affordable education.

The WGU's impact has been palpable: the early marketing attempts reveal an eager potential student body of learners who have the interest in programs that are currently not available in their region—learners who are not available to travel to, and live in, the far-away city where the program is offered. The effect of the WGU is also observable at traditional colleges: administrators at smaller colleges are expressing deep concern about their institutions' longevity in the face of an institution such as the WGU. In response, those colleges are beginning, as never before, to review their strengths, weaknesses, and opportunities, and to develop and refine the niches for their colleges.

The Southern Regional Electronic Campus (SREC), a service of the Southern Regional Education Board, has expanded its "commonwealth" to all fifteen states in its service area, which comprises the southeastern states. The SREC is a marketplace for courses and programs offered by colleges and universities through electronic methods. Unlike the WGU, the SREC has not established a new accredited college, but offers an opportunity for students to take courses electronically and transfer the credits to any participating institution.

All of the "virtual" institutions face common challenges in serving their student clientele: market research, faculty training, and student services. Market research becomes a more pressing need as the institutions attempt to offer services that extend well beyond community or state boundaries for delivery via the Internet. If courses are to be offered via distance learning, faculty need to be trained in the use of technology for course design and management. Some universities are training hundreds of faculty each semester. Along with course material, online students need resources that are typically available to on-campus learners, such as advising, financial aid, and especially library services.

The availability of the Internet has changed K-12 school priorities. Much of the enthusiasm for distance learning, particularly interactive video, in the early 1990s temporarily evaporated with the overwhelming focus on "getting the Internet" into the schools. A large proportion of technology spending in schools has supported links to the Internet, in-school wiring, and computers to access the Internet in each classroom. Purchasing content for the schools is a second priority, and staff training is a third, but growing, priority. It is expected that interest in distance learning will return after schools have completed their Internet connections, both internally and externally.

In the next few years, the focus on technology building will be overtaken by a focus on the development and acquisition of content. Already there is evidence of content publishers making substantial investments in the development of nonprint materials to be delivered on the Internet and on CD-ROM, in more than just an extension of printed textbooks. Indeed, some corporations envision themselves as partners with accredited postsecondary institutions that will offer the software as the course, much as PBS for years has offered telecourses in league with community colleges in the United States.

The Nationalization and Internationalization of Distance Learning

Distance learning can't be stopped at borders—state or national. State higher education commissions that place geographic boundaries on colleges in-state actually impede the potential of those in-state colleges to compete with out-of state providers. States like Maryland and California are struggling with geographical restrictions on community colleges and state universities at a time when the University of Phoenix and Stanford University have no such restrictions.

Whereas public institutions have been established to serve their community or state constituencies, like private colleges, they now envision new revenues, and even profitability, in delivering their specialized programs out-of-state or out-of-country. The last two years have seen a gaggle of higher-education administrators flying in all directions to establish foreign offices, especially in Asia, at least prior to the 1998 slump there. Unarguably, the United States, with the most extensive, most widely available higher-education system in the world, is a target destination for students in many foreign nations. U.S. institutions are seeking to make that education system available at sites around the world. Just as the Internet has made education available across state lines, it will permit colleges to serve the international market.

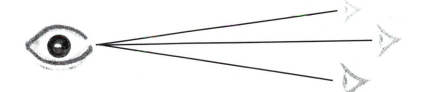

Appendix B: General Resources—Associations, Publications, Research Studies, and Other Information Sources

Here is a list of noncommercial organizations, books and periodicals, research studies, and Web sites that provide information for the successful deployment of videoconferencing systems.

Associations

Most of the following organizations provide a variety of conferencing and visual communications-related services, including publications, conferences, technical data, employment resources, and online communities. Their Web sites, in particular, can be very informative and helpful.

Association for Computing Machinery (ACM)
One Astor Plaza
1515 Broadway
New York, NY 10036-5701
(212) 869-7440
www.acm.org
The world's oldest educational and scientific computing society, with over 80,000 members in dozens of major special interest groups—including ACM SIGGRAPH (computer graphics and interactive techniques), the premiere forum for computer, video, and interactive graphics; and ACM SIGCOMM (data communications and computer networks).

Association for Applied Interactive Multimedia (AAIM)
P.O. Box 1635
Goose Creek, SC 29445-1635
www.aaim.org

Supports professionals who use and develop interactive multimedia for education training, commerce, and information. Workshops, conferences, and a useful Web site for practicing multimedia professionals, educators, trainers, and those interested in the professional use of multimedia.

Association of Telehealth Service Providers (ATSP)
4702 S.W. Scholls Ferry Road, Suite 400
Portland, OR 97225-2008
(800) 852-3591 or (503) 222-2406
Fax: (503) 223-7581
www.atsp.org
An international membership-based organization dedicated to improving health care through growth of the telehealth industry. It strengthens its members and the business of telehealth through advocacy, education awareness programs, and business support services.

The ATM Forum
Worldwide Headquarters
2570 W. El Camino Real, Suite 304
Mountain View, CA 94040-1313
www.atmforum.com
An international nonprofit organization with the objective of accelerating the use of asynchronous transfer mode (ATM) products and services through a rapid convergence of interoperability specifications. The ATM Forum Web site is a good source for technical and application information. ATM Forum "Ambassadors" are available to deliver presentations to groups regarding the Forum and ATM technology.

Audio Engineering Society (AES)
60 E. 42nd Street, Room 2520
New York, NY 10165-2520
(212) 661-8528
www.aes.org
A professional society devoted exclusively to audio technology with a membership of engineers, scientists, and other authorities. It has authoritative and interesting publications including the *Journal of the Audio Engineering Society*, and AES conferences offer the most interesting and exciting displays of audio technology.

Communications Managers Association (CMA)

1201 Mt. Kemble Avenue
Morristown, NJ 07960-6628
(800) 867-8008
www.cma.org
The association's membership includes telecom/IT professionals from two hundred of America's largest corporations. The CMA's annual conference and exposition, Corporate Networks (formerly CMA Telcom), is held at Hilton New York and Towers. It provides a good opportunity to learn more about the latest developments in telecommunications and offers telecom/IT professionals valuable networking opportunities.

Educause

1150 18th Street NW, Suite 1010
Washington, D.C. 20036
(202) 872-4200
www.educause.edu
Two major educational groups, CAUSE and Educom, have combined to create a new consolidated association "at the intersection of higher education and information technology." EDUCAUSE's mission is to "help shape and enable transformational change in higher education through the introduction, use, and management of information resources and technologies in teaching, learning, scholarship, research, and institutional management." Currently, membership includes more than 1,700 colleges and other educational organizations, more than 150 corporations, and is open to institutions of higher education, corporations serving the higher education technology market, and related associations and organizations. EDUCAUSE programs include excellent electronic and print publications, professional development activities, and a wealth of online information services.

Electronic Frontier Foundation (EFF)

1550 Bryant Street, Suite 725
San Francisco CA 94103
(415) 436-9333
www.eff.org
The EFF is a nonprofit, nonpartisan organization working in the public interest to protect fundamental civil liberties, including privacy and freedom of expression in the arena of computers and the Internet. The EFF has a highly informative Web site, and the organization's lawyers have played a key role in several landmark legal battles. The EFF was founded in 1990 and is based in San Francisco, California, with a satellite office in Washington, D.C.

International Communications Industries Association (ICIA)
11242 Waples Mill Road, Suite 200
Fairfax, VA 22030
(703) 273-7200
Fax: (703) 278-8082
www.icia.org
The ICIA is the primary organization for manufacturers, integrators, and other providers of video and audio communications equipment and services. The ICIA conducts extensive training and certification programs for technicians, system designers, salespeople, and consultants, and sponsors some of the largest and best trade shows in the field. Its INFOCOMM conferences provide the best environment for the investigation of new and competitive A/V technologies.

The Institute of Electrical and Electronics Engineers, Inc. (IEEE)
IEEE Communications Society (ComSoc)
305 E. 47th Street
New York, NY 10017
(212) 705-8900
www.comsoc.org
The "eye-triple-E" promotes the engineering process of creating, developing, integrating, sharing, and applying knowledge about electrical and information technologies and sciences for the benefit of humanity and the profession. IEEE's Communications Society, ComSoc is a diverse group of industry professionals interested in advancing all communications technologies by sponsors publications, conferences, educational programs, local activities, and technical committees.

International Multimedia Teleconferencing Consortium (IMTC)
Bishop Ranch 2
2694 Bishop Drive, Suite 105
San Ramon, CA 94583
(510) 277-8110
www.imtc.org
The IMTC is involved in the development and testing of IP and switched network multimedia interoperability specifications including: T.120, H.320, H.323, H.324, and Voice-over-IP products and services. Over the years, the IMTC has hosted more than forty interoperability testing events. Its 150-plus member organizations include vendors of audio, document, and VTC hardware and software; service providers; end users; academic institutions; government agencies; and nonprofit organizations. The IMTC's Web site is a good source of information on standards and the standardization process, from a practical business and technical point of view.

International Organization for Standardization (ISO)

ISO Central Secretariat
1, rue de Varembé, Case postale 56
CH-1211 Geneva 20
Switzerland
(+41) (22) 749-0111
www.iso.ch

A worldwide federation of national standards bodies from some 130 countries, involved in the establishment of international standards for everything from paper sizes to quality management, and film speed to video communications practices. ISO collaborates with the International Telecommunications Union (ITU) on standardization in the fields of information technology and telecommunications. Its mission is to promote the development of worldwide standardization to facilitate the international exchange of goods and services, and to foster cooperation in the spheres of intellectual, scientific, technological, and economic activity.

The International Telecommunications Union (ITU)

Place des Nations
CH-1211 Geneva 20
Switzerland
(+41) (22) 730-5852
www.itu.int/ITU-T

Headquartered in Geneva, Switzerland, the ITU is an international organization designated by the United Nations to coordinate global telecom networks and services. The International Telecommunications Union Standards Sector (ITU-T) studies technical, operating, and tariff questions, and adopts recommendations on them with a view to standardizing telecommunications on a worldwide basis. Recommendations and standards include the H Series (H.323, H.320, etc.) that pertain to audiovisual and multimedia systems such as videoconferencing equipment. The ITU-T Web site is the authoritative source for information and publications relating to these standards and proposed standards. The ITU-T also publishes the standards and recommendations, as well as guidebooks and other support materials.

The International Telework Association and Council (ITAC)

204 E Street NE
Washington, D.C. 20002
(202) 547-6157
Fax: (202) 546-3289 or (202) 547-6348
www.telecommute.org

The ITAC is a nonprofit organization dedicated to promoting the economic, social, and environmental benefits of telework. Members share information and research about the design and implementation of telework and telecommuting programs, and the development of the worldwide telework sector. The organization's Web site offers good resources to support the planning and formation of a telework or telecommuting program.

The Institute for Telecommunication Sciences (ITS)
325 Broadway
Boulder, CO 80305-3328
(303) 497-5216
www.its.bldrdoc.gov
The ITS is the chief research and engineering arm of the National Telecommunications and Information Administration (NTIA). The ITS supports such NTIA objectives as promotion of advanced telecommunications and information infrastructure development in the United States, and enhancement of domestic competitiveness. The ITS also serves as a principal federal resource for solving the telecommunications concerns of other federal agencies, state and local governments, private corporations and associations, and international organizations. Cooperative research agreements based upon the Federal Technology Transfer Act of 1986 are the principal means of aiding the private sector. This act provides the legal basis for and encourages shared use of government facilities and resources with the private sector in advanced telecommunications technologies. These partnerships aid in the commercialization of new products and services.

The Internet Society (ISOC)
11150 Sunset Hills Road, Suite 100
Reston, VA 20190-5321
(800) 468 9507
www.isoc.org
The ISOC is a professional society with more than 150 organizational and 6,000 individual members in over one hundred countries. It addresses issues involving the future of the Internet and is the organization home for the groups responsible for Internet infrastructure standards, including the Internet Engineering Task Force (IETF) and the Internet Architecture Board (IAB).

The Internet Engineering Task Force (IETF)
www.ietf.cnri.reston.va.us
The IETF is a large, open, international community of network designers, operators, vendors, and researchers concerned with the evolution of the Internet architecture and the smooth operation of the Internet. It is the principal body

engaged in the development of new Internet-standard specifications. The IETF is not a membership organization (no cards, no dues, no secret handshakes), and participation is open to any interested individuals. The IETF "Working Group" are the folks who actually deal with the hard-core issues relating to the state of the Internet and develop the solutions that will determine the Internet's future.

The MultiMedia Communications Forum (MMCF)

(301) 540-2600

www.mmcf.org

The MMCF is a nonprofit research and development organization of telecommunications service providers, endusers, multimedia application and equipment developers that is focused on QoS related issues. Forum members are dedicated to accelerating the market acceptance of multivendor, multimedia solutions that can interoperate easily across different types of networks. The MMCF Web site has some interesting white papers and other technical information not readily available elsewhere.

The MultiMedia Telecommunications Association (MMTA)

2500 Wilson Boulevard, Suite 300

Arlington, VA 22201-3834

(703) 907-7478

www.mmta.org

A subsidiary of the Telecommunications Industry Association, the MMTA focuses on the convergence of communications and computing business applications. The MMTA strives to "ensure a high level of competency and creativity in the delivery of new technology-based solutions to the business community" through communication, research, education, and professional certification programs. Its membership is comprised of over two hundred vendor and user organizations.

National Association of Broadcasters (NAB)

1771 N Street NW

Washington, D.C. 20036

(202) 429-5343

www.nab.org

The NAB is a full-service trade association that promotes and protects the interests of radio and television broadcasters in around the world. The NAB's annual convention includes the largest exhibition of tools for the creation and transmission of video and multimedia content.

Society of Motion Picture and Television Engineers (SMPTE)
595 W. Hartsdale Avenue
White Plains, NY 10607-1824
(914) 761-1100
www.smpte.org
The SMPTE is the premiere technical society for the motion picture and television industries. Membership consists of 10,000 members and 250 sustaining (corporate) members worldwide. The organization is devoted to advancing theory and application in motion imaging, including film, television, video, computer imaging, and telecommunications. Several industries rely on SMPTE to generate standards, engineering guidelines, and recommended practices to be followed by respective field professionals.

The Society of Telecommunications Consultants (STC)
13766 Center Street, Suite 212
Carmel Valley, CA 93924
(800) 782-7670
www.stcconsultants.org
The STC is an international organization of voice and data communications professionals who serve clients in business, industry, service organizations, and government. STC members adhere to strict professional standards and a rigorous code of ethics.

Telemedicine Research Center (TRC)
2121 S.W. Broadway, Suite 130
Portland, OR 97201
(503) 221-1620
http://trc.telemed.org
The TRC is a nonprofit public service research organization that promotes telemedicine research and creates, manages, and disseminates information about telemedicine-related issues. Major TRC resources include the Telemedicine Information Exchange (http://tie.telemed.org), a major source of information on all aspects of telemedicine and links to other resources.

The Telecommunications Industry Association (TIA)
2500 Wilson Boulevard, Suite 300
Arlington, VA 22201
(703) 907-7700
www.tiaonline.org
The TIA is a major national trade organization with membership of more than one thousand companies that provide communications and information technology

products, systems, distribution services, and professional services. It is active in standards development and domestic and international advocacy, as well as market development and trade promotion programs. The TIA sponsors SUPER-COMM, one of the world's biggest annual communications and information technology industry events. The TIA's Web site offers online access to a large amount of useful information, including telecommunications market data, standards information, a discussion forum, an events calendar, and links to related Web sites.

United States Distance Learning Association (USDLA)

140 Gould Street
Needham, MA 02494-2397
(800) 275-5162
www.usdla.org
The association's purpose is to promote the development and application of distance learning for education and training. The USDLA has become a leading source of information and recommendations for those entering the development of distance learning programs. Activities include research, conferences, and advocacy.

Women in Cable and Telecommunications (WICT)

230 W. Monroe, Suite 2630
Chicago, Illinois 60606
(312) 634-2330
www.wict.org
Founded July 1979, the organization's mission is educating and empowering women in telecommunications and related fields to achieve their professional goals by providing opportunities for leadership, networking, and advocacy. The WICT's vision is an environment at work, home, and in our society where women are valued for their contributions, absent of inequities in opportunities and recognition.

Publications

Books

Videoconferencing and Videotelephony: Technology and Standards (Second Edition)

By Richard Schaphorst
Published 1999 by Artech House, Boston
A comprehensive, understandable, and interesting book that includes everything you might need to know about the technical side of videoconferencing.

Guide to Teleconferencing and Distance Learning (Third Edition)
By Patrick S. Portway and Dr. Carla Lane
Published 2000 by Advanstar
A useful compendium of information and advice regarding distance learning and other aspects of teleconferencing.

Personal Videoconferencing
By Evan Rosen
A comprehensive and informative look at desktop videoconferencing and related applications. Includes a discussion of implementation strategies and issues, and a good description of the technologies available at the time the book was last revised.

Mainstream Videoconferencing: A Developer's Guide to Distance Multimedia
By Joe Duran, Charlie Sauer (Contributor)
Published 1997 by Addison-Wesley

A Telemedicine Primer: Understanding the Issues
By Jim Reid, PA-C
Published 1996 by Innovative Medical Communications
E-mail: reidjim@aol.com
An excellent book with lots of practical information for administrators, health care providers, and others (technical or nontechnical) who has an interest in telemedicine.

Videoconferencing: The Whole Picture
By Toby Trowt-Bayard
Published 1997 by Miller Freeman Books

Effective Videoconferencing: Techniques for Better Business Meetings
By Lynn Diamond, Kay Keppler (Editor), Stephanie Roberts (Contributor)
Published 1996 by Crisp Publications

Periodicals

Business Communications Review Magazine
BCR Enterprises, Inc.
999 Oakmont Plaza Drive, Suite 100
Westmont, IL 60559-5512
(800) 227-1234
www.bcr.com

This magazine is directed at enterprise network managers and other communications professionals. Published since 1971, the magazine has maintained a good reputation for objectivity, thoroughness, and accuracy. BCR Enterprises, Inc., also runs several conferences, including MultiMediaCom; conducts extensive training sessions and seminars; and publishes other periodicals on various aspects of telecomunications and related technologies.

Communications News Magazine

Nelson Publishing, Inc.
2500 Tamiami Trail N.
Nokomis, FL 34275
(941) 966-9521
www.comnews.com
A monthly magazine for communications and network managers. Features case histories on the successful implementation of emerging technologies. Informative Web site.

ED

United States Distance Learning Association
3345 Pahappa Hill
Riverside, CA 92606
(909) 369-4059
www.usdla.org/ED_magazine/illuminactive
This magazine and journal is the official publication of the United States Distance Learning Association (USDLA). Electronically published monthly, *ED* covers the latest developments in the field of distance learning with thoughtful articles.

Network World

118 Turnpike Road
Southborough, MA 01772-9108
(800) 622-1108
www.nwfusion.com
Network World is a good technical and business magazine for network managers and general managers responsible for network-related decisions. The magazine also maintains a very useful and comprehensive Web site.

Telespan

(626) 797-5482
www.telespan.com
An informative bulletin on teleconferencing technology, business, applications,

and trends. Covers developments in videoconferencing, collaborative computing, audioconferencing, and related areas. Published for eighteen years by industry insider (and scoutmaster) Elliot Gold, who also maintains a very interesting and entertaining Web site. Bulletin subscriptions are a bargain at $377 per year for forty issues.

Teleconference Magazine
201 Sandpointe Avenue, Suite 600
Santa Ana, CA 92707
(714) 513-8400
www.teleconferencemag.com
Published six times a year by Advanstar, Teleconference covers the applications, technology, and business of audio, video, and dataconferencing. Includes good articles by users, consultants, and manufacturers.

T.H.E. Journal
17501 E. 17th Street, Suite 230
Tustin, CA 92780
(714) 730-4011
www.thejournal.com/magazine
T.H.E. Journal contains articles from educators involved in integrating technology on their campuses and into their curricula and administration. The magazine also contains product reviews and other useful information. A companion Web site is even better. T.H.E. also offers online instruction for educators and an annual market research study.

Research Studies

The following organizations conduct research studies. Several post summaries of the studies on their Web sites.

The Association of Telehealth Service Providers (ATSP)
(800) 852-3591; (503) 222-2406
www.atsp.org
The ATSP is a reliable source for accurate, well analyzed data on Telemedicine and Telehealth issues. They recently issued *The 1999 ATSP Report on Telemedicine in the United States*.
Price: $300

Forward Concepts

(480) 968-3759

www.forwardconcepts.com

A leading research firm in VTC and networking areas. Their latest report is *Set-Top and PC-Centric Group Videoconferencing—The Enterprise Systems Goldrush.*

Forward Concepts, Report No. 911

Price: $1,795

Frost and Sullivan

(408) 392-2000

www.frost.com

This major research firm publishes a number of useful studies in this area, including *Video Streaming—Impact on Video Conferencing (U.S.)*

Frost & Sullivan, Code: 2044-64, Pub. 04/19/2000

Price: $2,950.

Another interesting report is *U.S. Distance Learning System and Service Markets Proliferation of Data Networks Changes Distance Learning Landscape.*

Frost & Sullivan, Code: 2103-64; Pub. 01/03/2000, 238 pages

Price: $3,450

Hezel Associates

(800) 466-3512

www.hezel.com

Dr. Richard Hezel has conducted research and consulted in the areas of distance learning and telemedicine for thirty years. Hezel Associates publishes reliable research studies and an informative online newsletter. The firm also offers "Business Model for Developing Distance Learning in Higher Education," a spreadsheet tool for cost-benefit analyses in developing distance learning programs. Their latest report is *Educational Telecommunications and Distance Learning: The State-by-State Analysis.*

Price: $97.50

Wainhouse Research

617-975-0297

www.wainhouse.com

The firm's flagship product is a multivolume market research report, *Teleconferencing Markets and Strategies*, which provides key insights on the videoconferencing, visual collaboration, and multimedia communications industries. The Wainhouse Web site contains several important white papers and other useful information. The firm also publishes a free, weekly news update, *The Wainhouse Research Bulletin*.

Other Information Sources

FAQs and White Papers

"H.320 Overview" from the International Multimedia Teleconferencing Consortium
http://www.imtc.org/h320.htm

"H.323 Info and Explanations" from RadVision
http://207.201.151.179/info/standard.html

"H Series Recommendation," the official ITU information page
http://www.itu.int/itudoc/itu-t/rec/h/

"MPEG FAQ," by Frank Gadegast
http://ftp.sunet.se/mpeg1/mpegfaq/

"Higher Level Protocols Used with IP Multicast: An IP Multicast Initiative White Paper"
http://www.ipmulticast.com/community/whitepapers/highprot.html

Portals

www.videoconferencing.com
A well-organized portal and service for information about videoconferencing.

www.getcommstuff.com
Tons of useful information on telecommunications (e.g., 520 white papers) and links to other useful Web sites.

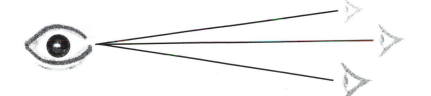

Appendix C: Commercial Resources—Service Providers, Manufacturers, Consultants, and Integrators

Here is a list of commercial organizations that could be helpful to anyone involved in the deployment of videoconferencing systems. The absence of an organization from this appendix should not be construed to have any negative meaning—chances are I just don't have any current information about their activities, or I forgot to put them on the list. Likewise, the presence of any organization in this listing does not imply an endorsement on my part, unless I have referred to them using terms such as "great," "first rate," or "spiffy."

Service Providers

Videoconferencing Service Providers

Most of the following organizations provide a variety of conferencing-related services, including multipoint bridging and the booking of public VTC rooms.

ACT Teleconferencing
Audioconferencing, videoconferencing, dataconferencing, and Internet conferencing products and services.
(800) 228-3719
(303) 233-3500
www.acttel.com

AT&T Teleconference Services
(888) 950-8433
(973) 564-2213
www.att.com/videoconferencing

Evoke Communications
Web conferencing and Webcasting
(800) 878-7326
www.evoke.com

Global Crossing Conferencing
A major provider of video, audio, and Web conferencing services.
Formerly known as Frontier Videoconferencing and Frontier ConferTech.
(800) 252-5150
www.themeetingson.com

Intellispace
Innovative provider of wide area Ethernet services, Internet access, and video-conferencing systems.
(212) 536-7900
www.intellispace.net

InView Videoconferencing
Major provider of global multipoint videoconferencing bridging with centers in the United Kingdom and the United States. Offers end-user training seminars.
(800) 603-9402
www.inview.net

PlaceWare, Inc.
Provides Web conferencing and distance learning services.
(650) 526-6168
www.placeware.com

Sprint
Offers a broad selection of conferencing services and products.
(972) 405-5000
www.sprint.com/icc

V-SPAN
Major provider of gateway services, multipoint bridging, videoconferencing, Web conferencing, and managed events.
(888) 44V-SPAN; (610) 382-1000
www.vspan.com

WebEx Inc.
Advanced Web conferencing services.
(408) 435-7221
www.webex.com

Public Room Videoconferencing Services

Most of the service providers listed above can also arrange for rooms in distant locations.

Affinity VideoNet
Provides access to affiliated VTC rooms around the world.
(800) 370-7150
www.affinityvnet.com

Aloha Conferencing
Rooms and other services in Hawaii.
(800) 316-4548
www.alohaconferencing.com

CMA Centre
Public VTC rooms in Australia and New Zealand.
(61) (411) 336-384
www.cma@ozonline.com.au

Connexus, Inc.
Public VTC room and training facility in Dallas, Texas.
(800) 938-8888
www.connexus-evn.com

MIVNET
Consortium of nonprofit VTC rooms around the world.
(800) 4-MIVNET
www.mivnet.com

Proximity, Inc.
Provides access to more than 2,000 rooms, worldwide.
(800) 433-2900
www.proximity.com

Manufacturers

System and Codec Manufacturers

Many system manufacturers also manufacture or sell cameras, video monitors, audio systems, and other peripherals.

Aethra Inc.
Full line of well-designed videoconferencing systems and codecs.
(305) 375-0010
www.aethrausa.com

AG Communications
MPEG-2 systems for distance learning and other applications.
(888) 768-7480

Array Microsystem
H.323 codec card for use with MS NetMeeting and similar products.
(800) 741-4461
www.array.com

Cabletime
Manufactures Media Star systems for video distribution and videoconferencing over Cat 5 cabling.
(44) (16) 353-5111
www.cabletime.com

CUseeMe Networks
Popular software-based system for videoconferencing on the World Wide Web.
(603) 886-9050
www.cuseeme.com

General DataComm Inc.
Manufactures MPEG-2 codecs, concentrators, and related equipment for VTC use.
(800) 794-8246
www.gdc.com

Litton Network Access Systems
MPEG-2 video products, including CAMVision-2 codec, which delivers a high-resolution image at bandwidth rates from 2 to 15 Mbps and interfaces with both

IP and ATM networks, and the Video Node package—a turnkey video cart that can create a videoconference in any location with a network connection.
(800) 537-6801
www.netaccsys.com

Lucent Technologies

Designs, builds, and delivers a wide range of networks, communication systems, software, telephone systems, and microelectronics components including MCUs, IMUXs, and turnkey desktop and group video systems.
(908) 582-8500
www.lucent.com

Minerva Communications

MPEG-2 video solutions including carrier-class video networking and management products for delivery of video services over broadband Internet protocol (IP) networks. Minerva also offers services to facilitate the deployment of end-to-end video networking solutions.
(800) 806-9594
(650) 940-1383
www.minervasys.com

Motion Media

Videophones for use with ISDN.
(44) (1454) 313-444 (U.K.)
www.motionmedia.com

NEC America, Inc.

The NEC VideoWorks product family includes group systems and specialized systems for telemedicine and distance learning.
(800) TEAM-NEC
www.cng.nec.com/marketing/video/index.htm

One Touch Systems, Inc.

Manufactures interactive distance learning systems.
(408) 436-4600
www.onetouch.com

Optivision, Inc.

Major supplier of MPEG over IP streaming video solutions for distance learning, content distribution, corporate training, e-commerce, telemedicine, and surveillance.

(800) 239-0600
www.optivision.com

Panasonic

Manufactures codec systems (Vision Pro Series 7800), pan/tilt cameras, video-phones, and other equipment for use in videoconferencing.
(800) 211-7262
www.panasonic.com

PictureTel Corp.

Major manufacturer of videoconferencing systems.
(978) 292-2100
www.picturetel.com

Polycom, Inc.

Best-selling line of versatile video, audio, and dataconferencing systems and appliances.
(877) POLYCOM
www.polycom.com

RSI Video Conferencing

Manufacturers, sells, and leases videoconferencing systems, including the popular, economical Video Flyer.
(612) 896-3020
www.rsisystems.com

Sony

Manufactures a full line of high-quality videoconferencing systems and peripherals.
(800) 472-Sony
(201) 930-7054
www.sony.com/videoconferencing

Sorenson Vision

Manufactures and develops innovative video communication systems and solutions, including EnVision and the Sorenson Video Codec.
(435) 716-8800
www.sorensonvision.com

Tandberg

Major manufacturer of high-quality VTC set-top, rollabout, and room systems.

(972) 243-7572 (NuVision)
www.tandbergusa.com

VBrick Systems, Inc.
Manufactures video network appliances for video distribution and conferencing over IP networks.
(203) 265-0044
www.vbrick.com

VCON
Technically advanced H.320/323 desktop and group systems, and conferencing appliances.
www.vcon.com

VTEL
A major manufacturer of videoconferencing systems. Particularly strong in distance learning and telemedicine application areas. Also provides high-level integration and technical services.
(512) 437-2700
www.vtel.com

Zydacron
Manufacturer of first-rate desktop videoconferencing and integrated video/data group systems.
(603) 647-1000
www.zydacron.com

Multipoint Controllers and Switching Equipment

Accord Networks
Enterprise and carrier-level multipoint controllers, gateways, and other equipment.
(770) 641-4400
www.accordtelecom.com

Compunetix
State-of-the-art multimedia multipoint telecommunications systems.
(800) 879-4266
www.compunetix.com

Ezenia!

Formerly called VideoServer, this company manufactures cost-effective, high-quality, standards-based multimedia communications servers (MCUs), Web interactivity servers, and related equipment.
(877) 923-9200
www.ezenia.com

FVC.com

Offers two-way video and streaming solutions managed by a common video portal, Click to MeetT, that operates across multiple network technologies, including IP, ATM, and the PSTN. Click to MeetT is available as a systems solution for enterprises, and as a service from FVC.com's service provider partners.
(800) 351-8539
(408) 567-7230
www.fvc.com

Latitude Communications

Its MeetingPlace system is a server-based e-conferencing platform that enables real-time collaboration applications designed for deployment over an organization's existing voice, data, and Internet network.
(408) 988-7200
www.latitude.com

Lucent Technologies

Manufactures a broad range of video networking equipment and systems including MCUs, switches.
(908) 582-8500
www.Lucent.com

Madge Networks

Video networking switches and other reliable equipment for the deployment of sophisticated video networks.
(800) 876-2343
www.madgenetworks.com

RADVision

Top-drawer hardware and software building-block solutions for H.323 videoconferencing.
(201) 529-4300
www.radvision.com

Audio Systems, Echo Cancellers, and Acoustical Treatment

Acoustics First
Soundproofing supplies.
(804) 342-2900

Gentner Communications Corp.
Best known for its high-quality echo cancellers and other audio equipment, Gentner also recently introduced the APV200-IP Videoconferencing Codec.
(800) 765-9623
www.gentner.com

Shure, Inc.
Manufactures a complete line of audio mixers, processors, and microphones.
(847) 866-2200
www.shure.com

Sound Control Technologies
Manufactures high-end audio processing equipment for videoconferencing and other applications. Products include echo cancellers, mixers, switches, and a flush-mounting ceiling microphone.
(203) 854-5701
www.soundcontrol.net

Cameras (VTC and Copy-stand)

Canon USA
Manufactures a wide range of high-quality cameras and lenses. Products include document cameras, the VCC-3 pan/tilt camera, and the Canobeam system for secure and confidential wireless transmission of video over distances up to four kilometers.
www.usa.canon.com

Elmo
Provides a broad line of excellent copy-stand cameras, as well as projectors and other related presentation and VTC gear.
(800) 947-3566
www.elmousa.com

Howard Enterprises
Cameras for desktop videoconferencing and related applications.
(805) 383-7444
www.howent.com

JVC Professional Products
Manufactures a broad range of video cameras and high-quality video equipment.
(800) JVC-5825
www.jvc.com/pro

Pixera Corporation
Pixera manufactures innovative, high-quality digital and analog CCD cameras for videoconferencing, telemedicine and other applications.
(408) 341-1800
www.pixera.com

Samsung
Manufactures a complete line of high-quality "Presenter" copy-stand cameras.
(800) 762-7746
www.simplyamazing.com

VideoLabs, Inc.
Manufactures of copy-stand and special purpose cameras including the popular FlexCam, VTC furniture and other peripherals.
(612) 542-0061
www.videolabs.com

Electronic Whiteboards and Collaborative Tools

MicroTouch
Manufactures a selection of high-quality touch-screen, whiteboard, and related products to facilitate collaborative, conferencing, and remote kiosk operations.
(978) 659-9000
www.microtouch.com

SMART Technologies, Inc.
Manufactures a full line of high-quality interactive whiteboards, multimedia cabinets, and software that facilitate meeting, teaching and training.
(403) 245-0333
www.smarttech.com

Virtual Ink

Manufactures innovative, cost-effective products to enhance videoconferences and collaborative computing. These include mimio, a product that converts any whiteboard into an electronic interactive tool; and flipChart, that does the same for a paper flip chart.
(877) 696-4646; (617) 623-8387
www.virtualink.com

Lighting and Furniture

Alpha Lighting

Design and installation of VTC lighting systems.
(925) 945-8690
www.trendonline.com/ncal/alpha

LightTech Group Inc.

Compact fluorescent fixtures for VTC.
(718) 525-2900
www.lighttech.com

Lutron Electronics Co., Inc.

Manufactures commercial dimmers and lighting control systems.
(610) 281-38000
www.lutron.com

MTI

Forty-five-degree louvers for ceiling fluorescent lighting fixtures.
(636) 230-3365
www.mtit.com

Navitar

Manufactures Hi-Lites videoconferencing lighting fixtures, as well as copy-stand cameras and slide projectors for VTC use.
(800) 828-6778
www.navitar.com/av/av.htm

VFI

Manufacturer of custom and special-purpose furniture for videoconferencing, including tables, podiums, lecterns, and rollabout stands.
(905) 946-1459
www.video-furn.com

VideoLabs, Inc.
Manufacturer of special-purpose VTC and presentation furniture, in addition to its excellent cameras.
(612) 542-0061
www.videolabs.com

System Controllers (Touch-screen and Others)

Crestron Electronics, Inc.
Manufactures a full line of high-quality, programmable, touch-screen controllers for VTC systems and other applications.
(800) 237-2041
www.crestron.com

Panja
A broad range of high-quality touch-screen and other control systems for VTC, conference rooms, building automation, and other applications. Includes the product line formerly known as AMX.
(800) 222-0193
www.panja.com

Video Switches, Screen Splitters, and Scan Converters

Communications Specialties, Inc.
Makes the famous Scan Do scan converters and other video/computer interface devices.
(631) 273-0404
www.comspecial.com

Covid, Inc.
Manufactures a number of high-quality video switches, screen splitters, video/computer display interfaces and related equipment for VTC systems.
(800) 638-6104
www.covid.com

Extron Electronics
Manufactures a complete line of reliable video/computer display interface, control and conversion equipment.
(800) 633-9876; (714) 687-6311
www.extron.com

Focus Enhancements

Manufactures high-quality, cost-effective Tview line of professional computer/video down converters for VTC use.
(978) 988-5888
www.focusinfo.com

Hotronics, Inc.

Manufactures computer/video display converters and related equipment.
(408) 378-3883
www.hotronics.com

Consultants, Integrators, VARs, and Resellers

You can also contact manufacturers for the names of authorized resellers in your area and refer to the ICIA Web site (www.icia.org) for certified integrators and consultants.

CDAI Integrated Technical Solutions

Design, engineering and consulting company in Atlanta.
(404) 633-8861
www.cdai.com

CMS Innovative Consultants

High-level system design and project management firm in the New York City area, with special expertise in multimedia and video distribution systems.
(516) 933-0747
www.cmsav.com

Criticom, Inc.

Experienced Maryland-based integrator of videoconferencing systems.
(301) 306-0600
www.criticom.com

Delta Information Systems, Inc.

Visual Communications Systems group offers high-level consulting services, system design, engineering, and integration.
(215) 657-5270
www.delta-info.com

Hoffman Video Systems
Experienced integrator of video and VTC systems in southern California.
(800) 550-0225
www.hoffmanvideo.com

Media Resources
Consulting services for VTC and other new media applications. The author of this book is one of the principals of this organization.
(914) 997-8809
johnr@bestweb.net

NuVision Technologies
Turnkey rentals/leasing of Tandberg and other VTC Systems.
(972) 241-2225
www.nuvisiontech.com

PicturePhone Direct
Web and mailorder reseller of a wide range of videoconferencing products and peripherals. Knowledgeable phone sales staff.
(800) 521-5454
www.picturephone.com

Pinacl Communication, Inc.
U.S. integrator for Cabletime's Mediastar video distribution and video-conferencing systems.
(914) 345-8155
www.pinacl.com/us

Todd Communications, Inc.
Respected Midwest integrator of video and VTC systems.
(612) 941-0556
www.toddcommunications.com

Walsh-Lowe
Major consulting firm with practices in many fields, including videoconferencing and data communications.
(201) 216-1100
www.walsh-lowe.com

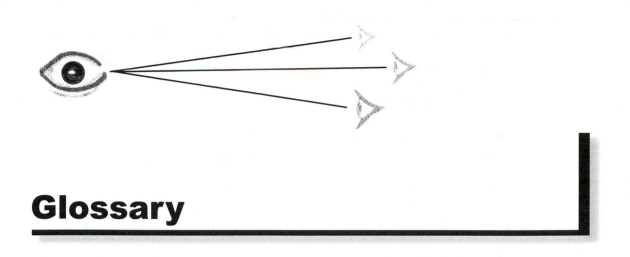

Glossary

This glossary is intended to provide a practical, nontechnical understanding of some common videoconferencing terms. For precise technical or legal definitions of these terms, please refer to the Web sites or publications of the appropriate organizations, regulatory bodies, and experts listed in Appendix B.

4CIF—Four times common intermediate format. An optional high-resolution format (in H.263) for the transmission and display of a picture consisting of 704 x 576 pixels.

10Base-T—10 Mbps Ethernet LAN technology.

100Base-T—100 Mbps Ethernet LAN technology.

A-D—Analog-to-digital conversion.

ADPCM—Adaptive differential pulse-code modulation. An audio coding technique used in G.728.

ADSL—Asymmetric digital subscriber line. A high-bandwidth network technology that transmits at a higher rate in one direction than the other. Uses conventional copper telephone wiring for bandwidths of up to several Mbps.

AGC (Automatic gain control)—A circuit or algorithm that normalizes a signal (e.g., voice or video) regardless of the amount of light or sound.

A-V (Audio-visual)—Usually refers to a system or application that involves the simultaneous use of both media, audio and video.

Aggregation—Method for sending data down two or more parallel channels.

A-law—European PCM compression method for digital voice communication.

Algorithm—A mathematical formula or program intended to perform a specific task (e.g., compressing video or encrypting data).

Analog—The conventional method of recording or transmitting audio and video. Usually employs continuously variable amplitude or frequency (corresponding to some characteristic of the original signal) to convey information.

Analog overlay systems—Video distribution and conferencing systems that transmit analog video and audio over extra or unused pairs of Category 5 LAN cabling. They typically deliver high-quality video and audio, with little if any impact on network performance.

Annex D—Still-image graphics mode for H.261. Can support maximum 704 x 576 resolution.

ANSI—American National Standards Institute.

API—Application programming interface. This is a programming tool or environment provided by the manufacturer of a program or system to allow relatively easy customization and extension of its product's original function.

Artifact—A coding error found in (or introduced into) a compressed audio or video signal. Artifacts common to videoconferencing include tiling and blurring (video) or clipping and lisping (audio).

Aspect ratio—The ratio of horizontal to vertical picture size. For example, the emerging wide-screen format has an aspect ratio of 16:9, while conventional TV and VTC have an aspect ratio of 4:3.

Asynchronous—A data transmission method that allows bytes to be sent at variable intervals, bracketed by start/stop bits that enable the receiving machine to reestablish synchronization (timing).

Asynchronous transfer mode (ATM)—A high-speed switching and multiplexing method using fixed-length cells (packets) of 53 bytes to support multiple types of traffic. ATM is designed to reliably route multimedia traffic over the network. ATM currently supports data transfer rates from 25 to 622 Mbps, and is a natural platform for the delivery of videoconferencing. It provides guaranteed QoS at various levels and variable bit rate (VBR).

Audioconference—A live audio-only conference call between two or more locations. When more than one person participates from a single location, a full-duplex speakerphone is usually employed. When three or more locations are involved, it is advisable to use an audioconferencing bridge or a bridging service. This optimizes the level (volume) of the signals from all locations for maximum quality and intelligibility, and makes it easier for people to join (and leave) the call. Audioconferences can also be enhanced through the use of graphics and collaborative computing.

Audiographic conferencing—The use of a variety of graphics transmission and display technologies in conjunction with an audioconference. *See* Collaborative computing.

B-channel—A 64 kbps "bearer" channel used for digital video, voice, or data communication. A basic building block of ISDN.

Bandwidth—The maximum amount of data that can be sent over a transmission channel in a specific amount of time. Usually expressed in thousands (kbps) or millions (Mbps) of bits per second. Sometimes referred to as the speed or capacity of a channel or circuit.

Basic rate (BRI)—The interface used in ISDN service. It provides two B (bearer) channels of 64 kbps each for video voice or data communication (total usable bandwidth 128 kbps), and a D (data) channel usually employed for signaling.

Baud rate—The rate of code elements or symbols per second. For example, if the symbol standard used captures 6 bits of data, a typical 2400-baud modem will be theoretically capable of communicating 14,400 bps.

B-ISDN—Broadband ISDN. Based on ATM, it can carry up to several hundred Mbps.

Bit rate—A unit of information that contains one of two states: on or off. This is the unit of counting in the "digital" binary system.

Blocking—An artifact found in H.261, H.263, MPEG and other DCT video coding methods. The effect is sometimes called tiling, in that portions of the picture appear to freeze or flicker in the shape of small squares. It usually occurs when the codec does not have enough information to produce a complete picture—due to processor overload or transmission error.

Blurring—An artifact seen in digitized video when the high frequencies (detail), or the moving edge of an object are not accurately coded. Seen frequently at lower bit-rates or with less robust codecs.

BONDING protocol—An industry standard protocol for the aggregation of B channels through the use of an inverse multiplexer (IMUX). Developed by the Bandwidth on Demand Interoperability Group, BONDING enables the combination of multiple BRI circuits (usually three) to provide a single high bandwidth (e.g., 384 kbps) virtual dial-up circuit.

Bits per second (bps)—The speed of a network connection expressed in the number of bits that can be transmitted every second.

BRI—The basic rate interface used in ISDN service. It provides two B (bearer) channels of 64 kbps each for video voice or data communication (total usable bandwidth 128 kbps), and a D (data) channel usually employed for signaling.

Bridge—A device that links two or more networks or devices of compatible protocols. In VTC, a multipoint control unit (MCU) is a bridge that connects anywhere from three to dozens of videoconferencing locations in a multipoint call.

Broadcast—A mode of communication in which the signal from one endpoint is transmitted to many others. Because this method usually requires no acknowledgment, it is simpler to implement and typically requires less bandwidth.

Business television (BTV)—An application that employs either satellite or terrestrial multicast technologies for the distribution of private television programming. BTV often includes some interactive elements, such as two-way audio and audience polling capabilities.

CCD—Charge-coupled device. A solid-state camera technology that captures visual images for conversion into video signals.

CCIR-601—Broadcast and commercial production standard format for digital video. Consists of 720 x 480 pixels at 30 frames per second (NTSC), or 720 x 576 at 25 frames per second (PAL).

CELP—Code excited linear prediction. Audio compression method used in G.728.

Channel—An electronic path for transmitting and/or receiving a signal.

Channel bank—Equipment in a telephone central office, or a private exchange, that multiplexes (combines) lower-speed digital channels into a single higher-speed composite channel. The channel bank also handles signaling and framing information for each individual digital channel.

Channel service unit (CSU)—A type of customer premises equipment (CPE) that terminates the carrier's circuit, and provides diagnostic services and protects the wide area network from damage.

Chrominance (chroma)—The level of color information in a video image.

CIF—*See* FCIF.

Circuit switched—A type of digital network or service that establishes a temporary "dedicated" communications channel between two or more locations (e.g., ISDN, POTS). Circuit switching enables data to be sent in a continuous stream, at a constant data rate, and with a delay (or latency) limited to the propagation time (approx. 186,000/distance in miles). *See* Packet switched.

Clear channel—A channel in which all 64 kbps are used for transmission of content data.

CO—Central office. The local phone company switching facility, where the subscriber's local loop terminates and is switched or routed for local and long-distance connections. The CO is usually identified by the first three digits of the local telephone number. Distance to the CO is an important factor in the provisioning of digital subscriber lines (DSL) and other distance-sensitive digital services.

Coaxial cable—A cable with a central conductor surrounded by an insulating layer and a conducting shield layer. Coaxial cable was originally developed to carry RF (radio frequency) of hundreds of megahertz (MHz) for considerable distances. Various types of "coax" (RG-58, RG-59, etc.) are used for cable TV transmission, video interconnection, and (less frequently) data transmission.

Codec—Originally an acronym for coder-decoder, a codec is any device that compresses and decompress information. In VTC, it is a hardware or software device that digitizes and compresses analog video and audio for transmission, and decompresses and converts digital audio and video signals for reception and output. An uncompressed video signal can require as much as 90 Mbps of bandwidth for transmission. A typical videoconferencing codec will compress the information that make up the signal so that it requires much less than 1.54 Mbps but still delivers a very usable picture.

Collaborative computing—The use of a variety of interactive technologies that enable computer users to share data, in real time, over a local or wide-area network. Usually employed in conjunction with an audioconference or point-to-point voice call. Collaborative computing employs a wide range of techniques, including screen sharing, which allows multiple users to view a common computer screen; screen annotation, which allows distant users to draw on a common whiteboard; and application sharing that enables users to enter, edit, view, and save data on a shared file (e.g., an Excel spreadsheet). Common collaborative computing software includes MS NetMeeting and Lotus Notes.

Compression—The use of an algorithm to reduce the number of bits required to transmit or store data. Lossless compression allows the data to be reconstituted without any loss of information. Lossy compression eliminates data judged to be redundant or otherwise unnecessary for the particular application.

Continuous presence—The ability to see more than one distant location at the same time during a multipoint conference. Sometimes called *Hollywood Squares*, after the TV show of that name, continuous presence is a function of the multipoint control unit (MCU) or the conference bridging service.

Copy-stand camera—A CCD video camera that is built into a graphics copy-stand. These units are used to shoot or capture images of printed and three-dimensional objects for transmission over a videoconferencing system.

CPE—Customer premises equipment. A generic term for communications hardware located at a customers premises. Includes VTC equipment (codecs, cameras, etc.), multiplexers, switches, and other equipment. Unless otherwise specified, the proper functioning of this equipment is not the responsibility of the phone company or other provider of wide-area connectivity.

CS-ACELP—Conjugate structure algebraic code excited linear prediction. Audio compression method used in G.729.

CSU—*See* Channel service unit.

D-channel—The ISDN channel that carries signaling information to control the call setup, teardown, or activation of supplementary services. The D-channel may also be used to provide packet mode data service.

D-A—Digital-to-analog.

Data compression—*See* Compression.

Data service unit (DSU)—An electronic device providing interface between a data terminal, codec, or other data communications device and a digital access line such as ISDN. Often combined with a channel service unit.

DCT—Discrete-cosine transform. A basic method used in many codecs, including H.261, H.263, MPEG, and JPEG, to compress visual information.

DES—Data encryption standard. A common method for encrypting videoconferencing communication to provide additional security. DES is built into many codecs and requires that the connecting parties both possess an encryption key composed of a series of letters and/or numbers.

Desktop videoconferencing (DVC)—The use of a PC to serve as a videoconferencing terminal, with the picture from the distant location being displayed on the PC's monitor. One major advantage of DVC is the ease with which users can integrate collaborative computing functions into their conferences. Typically, a small camera is mounted directly atop the computer screen, and a PCI board is installed in the computer to serve as a codec and communications interface. However, some newer models (particularly lower-cost H.323-based units), use the PC's own CPU to perform codec functions, and connect directly to the LAN (local area network) through a standard network interface card (NIC).

Digital—An electronic signal coded in binary format (ones and zeros, on and off), as opposed to the continuously variable flow of an analog signal.

Digital loopback—A remote diagnostic technique for communications devices such as codecs or VTC terminals. The device being tested typically decodes and reencodes the signal, then echos it back to the originating location for analysis or comparison with the original signal. Conversely, a codec at a remote site can transmit a signal to a specially configured site, for loopback and confirmation of proper functioning.

Distance learning—A type of instruction or training in which the instructor is not in the same location as the student or students. A broad continuum of media and methodologies are used for distance learning. These range from the simple broadcasting of lectures to the highly interactive use of live, recorded, and computer-assisted video and multimedia content over the Internet.

DPCM—Differential pulse code modulation. An audio coding technique.

DS3—A dedicated digital connection supporting data transfer rates of up to 43 Mbps. It is composed of 672 channels, each supporting a data transfer rate of 64 kbps. DS3 service is sometimes referred to as T3, and is widely used by ISPs for their connection to the Internet backbone, large financial institutions for data and video traffic, and by TV networks for the transmission of programming.

DSL—Digital subscriber lines, which include several distinct telecommunications services. Under the proper circumstances, they all are capable of delivering high-speed digital service over the installed base of copper wires. Maximum speeds available with DSL services are as high as 9 Mbps downstream/640 kbps upstream for ADSL (asymmetric DSL), 3 Mbps both ways for SDSL (symmetric DSL), and up to 32 Mbps downstream/1 Mbps upstream for xDSL.

DSP—Digital signal processor. An integrated circuit (chip) that performs various functions related to the digital processing (e.g., compression, equalization) of a video or audio signal.

DSU—*See* Data service unit.

DTMF—Dual tone modulated frequency. The sounds created by dialing an ordinary touch-tone keypad, used for signaling within a phone system.

DVC—*See* Desktop videoconferencing.

E1—The European equivalent of the T1 circuit. It consists of 30 channels, each supporting data transfer rates of up to 64 kbps.

Echo canceller—A device that electronically eliminates or minimizes echo that is caused by room acoustics and system/transmission related signal delay while maintaining full-duplex audio communications.

Ethernet—A standard group of protocols (IEEE 802.x) for data communication over a local area network (LAN) using a variety of transmission media and protocols. See 10Base-T, 100Base-T, and Gigabit Ethernet.

FCIF—Full common intermediate format (also CIF). An "optional" format in H.261 and H.263 that is supported by virtually all current equipment. Displays 352 x 288 luminance pixels (and 25 percent that number of chromanance pixels), at up to 30 fps (frames per second).

Frames per second (fps)—The number of frames or video pictures that can be transmitted and displayed by a specific system. Many H.261 and H.263 compliant codecs will deliver 30 fps at 384 kbps. This is roughly equivalent to the refresh rate of a standard NTSC video picture, which displays 30 fps (composed of 60 alternating-line, interlaced fields).

Frame relay—A network service that employs a packet-switching protocol for connecting devices on a wide area network (WAN) and supports data transfer rates of up to DS3 (43 Mbps). In the United States, frame relay service is widely available for data transfer at rates of 56 kbps to 1.544 Mbps.

Full-duplex—Simultaneous two-way communication over a single communication link as opposed to one-way or simplex communications. Generally refers to full-duplex audio, which allows both sides of a conference to talk and be heard at the same time.

G.711—An ITU standard PCM-based compression algorithm used for the transmission of audio signals at speeds of 48 to 64 kbps with an audio bandwidth of up to 3 kHz.

G.722—An ITU standard ADPCM-based compression algorithm used for the transmission of audio signals at speeds of 48 to 64 kbps with an audio bandwidth of up to 7 kHz.

G.728—A lower-quality LD-CELP-based compression algorithm used for the transmission of audio signals at speeds of 16 kbps with an audio bandwidth of up to 3 kHz.

Gateway—In an H.323-compliant system, this device (or entity) permits the use of an H.320 VTC terminal (e.g., a legacy room system) on an H.323 network. They also facilitate connection of H.323 terminals and other devices to a circuit-switched WAN (e.g., ISDN).

Gatekeeper—In an H.323-compliant system, this device (or entity) controls the traffic of a group of H.323 terminals and other equipment on a network. Gatekeepers may allow the network administrator to manage the various devices on the network, set privileges, bandwidth allocations, and parameters for traffic control that will ensure proper functioning of the H.323 devices and the rest of the network. Gatekeeper functions also include address translation to simplify a variety of user operations.

Gigabit Ethernet—An Ethernet LAN that operates at speeds of up to 1 Gb per second in compliance with the IEEE 802.3z standard.

H.231 and H.243—International Telecommunications Union (ITU) standards for multipoint conferencing.

H.248—An emerging standard for the switching of video, voice, fax, data, and multimedia calls between packet switched (e.g., TCP/IP) and circuit-switched (e.g., ISDN) networks. Also called Megaco, H.248 is a joint project of the ITU and the IETF Internet Engineering Task Force (IETF).

H.261—An ITU standard, DCT-based interframe compression algorithm used for H.320-based videoconferencing. Most effective in the range of 112 kbps to approximately 2 Mbps. It defines two picture sizes/resolutions, the most widely used of which is full common intermediate format (FCIF) with an effective resolution of 352 x 288.

H.263—The primary video coding standard for H.323 videoconferencing. It specifies the video coding algorithm (a type of DCT), the picture formats (SQCIF, QCIF, FCIF, 4CIF, 16CIF), and other required and optional techniques that can be employed.

H.320—An umbrella designation for a group of standards and recommendations from the ITU regarding methods of audio, video, and multimedia conferencing over ISDN networks.

H.323—An umbrella designation for a group of standards and recommendations from the ITU regarding audio, video, and multimedia conferencing over packet-switched networks. This includes point-to-point and multipoint videoconferencing over Ethernet LANs, WANs, and the Internet; Internet Telephony (VoIP) and other related applications.

226

IMUX—*See* Inverse multiplexer.

Interframe—Any of a number of compression methods that compare information in two or more frames of a video picture in order to provide visually equivalent picture quality at higher compression ratios.

Inverse multiplexer (IMUX)—A device that allows users to aggregate lower-bandwidth channels to create a higher-bandwidth channel than might otherwise be available on the network. A typical BONDING-compliant IMUX, for example, can combine three 128 kbps BRI-ISDN lines into a single 384 kbps communication channel.

IP—*See* TCP/IP.

ISDN (Integrated services digital network)— A digital network in which the same time-division switches and digital transmission paths are used to establish connections for a wide range of services, including telephone, data, electronic mail, fax, and videoconferencing.

ISO (International Organization for Standardization)—An international organization, affiliated with the United Nations, that has as its members the national standards bodies of most of the countries of the world. The ISO is responsible for the development and publication of international standards in various technical fields.

ITU (International Telecommunications Union)—Formerly called the CCITT, the ITU is the specialized agency recognized by the United Nations that has the task of developing worldwide standards and extending international cooperation in the field of telecommunications.

JPEG (Joint Photographic Experts Group)—The standard for the compression of still images developed by the group. JPEG is an intraframe compression method that uses several algorithms, most essentially DCT, and a wide range of compression ratios to achieve optimal image compression for various uses. *See* MJPEG (Motion-JPEG).

Leased line—A dedicated circuit, connecting two points, which is leased from a telecommunications provider to furnish continuously available service.

Local loop—The communications circuit that connects the subscriber's premises to the switching equipment at the telecommunications provider's central office (CO) or point of presence (POP).

Luminance—The part of a video signal (Y) that provides monochromatic information about the brightness of different parts of that image.

Megaco (H.248)—An emerging standard for the switching of video, voice, fax, data, and multimedia calls between packet switched (e.g., TCP/IP) and public switched telephone (PSTN) networks. Megaco is a joint project of the International Telecommunications Union (ITU) and the Internet Engineering Task Force (IETF).

MJPEG—A "motion" version of JPEG, an ITU standard, DCT-based, intraframe (no frame to frame comparison) compression algorithm, developed initially for storage and transmission of still photographic images.

MPEG-1—An ITU standard, DCT-based interframe compression algorithm, developed initially for video recording on CD-ROM but primarily used today for streaming video applications and the posting of video files on Web sites. MPEG stands for Motion Picture Experts Group.

MPEG-2—An ITU standard, DCT-based interframe compression algorithm, developed initially for transmission of "broadcast" quality video via digital satellite and land lines at speeds of 2 Mbps to 25 Mbps and higher. Widely used today for the encoding of video movies on DVD. MPEG-2 and related algorithms are also being used for very-high-quality videoconferencing in such applications as distance learning.

Mux (Multiplexer)—A telecommunications device that either combines two or more channels into one channel, or separates the channels of a circuit that are to be used for different purposes.

NTSC—Acronym for the standard form of television picture used in the United States and Japan that was developed by the National Television Standards Committee. Some engineers say that it stands for Never Twice the Same Color, a reference to the relative instability of the color information in NTSC, as compared with the European PAL and other systems.

Pan/tilt cameras—A video camera that is integrated with a motorized pan/tilt mechanism, and is usually equipped with a zoom lens and some means of remotely controlling all these functions. Additional features include preset positioning for programmed shot selection and a variety of auto-tracking schemes that attempt to focus the camera on the person currently addressing the meeting. Pan-tilt cameras are standard equipment on virtually all set-top and rollabout systems and are available as an option with most desktop video systems.

POTS (Plain old telephone service)—Circuit switched, analog local phone service over copper twisted-pair wires.

PRI-ISDN—Primary rate interface or primary rate ISDN is a digital circuit providing 24 B channels (in the United States and Japan), one of which is typically reserved for signaling purposes. This leaves at least 23 B or 1.472 Mbps for communications purposes, and they can be parceled out for various uses by a multiplexer (Mux). For example, six channels (384 kbps) can be dedicated for videoconferencing, two channels (128 kbps) for remote access to the internet through an ISP, and the remaining 15 channels can be connected to a PBX (internal phone system).
Note: PRI uses the T1 (24 B) signaling structure in the United States and Japan, and the E1 (30 B) structure in Europe and elsewhere in the world.

QCIF (Quarter common intermediate format)—A video format defined in H.261 and other standards that provides for a picture with up to 176 x 144 pixels of luminance information. Intended for use with videophones and other low-bandwidth applications. *See* also FCIF.

QoS (Quality of service)—As used in video networking, it refers to the guaranteed level of throughput, end-to-end, that can be expected from a particular network connection. This generally takes into consideration the stability of the data rate, the bit error rate, jitter, latency (delay), and other factors. The QoS of ISDN and ATM can be guaranteed, while on packet-switched networks this is not usually the case.

RFI (Request for information)—A document issued by a prospective customer seeking preliminary input regarding possible solutions for a perceived need or a planned project.

RFP (Request for proposal)—A document requesting the submission of bids or proposals for the delivery or completion of a specified product, system, or service.

Rollabout videoconferencing systems—These usually consist of a variety of audio, video, telecommunications, and control systems electronics mounted in a wheeled cabinet, topped by one or two monitors, and crowned with a pan-tilt camera. The integrated, modular construction of rollabout systems make them a flexible, easy-to-maintain solution for applications ranging from workgroups to boardrooms, and distance learning to telemedicine.

Set-top videoconferencing systems—These compact units integrate camera, microphone, speakers, codec, network interface, and other components into a single box that sits, as the name implies, on top of a TV set or monitor. They are a good choice for small groups (two to six people) and routine meetings. Though originally aimed at the low-cost workgroup market, these units (like the compact car) keep getting bigger and more powerful, and the latest offerings in this category are equal to many rollabout systems in cost and capabilities.

SONET (Synchronous optical network)—A U.S. standard for connecting fiber-optic transmission systems that defines a hierarchy of interface rates allowing data streams at different rates to be multiplexed or combined without interference. It describes optical carrier (OC) levels from 51.8 to 2.48 Gbps—the equivalent of over 1600 T1 or PRI circuits.

Synchronous — A data transmission method in which bytes of information and control characters are sent at regular intervals in order to maintain the continuity of data.

T1—A dedicated digital connection supporting data rates of 1.54 Mbps. A T1 circuit (sometimes called a DS1) consists of 24 individual channels supporting data transfer rates 56 or 64 kbps. Each channel can carry voice, data, or video traffic. A T1 connection can also be configured to support PRI-ISDN service with 24 B channels, one of which is usually reserved for signaling.

T.120—A group of ITU standards and recommendations for data conferencing and collaboration.

TCP/IP (Transmission control protocol/Internet protocol)—A full-duplex protocol used over packet-switched networks.

Touch-screen controllers—Available from a number of sources, most notably Crestron and Panja/AMX, these units allows even nontechnical users to control many system and room functions simply by touching illuminated icons on a small screen. They are available in both wired and wireless models, and cost between $500 and $5,000, depending on screen size and type.

Videoconferencing—Two-way, full-duplex, interactive video, voice, and graphic communications. Videoconferencing is usually conducted over a digital network and often includes elements of collaborative computing.

Videophone—A desktop device that combines the functions of a telephone and videoconferencing terminal. Typically, these units are equipped with a small (4" to 9" diagonal) LCD screen, operate over a single BRI-ISDN line or LAN connection, and utilize a modified phone-keypad layout rather than a computer-style keyboard.

VPN (Virtual private network)—Any of several types of networks that use public or insecure networks (e.g., the Internet or ISDN) at some point in the connection of nodes, but provide a secure, private communications link between them. Techniques employed to ensure privacy and security include encryption, authentication, and tunneling (or encapsulation).

VTC (Video teleconferencing)—A common acronym for videoconferencing.

Web conferencing—The use of the Internet or other TCP/IP network to allow remote users to view PowerPoint slides and other presentation graphics with a Browser-equipped computer. Most Web conferencing systems and services include annotation and other collaborative computing functions, and some even provide two-way streaming audio and video communications.

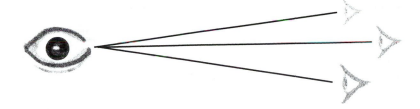

Index

About the Author

John Rhodes has been involved in the videoconferencing industry since its early days. In 1989, he was part of the team that initiated Sony's entry into the U.S. videoconferencing market, and was named marketing manager for Sony's Videoconferencing and Satellite Systems Division. He has been responsible for product development and marketing of videoconferencing solutions at Sony, IPC, and Pinacl Communications. He has also designed and/or managed the implementation of video communications systems for a wide variety of organizations—including Citicorp, Sony, Ralph Lauren, the U.S. Navy, and the New York City School for the Deaf. He has served as contributing editor for Teleconferencing Business, and written numerous articles on videoconferencing and multimedia communications for *AV Video*, *Multimedia Producer*, and *Inc. Technology Sourcebook Educational Guide*. Rhodes is president and co-owner of Media Resources, a West Harrison, New York-based company, specializing in the deployment of new media technologies and content for business communications applications.

His approach to systems development focuses on enabling users to communicate more easily and effectively, with technology that is easy to use and simple to support.

He enjoys most forms of sincere or humorous music, user-friendly technology, golf, ecology, multimedia, and the pursuit of truth.